Comparative Anthropology

Comparative Anthropology

Edited by
LADISLAV HOLY

Basil Blackwell

British Library Cataloguing in Publication Data
Comparative anthropology.
1. Ethnology—Methodology
I. Holy, Ladislav
306'.072   GN345
ISBN 0—631—15155—9

Library of Congress Cataloging in Publication Data
Comparative anthropology.

Papers of the Symposium on Comparative Method in
Social Anthropology, held at the University of
St. Andrews, December 15—18, 1983.
Bibliography: p.
Includes index.
1. Ethnology—Comparative method—Congresses.
2. Cross-cultural studies—Congresses. I. Symposium
on Comparative Method in Social Anthropology (1983 :
University of St. Andrews) II. Holy, Ladislav.
GN345.C65 1987   306   86—26380
ISBN 0—631—15155—9

Typeset in 10 on 12 pt Garamond
by Pioneer Associates, Perthshire
Printed in Great Britain by
T. J. Press Ltd, Padstow

Contents

List of Contributors   vi

Preface   vii

1 Introduction   1
   Description, Generalization and Comparison: Two Paradigms
   Ladislav Holy

2 Summer's Days and Salad Days: The Coming of Age of   22
   Anthropology? *Mark Hobart*

3 Comparison as the Search for Continuity *David Parkin*   52

4 Translation as a Creative Process: The Power of the Name   70
   Joanna Overing

5 History, Culture and the Comparative Method: A West African   88
   Puzzle *J. D. Y. Peel*

6 Anthropological Comparison *R. H. Barnes*   119

7 Caste in Bali and India: Levels of Comparison *Leo Howe*   135

8 Pastoralism and the Comparative Method *Philip Burnham*   153

9 'African Ethnogenesis': Limits to the Comparability of Ethnic   168
   Phenomena *Richard Fardon*

10 Khoisan Kinship: Regional Comparison and Underlying Structures   189
   Alan Barnard

11 The Use of Ethnographic Parallels in Interpreting Upper Palaeolithic 210
   Rock Art *Robert Layton (with an appendix by Malcolm Smith)*

   Index   240

List of Contributors

Alan Barnard is a lecturer in the Department of Social Anthropology and the Centre of African Studies, University of Edinburgh.

R. H. Barnes is University Lecturer in Social Anthropology, Oxford University.

Philip Burnham is Reader in Anthropology and Head of the Department of Anthropology at University College London.

Richard Fardon is a lecturer in Social Anthropology at the University of St Andrews.

Mark Hobart is Lecturer in Anthropology with reference to South-East Asia at the School of Oriental and African Studies in the University of London.

Ladislav Holy is Professor of Social Anthropology at the University of St Andrews.

Leo Howe is Assistant Lecturer in the Department of Social Anthropology, University of Cambridge.

Robert Layton is Reader in the Anthropology Department, University of Durham.

Joanna Overing is Senior Lecturer in the Social Anthropology of Latin America at the London School of Economics and Political Science.

David Parkin is Professor of Anthropology at the School of Oriental and African Studies in the University of London.

J. D. Y. Peel is Charles Booth Professor of Sociology in the University of Liverpool.

Preface

This volume is the result of the Symposium on Comparative Method in Social Anthropology held on 15—18 December 1983 at the University of St Andrews. The underlying idea of the symposium was to take stock of the present standing of comparison in social anthropology and to consider its role in ethnographic description on the one hand, and generalization on the other. At one time, comparison was considered to be the method of social anthropology. Indeed, it was built into the very definition of the subject as comparative sociology and this conceptualization of anthropology was duly reflected not only in its practice but also in the concentration on the problems of comparison in methodological discussion. The demise of structural-functionalism (comparison of forms) and the move away from structuralism (comparison of structural principles underlying and generating the observable forms) has been accompanied by the concentration on the problems of adequate description. In the methodological discussion, the question of comparison has been eschewed. However, this lack of attention given to comparison is clearly at odds with the subject's actual practice. In anthropological analysis, comparison continues to be widely used, although its style has changed considerably over the past few decades. This discrepancy between the lack of specific methodological attention paid to comparison and its continuing use in actual research practice defined the main problem of the symposium.

The participants were specifically invited to consider the ways in which comparison is employed nowadays in fieldwork and analysis. It was felt that this aim could best be achieved by bringing together anthropologists whose expertise lies in different substantive areas of the discipline and whose ideas on comparison are sufficiently different to generate discussion and debate. All participants have contributed papers to this volume except for A. Kuper and R. Willis who were unable to revise their contributions for publication due to the pressure of their other commitments. The papers were all written before the symposium and revised in light of the critical discussion at our meeting.

The symposium at St Andrews, as well as this book, would have never materialized without the enthusiasm of all the participants about the problems of comparison and their hard work before, during and after the meeting. From among them, special thanks are due to R. Barnes, P. Burnham, M. Hobart and J. Overing, who chaired individual sessions and skilfully guided the often heated discussion, and particularly to D. Parkin who summed up the discussion and provided helpful comments on the introduction to this volume. The symposium at St Andrews was made possible by a grant from the Economic and Social Research Council. Its interest in the topic and financial assistance are gratefully acknowledged. L. Howe's paper delivered at the symposium was subsequently published in *Contexts and Levels: anthropological essays on hierarchy* edited by R. H. Barnes, D. de Copper and R. J. Parkin (JASO Occasional Papers, No 4, Oxford 1985). I am grateful to the editors of JASO for their permission to reprint it in this volume.

Ladislav Holy

1

Introduction

Description, Generalization and Comparison: Two Paradigms

Ladislav Holy

In spite of the continually changing style of anthropology, a recurrent set of problems underlies all anthropological endeavour. One such problem concerns the relation between the anthropologists' description of particular cultures and societies and their generalization about human culture and society. Nowadays, the main question is whether description of particular societies is merely the means to generalization, or whether description itself is the key task and need not lead to generalization. The question has been asked as part of the recent paradigmatic shift in anthropology from a positivistic to a more subjective approach. As is evident from all the papers in this volume, many anthropologists no longer see description and generalization as means and end respectively. This leads them to question the received wisdom that comparison is the main method for arriving at generalizations and that in this sense description and comparison are in some way counterposed as they were, for example, for Goodenough (1970). They see as questionable that a functional link exists between comparison and generalization (see especially Barnes). Whether comparison is functionally linked to generalization or description depends rather on how the relationship between generalization and description is conceptualized.

This introduction addresses itself to this recurrent question of the relation between description and generalization and of the role of comparison in describing particular cultures and societies, and in generalizing about culture and society. In doing so it has two objectives: (a) to show that the role of cross-cultural comparison as the method for generating and testing hypotheses derives from the positivistic paradigm in anthropology which is no longer shared by all (and probably not even most) anthropologists; (b) to show that the notion of comparison as unified method also derives from this paradigm.

It further suggests that with the paradigmatic shift in anthropology, both the objectives and techniques of comparison have diversified to such an extent that there is no longer a 'comparative method' in anthrpology; it has been replaced by varying styles of comparison.

I appreciate that the practice of individual anthropologists is often not explicable in terms of their theoretical pronouncements and that the two paradigms in anthropology which I compare and contrast embrace various shades of theoretical opinions and a considerable diversity of research practices. Nevertheless, certain similarities underlie this diversity embodied in each paradigm which enable us to construe each paradigm as an ideal type. I concentrate on those features of each ideal type which I believe would be considered by most anthropologists as the defining ones and I compare and contrast the two paradigms at this ideal typical level.

DESCRIPTION AND GENERALIZATION
IN POSITIVISTIC ANTHROPOLOGY

The notion prevailing among positivists in anthropology was that the description of a particular culture, different in some significant respect from all others, had to be counterbalanced by concentrating attention on the similarity of many of its parts to those of other cultures. Thus, anthropology could become a generalizing science. Considering itself a branch of comparative sociology, anthropology followed Durkheim in his view that 'comparative sociology is not a particular branch of sociology; it is sociology itself insofar as it ceases to be purely descriptive and aspires to account for facts' (1964: 139). Description provided the facts, and comparative method was adopted to account for them; it was seen as the means of formulating and testing hypotheses or generalizations valid not only for one specific society or culture but cross culturally (Evans-Pritchard 1951: 89—90; Evans-Pritchard 1965: 31). Comparative method marked the distinction between anthropology as a generalizing science and ethnography as mere description of one particular society or culture. Radcliffe-Brown expressed this view quite clearly when he wrote: 'without systematic comparative studies anthropology will become only historiography and ethnography' (Radcliffe-Brown 1951: 16).

The possibility of generalizing from a single case was of course not ruled out, but the merits and deficiencies of this type of generalizing, in contrast to generalization on the basis of systematic comparison of several cases, were addressed as a methodological problem (Köbben 1970). World-wide comparisons establishing statistical correlations between phenomena were condemned because they failed to formulate useful generalizations. As Evans-

Pritchard expressed it, 'the method of statistical correlation can only pose questions, it cannot give us answers to them' (Evans-Pritchard 1965: 22—3). In Leach's view, 'Murdock's World Ethnographic Sample and all the work that derives from it . . . is producing tabulated nonsense' (Leach 1965: 299). Similar views were expressed by Steiner (1951), Schapera (1953), Needham (1962a) (see also Leach 1950; Köbben 1952). Although in Britain the statistical use of comparative method on a world-wide scale was abandoned for these reasons, it continued to flourish in America. Its shortcomings were recognized but the belief persisted that they could be overcome. Most British anthropologists (notably Schapera 1953; Evans-Pritchard 1965: 28—9) as well as some Americans (e.g. Eggan 1954) advocated rather an intensive comparison on a geographically or culturally limited scale. The disagreement among the world-wide and area-limited comparativists about what is the most useful scale of comparison was again generated by the disagreement about the kind of comparison which yields better generalizations (for a more detailed discussion of regional comparison and its relation to global comparison, see Parkin's paper in this volume).

The whole comparative endeavour was part of the anthropologists' emulation of what they understood to be the scientific method. Even Evans-Pritchard, who clearly expressed his doubts whether social anthropology can, or should be, science, saw comparison as anthropology's equivalent of experiment (Evans-Pritchard 1951: 89—90). 'Whether or not the method-ology of natural science has been fully comprehended — even writers like Popper have doubts — the question of the *appropriateness* of such methods has generally been pre-empted in the rush to be as "scientific" about society as about organisms and matter' (Silverman 1972: 184). Of course, if the scientific pretensions of anthropology were to be meaningful, fieldwork could not be an end in itself but had to generate a growing corpus of knowledge expressed in the formulation of theories. The logical outcome of this view of the research process was its overall conceptualization in terms of theory testing. Fieldwork found its place only within this overall scheme, and its raison d'être was to test existing generalizations. In this sense, it was itself seen as experimental and comparative (Evans-Pritchard 1951: 89—90; 1965: 30—1).

In its effort to be scientific, positivistic anthropology preoccupied itself with formulating and testing generalizations, which necessitated a focus on comparisons. Problems of comparison were virtually the only problems that ever entered the methodological discussion. A good half of all the papers assembled by Naroll and Cohen in their *Handbook of Method in Cultural Anthropology* (1970) are explicitly concerned with comparison, comparative method or specific problems of comparative studies. Validity and comparability of the primary data, reliability of the rating procedures, suitability, randomness and representativeness of the sample, control of the possibility of historical diffusion rather than functional relationship of phenomena (Galton's problem) and significance of the results were hotly disputed issues (see Driver 1973; Sarana 1975; and, for more recent discussion of these issues, Jorgensen 1979). The ultimate objective of any comparative research — whatever its scale — was to establish operationally defined variables which were then related together. It was seen as a problem whether the relationship between the variables should be conceptualized as a causal or functional one, but the variables themselves were hardly ever seen as problematic. They were institutions, institutionalized relationships, beliefs, states of affairs — 'held to have essences discernible independent of observers and frames of reference' (Hobart, this volume) and all treated as objectified manifestations or forms of objectively existing social and cultural reality. It was not recognized that it is discourses rather than objective forms that are compared (see Hobart's paper in this volume) and, in consequence, the construction of these 'objective forms' was not seen as being problematic. They were real and factual, and they were available to the anthropologist through direct observation. In consequence, the way in which the description of a particular society or culture or of some of its aspects had been arrived at, was, on the whole, not seen as problematic. It was accepted that the data were gathered by the anthropologist through his participant observation; this method of anthropological field research was, of course, also discussed alongside the methodological problems of comparison, but its discussion has been, for the most part, concerned merely with the technical problems it presents. The epistemological problems involved in data gathering through participant observation were largely eschewed.

In brief, while generalization was seen as problematic, description was not. Or, if it was problematic at all, it was such in terms of its adequacy for the formulation of generalizations through comparison. Thus, if the need to improve the standard of description was expressed at all, it was motivated by the demand to gather data which could be used in a future comparative analysis. For example, one of the problems of comparison stemmed from the recognition of the difference between normative patterns and actual behaviour which may differ from its norms. It led to the realization that the normative pattern of one society is incomparable with actual behaviour in another society. Considering this problem, Colson pointed out that 'the worker in the comparative field is hampered very badly because he does not have "adequate numbers of actual facts" upon which to base comparisons. Instead he must rely upon generalized statements about social institutions and compare them on an all-or-none basis, though the generalized descriptions may be incomparable in actual fact' (Colson 1967: 4). She concluded that 'the comparative method will contribute little further to our understanding of social organization and the field of cultural phenomena in general until we shift from the all-or-none classifications so largely used at present to a method based on the comparison of rates constructed from quantitative information collected in a systematic fashion. For this we need new standards of fieldwork' and what such fieldwork should provide is 'quantitative material to back up qualitative statements', i.e. 'material of a type that allows of a direct comparison of rates' (Colson 1967: 4—5). Driver, before her, expressed a similar view: 'If we are going to use more mathematics, we must organise fieldwork with that in mind. We must obtain more quantification of every kind whenever it is possible to do so. . . . If one of the goals of ethnography is to arrive at patterns, configurations or structures of cultures, these must be determined inductively from adequate numbers of actual facts if they are to satisfy the standards of science' (Driver 1953: 53).

DESCRIPTION AND GENERALIZATION IN INTERPRETATIVE ANTHROPOLOGY

I started with a brief review of the conceptualization of the relationship between description and generalization in positivistic anthropology to indicate that it was generalization that attracted methodological attention and was seen as problematic while the description was removed from the main focus of methodological attention. On the whole, description was subordinate to the demands of generalization and the standard of adequate description was determined by the demand of comparison which was seen as the main method of generating and testing hypotheses.

This is a direct reversal of the way in which the relation of description and generalization is perceived today.

Behind the apparent proliferation of the recent approaches to theory in social anthropology lies a general move from the theory of social facts as things to a theory of them as constructions. This theory holds that facts exist only within a frame of reference, that there is no such thing as 'pure experience' and no such things as facts that are recorded directly from the objectively existing outside reality. This move is logically accompanied by a move away from the notion of the methodological unity of the natural and social sciences towards the realization that the social sciences require different methods of inquiry from those used in natural science investigations due to the subjective quality of social phenomena. These are not external to man in the way in which phenomena of the natural world are; they are constituted by meaning in the sense that they do not exist independently of the cultural meanings which people use to account for them and hence to constitute them. These notions are not specific to anthropology but are shared by much of the present-day social science. In the sense of a paradigm as 'the entire constellation of beliefs, values, techniques and so on shared by the members of a given community' (Kuhn 1970: 175), it is possible to characterize the present situation as that of a new paradigm replacing the paradigm of positivistic social science. In sociology, this new paradigm is found in symbolic interactionism (Blumer 1969; Stryker 1980), ethnomethodology and phenomenological sociology (Cicourel 1964; Garfinkel 1967; Glaser and Strauss 1967; Douglas 1971; Filmer et al. 1972), in anthropology in the approaches that describe themselves as humanistic or cultural, in the recent interest in ethnoscience and cognitive anthropology and in the preoccupation with meaning and the growing strength of what is usually called symbolic or semantic anthropology (Crick 1976; Dolgin, Kemnitzer and Schneider 1977; Parkin 1982). The notions briefly outlined above seem to be shared to a greater or lesser extent by them all and in referring to this common ground I use the term 'interpretative anthropology': this label derives from the fact that anthropologists sharing these notions are not simply observing things but interpreting meaning.

With the move to the new paradigm, the emphasis in methodological discussion has shifted radically from the problems of generalization to the problems of description (Parkin 1982: xiii; see also Overing's paper in this volume). The major problem is no longer how the data should be handled after they have been collected so as to generate generalizations, but rather how they should be gathered in the first place so that they can legitimately be taken for data on (a) social reality as constructed through actors' practical accomplishments and (b) the meaning of social phenomena as resulting from actors' construction and negotiation of their interpretations. In the realm of methodology, there is a logical corollary of the theory of a social world as constructed through its members' interactions and as intrinsically meaningful. This is a theory of its cognitive availability through the participation in the construction of its meaning. Here the notion of the researcher's participation in the subjects' activities replaces the notion of their simple observation as the main data-yielding procedure. In interpretative sociology, the discussion of the epistemological problems of and reasons for the researcher's participation as the main data-gathering method (Cicourel 1964; Bruyn 1966; Blumer 1969; Filmer et al. 1972; Spradley 1980) has replaced the former discussion of the methodological problems of comparison. It has done so to such an extent that the comparative research is not even broached and the word comparison itself has completely disappeared from the vocabulary of methodological discourse: a subject index in which 'participant observation' is a prominent entry does not even list 'comparison'. The fact that these two terms appear to be mutually exclusive indicates a complete shift of emphasis from sociological generalization to adequate description.

The effort is directed not at what to do with what we know about particular societies and cultures so that we learn more about society and culture in general but rather at making explicit how the researcher has come to know what he claims to know about a particular society or culture. This development has been fully paralleled in anthropology. The emphasis on adequate description of culturally specific cognitive worlds and a retreat from cross-cultural generalizations about cognitive systems has characterized the whole development of cognitive anthropology. The description and analysis of people's cognitive worlds has, over the last 25 years or so, come to be recognized as an aim in itself, so much so that methods adopted specifically for this purpose were heralded as the 'new ethnography' (Sturtevant 1964: 99, 101; see Colby 1966). Analyses aimed at understanding a culture 'internally' (Hanson 1975), 'in its own terms' (Geertz 1973) or 'from the actor's point of view' (Cancian 1975; Basso and Selby 1976) have characterized most of symbolic or semantic anthropology, resulting again in the proliferation of descriptions and analyses of particular societies and cultures.

Underlying the anthropologists' current preoccupation with the culturally specific meaning is the awareness that anthropologists are not 'neutral scientists collecting unambiguous data' and that the people they are studying are not 'living among various unconscious systems of determining forces of which they have no clue' (Rabinow 1977: 152), and to which only the anthropologists holds the key. Rabinow adds: 'Anthropological facts are cross-cultural, because they are made into facts during the process of questioning, observing and experiencing — which both the anthropologist and the people with whom he lives engage in' (p. 152). This notion of facts as joint constructions of the anthropologist and the people studied has shaped the current methodological discussion in anthropology: it concentrates distinctly on the epistemological problems of anthropological fieldwork and on the role of the anthropologist's own experience as the source of his knowledge of the studied culture. There is now a wealth of personal accounts of fieldwork which address themselves to these issues (Read 1965; Kimball and Watson 1972; Beteille and Madan 1975; Okely 1975; Rabinow 1977; Cesara 1982; see also Ellen 1984: 87—132; similar issues have been addressed by other social scientists: Kaplan 1964: 141ff.; Wilson 1970; Phillips 1971; 1973: 164; Phillipson 1972).

The basic methodological problems of the discipline are thus markedly different from those of the 1950s and 1960s. Then it was generalization through comparison that was problematic, now it is description. What is seen as the basic methodological problem at a given time is, of course, a reflection of what is seen as the objective of empirical research. In the 1950s and 1960s, it was to formulate universally valid generalizations; currently the emphasis is placed on producing accounts of specific cultures which do not alter the cultural reality studied through the imposition of criteria external to it.

These days, a great proportion of empirical research is distinctly non-comparative. This is probably most clearly visible in cognitive anthropology. If anything, it is methods of research that are compared rather than its substantive results. The practice of anthropology parallels here clearly the methodological concern with description and the disregard for comparative generalizations. One of the reasons for this shyness of comparison stems from the fact that comparative research has obviously lost the function of theory testing which it had for the positivists. The importance attached to comprehending the actors' meanings, experiences and views of reality brings into question all a priori definitions and hypotheses. In consequence, the role of fieldwork is no longer seen as that of testing theory as rather generating 'grounded theory' (Glaser and Strauss 1967), which instead of forcing data into preconceived analytical categories, mobilizes as a research tool the categories which the actors themselves use to order their experience. If the theory generated in anthropological fieldwork is grounded, it cannot be tested by the application of the criteria which the scientific community has itself devised for this purpose; it can only be tested against the experience of the community of people during the actual process of data gathering.

The high value ascribed to non-comparative analytical description reflects the redifinition of anthropology as an interpretative humanity concerned with cultural specificity and cultural diversity, rather than as a generalizing science. Instead of explaining general processes, it is interested in culturally specific processes of meaning construction, thereby emulating the methodology of historiography and developing in a direction urged upon it by Evans-Pritchard a long time ago.

Another reason for the retreat from comparison is practical. The concern with ethnographic specificity has produced data which in their quality of detail differ considerably from those with which anthropologists worked some twenty years ago. The accumulation of more and more detailed data makes general comparison much less feasible. Needham clearly stated this problem in his discussion of the study of kinship terminologies: 'while analysis is made more exact, comparison is made more intricate and difficult' (1974: 60). He himself sees the increased difficulty of comparison as 'a price that simply has to be paid' (Needham 1975: 358). Not everybody nowadays seems to be prepared to pay the price and the line between comparativists and non-comparativists (Köbben 1970) is probably more sharply drawn than ever before.

STYLES OF COMPARISON

Comparative research in positivistic anthropology varied considerably in the scope of comparison (regional or global) but it was basically unitary in terms of its objectives and methods. This is not the case of comparative research today: it differs both in its objectives and methods to such an extent that at least three different styles of comparison are discernible.

Comparison Establishing Functional Correlations

This type of comparison shares the objectives and methods of the comparative research in positivistic anthropology: its aim is to generate or test hypotheses through establishing functional correlations between variables treated as objective facts that differentiate one type of society from another. Why should this type of comparison continue? Methodological inertia, belief that any comparison is better than no comparison may be the reasons as well as the conviction that decontextualization of the phenomena compared is inevitable and that it is a fair price to pay for the knowledge gained in the move from description to generalization.

The unending attraction of this type of comparison indicates that if there is a paradigmatic shift in anthropology, it is a gradual one. While the notion of social facts as things is explicitly denied in analytical descriptions of particular cultures, it is tacitly acknowleged in the practice of comparative research. And similarly, though it may be true that the search for the functions of social and cultural phenomena has been replaced by the search for their meanings in the analyses of particular cultures, the concept of function informs much of the cross-cultural comparison (see for example Goody 1976).

In its turn, this situation indicates that if the paradigmatic shift is to be completed, the methodological attention given to the problems of adequate description needs to be counterbalanced by addressing the methodological problems of the role of comparison in generating adequate generalizations.

Cross-cultural Comparison Facilitating Description

I suggested that the demands imposed on description in positivistic anthropology derived basically from the wish to generalize through comparison, i.e. from what was perceived as the goal of any science, anthropology included. The descriptive analysis of one society and its cross-cultural comparison were informed by the same assumptions about the nature of the reality studied. As long as the phenomena studied were conceptualized as social facts existing independently of the way actors defined them, they did not change in any way whether they were seen as aspects of a single culture or of many. They were universally found, 'concretely' fixed objects. Moreover, comparison was a logical extension of description in that the two kinds of investigation had basically the same purpose, namely to establish a relationship between variables. As long as the analysis was not concerned with the meaning that the relation between the variables has for the participants or with how it bears on their experience, the problems of the comparative study of variables were merely technical ones; no epistemological problems were involved in the move from studies relating A to B in one culture to studies relating A to B cross-culturally.

When concerned with the relation of A to B, our analysis is now informed by the realization that A and B are not simply objective social facts separated from the defining activities of the actors but that they exist in any meaningful sense insofar as they are constructed and sustained by acts of interpretation. We begin from an analysis of the experience and meanings of the actors themselves and focus our attention on the processes through which social definitions arise, are sustained and change. Rather than studying, for example, '"sex-roles" — the differential participation of men and women in social, economic, political and religious institutions' (Ortner and Whitehead 1981: 1) in one culture, or cross-culturally, on the assumption that we know what 'men' and 'women' are (i.e. by treating them as given or natural objects), we are now primarily concerned with how gender and sexuality are conceptualized in a specific culture, how categories 'male' and 'female' are culturally constructed. We ask 'what male and female, sexual reproduction, *mean* in given social and cultural contexts, rather than assuming that we know what they mean in the first place' (Ortner and Whitehead 1981: 1).

The aim of much comparative research now being undertaken is to facilitate our understanding of such culturally specific meanings, i.e. to identify or bring into focus cultural specificity. This constitutes a complete reversal of the relationship between description and comparison in positivistic anthropology where the ultimate purpose of any description was to collect data for cross-cultural comparison. One of the important purposes of cross-cultural comparison now is to facilitate the definition of the culturally specific so that it may be fully understood. Barnes's paper in this volume is specifically concerned with this problem. I read in this way also, for example, Marilyn Strathern's comparisons of Hagen and Wiru gender constructions aimed at showing that womanness in these two societies has not only different symbolic content but that there is also difference in the techniques of symbolic construction. In her Malinowski lecture (1981), in which she was directly concerned with generalization and comparison, she pointed out that the focus of comparative analysis cannot be objects (not even objects 'so generally defined as "women's wealth"') but must be the processes through which the objects are given cultural value, i.e. the cultural logic through which they are constructed. In a similar way, Parkin's comparative study of the Mijikenda and Luo marriage patterns (1980) is aimed at describing the cultural logic through which the separation or non-separation of uxorial and childbirth payments is linked with the negotiability or non-negotiability of women's roles as wives and mothers and daughters and sisters.

Cultures of course would not be different if they were not built on different cultural logics. In consequence, this kind of comparison cannot achieve anything else than to posit difference; it has an heuristic rather than an explanatory value. It is a more explicit, self-conscious and systematic version of implicit comparison which is the basis of all cognition.

What this comparison shares with comparison establishing functional correlations is the identification of units of comparison as objects, forms or analytic rather than semantic domains (Schneider 1965) (gender, marriage payments, etc.). It differs, however, from that other type in that its objective is not to establish correlations of these forms and objects with other forms and objects, but rather to elucidate the processes of their construction or the cultural logic through which they are endowed with their culturally specific meaning. Any correlation between variables which is established in cross-cultural comparison (e.g. co-variation of marriage payments, filiation and divorce in Parkin's analysis) is not an end in itself in the sense of establishing what is then to be explained. It is only a means to an end, i.e. a step on the way to the description of the processes through which the variables acquire their cultural meanings.

The difference between the two types of comparison can be expressed not only in the difference of their objectives but also in the difference of what is being compared: in the former type of comparison it is the objects presupposed to be similar both in their form and meaning, in the latter type it is objects similar in form but presupposed to be different in meaning.

The difference in the objectives of the two styles of comparison, as well as in the presuppositions about the similarity and difference in the objects compared, accounts for the fact that generalizations can be arrived at through the first type of comparison but that the second one can lead only to the highlighting of cultural specificity. In this respect, comparative endeavour of the second type has more in common with non-comparative analytic description than with comparison aimed at establishing correlations between variables. It too is an enterprise embedded in the conceptualization of social anthropology as an interpretative humanity concerned with cultural specificity and diversity rather than as a generalizing science concerned with cultural and social universals (for a discussion of the role of comparison in describing ontologies incommensurable to our own, see Overing's paper in this volume).

Intra-cultural Comparison

Intra-cultural comparison reverses the assumptions underlying the attempt to compare processes of meaning construction between cultures. Instead of comparing similar forms, objects or constructs in two or more cultures with the objective of elucidating the defining processes through which their meanings are constituted, it compares apparently dissimilar constructs within one culture in an effort to establish to what extent the processes of meaning creation, which underlie them, are similar. Its purpose is not to establish the different cultural logics underlying apparently similar constructs in different cultures but to establish the common cultural logic underlying the analytically or ethically dissimilar constructs in the same culture. Schneider's (1969) study of American culture and Needham's (1962b) analysis of Purum dual symbolic classification, although substantially different in their theoretical orientation, can both be seen as examples of this type of comparison. It is a comparison which is concerned with the creation of similarity out of diversity by imposing native rules of an activity on the diversity of different activities in the studied society (cf. Parkin's paper in this volume).

COMPARISON AND GENERALIZATION IN INTERPRETATIVE ANTHROPOLOGY

I suggested earlier that much contemporary research in anthropology is geared towards the descriptive analysis of specific cultures which is careful not to violate the studied reality through the imposition of criteria of relevance external to it. This concern is indicated not only by the fact that much empirical research is non-comparative but also by the fact that a great deal of comparison is directly concerned with differences, diversity and cultural specificity. Such cross-cultural and intra-cultural comparisons aim to discover the cultural logic that underlies, articulates or generates the observable diversity of cultural forms and patterns. In this respect, they are part of the quest for adequate analytical description rather than cross-culturally valid generalizations.

Comparisons aimed specifically at generating cross-culturally valid generalizations seem to be conspicuous by their absence. In a way this is understandable, for the formulation of such generalizations through comparative research in interpretative anthropology is hampered by one basic problem which did not face the positivists, namely how to guarantee that the culturally specific meanings of phenomena are not altered or violated in the process of comparison by applying our culturally specific models to other peoples (see Hobart's paper in this volume). In practical terms, the problem facing the positivists was how to compare so that the explicit aim of comparison, i.e. to generate or test hypotheses, could be satisfactorily achieved. The problem facing us today is how to recognize and define our units of comparison (Hobart) before making generalizations.

We cannot start by assuming that such units of comparison are substantive variables or the like, for this would merely push us back into the conceptualization of social facts as things. If the theory of social facts as constructions is not to be anulled through comparative practice, it would at first seem that the things compared would have to be the processes of meaning creation themselves. But as these processes are built on different cultural logics in different cultures, it follows that they cannot be the units of comparison either: both in case of the processes of meaning construction and in case of their products we are merely confronted with differences. To carry out the comparison we need a vantage point that is not culturally specific. This has been recognized by those who argue that if comparison is aimed at formulating cross-culturally valid generalizations, its units have to be formal patterns rather than substantive variables. In the introduction to his *Cognitive Anthropology,* Tyler (1969: 15) wrote that 'comparison between systems can only be useful if the facts compared are truly comparable, and we cannot know what facts are comparable until the facts themselves are adequately described. When this is achieved, the units of comparison will be formal features rather than substantive variables'. From a different perspective Needham (1975: 358) argued that the 'consequence of the adoption of polythetic classification in social anthropology is that comparative studies, whether morphological, or functional, or statistical, are rendered more daunting and perhaps even unfeasible' if they are carried out in empirical terms. According to him, 'comparison stands a better and quite different chance of success if it is conducted in formal terms' (p. 356), i.e. in terms of relational 'analytical concepts that were appropriate to the phenomena under consideration but would not be merely derived from them' (Needham 1974: 16). Examples of such concepts he gives as 'symmetry', 'alternation', 'transitivity', 'complementarity', etc. Such concepts 'have formal properties which can be defined in purely formal terms . . . without reference to any classes of entities, however the classes may be composed, or to the characteristic empirical features of their members' (1975: 365). They are terms which 'are not peculiar to any particular linguistic and intellectual tradition, but denote properties which must be discernible (either conceptually or in social practice) by any cultural system of thought'. Alternatively, they 'denote mental proclivities and constraints which are universal to mankind in the fabrication (deliberate or not) of categories and articulatory relationships' (1975: 366).

That units of comparison should be formal features or that comparison should be conducted in formal terms may indeed move us in the direction of a culturally neutral viewpoint. But does not this approach presuppose its own reductionism? Stripped of their respective cultural guises, it is difficult to imagine what might be achieved by comparing 'symmetry' or 'alternation' cross-culturally or indeed how 'symmetry' or 'alternation' could at all be so compared. Should this be possible, however, the likely discovery would be that the culturally specific and particular processes of meaning construction are similar across cultures in being structured by the same formal principles. The above quoted statements therefore suggest that given the requirements of adequate (i.e. indigenously recognizable) description, or, given the polythetic nature of our analytic categories, our generalizations can only be expressed in culturally free formal terms. So expressed, they can only be generalizations about the formal features of universal cognitive processes.

This accepted, both styles of comparison carried out in interpretative anthropology can play their role in generating such generalizations for, although specifically geared towards description, they are at the same time generalizing. Schneider's comparative study of kinship, nationality and religion in American culture (1969) has shown that they are articulated by the cultural logic of symbols which unite the domains of nature and law, and by similar meanings carried in each of them by different epitomizing symbols that are transformations of one another. Parkin, although dealing with different ethnographic data, is very close to Schneider's position in his view that the restricted ranges of variation in the marriage pattern of the Luo and Mijikenda 'represent different transformations of a particular paradigm of concepts' (Parkin 1980: 199).

In one case, we have a generalization about the similarities in the structuring of different domains of the same culture, in the other one, a generalization about the similarities in the structuring of the same domain in different but regionally adjacent cultures. The next logical step is to move to a yet higher level of abstraction and to formulate the principles which articulate the observable similarity of structuring. This can be done in two ways: by formulating either (a) the cognitive categories which seem to be universally applied in the processes of meaning construction, or (b) the formal logical principles which interrelate the basic cognitive categories, whatever those may be. Any of these ways moves anthropology towards a direct concern with the processes of human cognition which, it would appear, has to be its ultimate concern if it does not want to give up its aspirations to becoming a generalizing discipline.

COMPARISON: CONTEMPORARY PROBLEMS

None of the papers in this volume is specifically concerned with the problem of formulating generalizations through comparison and none of them advocates the hard-core positivistic approach typified in comparative studies by search for statistical correlation among analytically defined categories, still manifest in the work of many American anthropologists using the data assembled in Murdock's *Human Relations Area File*. All the papers also clearly indicate that equally out of fashion is global comparison; many of them (Parkin, Peel, Barnes, Fardon, Barnard) put explicit emphasis on regional comparison.

Although the differing theoretical orientation of the papers assembled here leads to a different perception of the main problems of comparative research, all authors start from the acceptance of the fact that there is no field of empirical inquiry which does not use comparative analysis. This view, expressed by Peel in his paper, is echoed in different ways in most of the others (Barnes, Burnham, Howe, etc.). The problem of comparison turns on the problem of translation (Hobart) and all our analysis is ultimately comparative in that we have to translate to be able to describe (Overing). As Peel points out, comparison is implicit in any method of deriving understanding through explanation. In this endeavour, anthropologists are involved in a kind of comparison which is similar to that underlying our everyday judgement and decisions (Parkin) or to comparison in which every academic discipline (and everyone else) indulges when theorizing about the world.

The specific problems of this type of comparison derive from the fact that the main objective of the comparative method is no longer that of testing hypotheses but rather that of identifying or highlighting cultural specificity. This change can be seen as logically following the move from the assumption of social facts as things to their conceptualization as constructions. The same kind of move can be expressed as that from the interest in function to the interest in meaning, or a move from social structure to culture, as being the object of anthropological investigation and the consequent refusal to treat culture as a dependent variable (Peel).

Irrespective of the way in which the shift is conceptualized, or which aspect of it is stressed, the use of comparison in contemporary anthropology is more akin to the unselfconscious, commonsensical comparison of everyday judgement than to the formal, cross-cultural comparison of analytically defined variables. This being so, it also shares with everyday judgement its lack of rigour, which is often seen as stultifying (Overing).

Both comparisons underlying everyday judgement and those to which we resort as anthropologists are specific to our purposes at hand, i.e. to what we see as problems on which we want to shed some light. As these purposes differ from one analysis to another, the very notion of similarity and difference which underlies any comparison cannot be stipulated *a priori.* As Howe and Hobart argue, relations of similarity and difference are not given in the empirical phenomena themselves but are generated by people who act on them and decide, using criteria of their own choosing, to which class, category or concept they conform. The process of comparison, by virtue of the fact that certain criteria are selected to the exclusion of others, creates or establishes relations of similarity and difference in the first place. It also inevitably reifies constructs (Fardon).

In the process of the creation of similarity and difference, we are increasingly sensitive to differences. This is perhaps as it should be, for as Boon convincingly argues, cultures, like languages can only be known contrastively (1982: 136). The reasons are that to experience a culture 'as a culture' requires firstly that it materialize in contradistinction to another culture, and secondly that such comparison does not reduce cultures to platitudinous similarity but situates them apart as equally significant systems of differences (p. ix). Such comparison has to be one oriented towards the discovery of cultural logic that underlies, articulates or generates the observable diversity of cultural forms and patterns. On this point there is a remarkable degree of consensus among all the contributors to this volume. They also all agree on the scope of comparison deemed as useful or desirable. As already mentioned, none of them advocates systematic world-wide comparison of analytically defined variables and all of them concentrate on the problems of comparison between closely related cultures or comparison within a specific region.

Disagreement emerges with regard to how the observable diversity or variation should be conceptualized. On the one hand, it can be conceptualized as surface transformations of the underlying structure or set of rules which are presupposed to possess a generative capacity; the separation of essence from appearance and the stipulation of a hierarchical relationship between the two underlies this conceptualization. Layton is seeking some kind of such structure in his attempt to grapple with the meaning of prehistoric rock paintings — understandable enough, given that the analyst has no other access to the meaning the paintings might possible have had for their creators. Underlying structure is also postulated in Barnard's analysis in which the concept of transformation plays an important explanatory role. The main question which has to be asked of these approaches concerns the existential status of such structure: is the anthropologist creating it in his effort to account for the observable variation or can it be suposed to exist independently of his effort? Those whose analysis stays close to everyday comparative judgement stress the need to pay more attention to the question of the manner in which the formal relations of the postulated structure are recognized and talked about by the actors themselves (Parkin). In their view, unless the analyst pays sufficient attention to this problem, we cannot eliminate the possibility that he is himself creating structures to accommodate variation.

The view that comparative analysis should stay close to everyday comparative judgement is most clearly expressed by Parkin in his insistence that variations need not be seen as variations on a theme or as variations on one another: instead of conceptualizing them as systematic transformations of an underlying structure, he suggests that we treat them as chain-like sequences representing endless possible perspectives which are the manifestation of cultural creativity. That such creativity is in itself irreducible has been most forcefully expressed by Overing and Hobart and is a view to which Howe and Burnham also subscribe. Peel advocates the view that histories rather than structures should be compared; in assuming continuity rather than structural transformation, his analysis is closer to those which see no need to give the idea of a theme any specific status as underlying essence. So is Barnes's discussion of colour terms which does not presuppose any abstract scheme of formal logical relations; so too, in a different way, is Fardon's discussion of ethnicity which seizes upon the notion of the actors' view of the world as fully embedded in practice. Those who insist on the heuristic value of the concept of underlying structure (see especially Barnard's paper) point out that without the assumption of an underlying structure, which alone enables us to fix the similar in relation to the observable variability, we have no way of telling what is specific to particular cultural creativity and to particular cultural logic.

The notion of the generative power of underlying structure as well as the notion of culture as discourse or endless perspectives are presuppositions which the analyst adopts to make sense of the data which he seeks to explain. No analysis is possible without such presuppositions, and ultimately the reader has to judge for himself to what extent the differing presuppositions are justified by the analytical conclusions they yield. Burnham's paper makes it clear that there is an 'as if' notion underlying every analysis — examples are the notion of generative structure and that of endless perspectives. The value of the papers in this volume lies precisely in the fact that the assumptions underlying particular analyses have been made explicit. Only when that is done can the result of the analysis be properly evaluated and the usefulness of the assumptions themselves scrutinized. It seems that for some time to come both basic assumptions will be resorted to in comparative analyses. Those who prefer to see variations as endless perspectives point out that the notion of the generative power of the underlying structure can be rescued from its rigid formalism when more attention is paid to the way the actors themselves conceptualize, use, manipulate and interpret the phenomena which the structure is assumed to generate. Those who advocate the necessity of the notion of an underlying structure point out that endless perspectives are in fact finite and that only some perspectives from the endless multitude of the possible ones are adopted. To account for that, some notion of structural regularity has to be enetertained. The limitation on perspectives can be accounted for by discovering the structuring principles which have been recognized by any particular culture in question. Both sets of assumptions can thus become more useful if more consistent attention is paid to the notions of the actors themselves.

It seems that it is in this area of problems that comparative research plays its most prominent role today; of necessity this is also where the major problems of comparative analysis lie. This clearly suggests that the contemporary problems of comparison in social anthropology are neither methodological nor technical but epistemological: namely, the relationship to each other of structure and agency. In this respect, comparison in social anthropology is distinctly different from the comparative method as it was conceptualized some twenty years ago.

REFERENCES

Basso, K. H. and H. A. Selby (eds). 1976. *Meaning in Anthropology*. Albuquerque: University of New Mexico Press.

Beteille, A. and T. N. Madan. 1976. *Encounter and Experience: personal account of fieldwork*. Delhi: Vikas Publishing House.

Blumer, H. 1969. *Symbolic Interactionism*. Englewood Cliffs, New Jersey: Prentice-Hall.

Boon, J. A. 1982. *Other Tribes, Other Scribes: symbolic anthropology in the comparative study of cultures, histories, religions and texts*. Cambridge: Cambridge University Press.

Bruyn, S. 1966. *The Human Perspective in Sociology*. Englewood Cliffs, New Jersey: Prentice-Hall.

Cancian, F. 1975. *What are Norms?* Cambridge: Cambridge University Press.

Cesara, M. 1982. *No Hiding Place: reflections of a woman anthropologist*. London: Academic Press.

Cicourel, A. 1964. *Method and Measurement in Sociology*. New York: Free Press.

Colby, B. N. 1966. Ethnographic semantics: a preliminary survey. *Current Anthropology* 7: 20—23.

Colson, E. 1967. The intensive study of small sample communities. In *The Craft of Social Anthropology* (ed.) A. L. Epstein. London: Tavistock.

Crick, M. 1976. *Explorations in Language and Meaning: towards a semantic anthropology*. London: Malaby Press.

Dolgin, J. L., D. S. Kemnitzer and D. M. Schneider (eds). 1977. *Symbolic Anthropology: a reader in the study of symbols and meanings*. New York: Columbia University Press.

Douglas, J. D. 1971. *Understanding Everyday Life: toward the reconstruction of sociological knowledge*. London: Routledge and Kegan Paul.

Driver, H. E. 1953. Statistics in anthropology. *American Anthropologist* 55: 42—59.

—— 1973. Cross-cultural studies. In *Handbook of Social and Cultural Anthropology* (ed.) J. J. Honigman. Chicago: Rand McNally.

Durkheim, E. 1964. *The Rules of Sociological Method*. New York: Free Press.

Eggan, F. 1954. Social anthropology and the method of controlled comparison. *American Anthropologist* 56: 743—63.

Ellen, R. F. (ed.). 1984. *Ethnographic Research: a guide to general conduct*. ASA Research methods in Social Anthropology 1. London: Academic Press.

Evans-Pritchard, E. E. 1951. *Social Anthropology*. London: Cohen and West.

—— 1965. The comparative method in social anthropology. In *The Position of Women in Primitive Societies and Other Essays in Social Anthropology*. London: Faber.

Filmer, P., M. Phillipson, D. Silverman, D. Walsh. 1972. *New Directions in Sociological Theory*. London: Collier-Macmillan.

Garfinkel, H. 1967. *Studies in Ethnomethodology*. Englewood Cliffs, New Jersey: Prentice-Hall.

Geertz, C. 1973. *The Interpretation of Cultures*. London: Hutchinson.

Glaser, B. G. and A. L. Strauss. 1967. *The Discovery of Grounded Theory: Strategies for Qualitative Research*. New York: Aldine.

Goodenough, W. H. 1970. *Description and Comparison in Cultural Anthropology*. Cambridge: Cambridge University Press.

Goody, J. 1976. *Production and Reproduction: a comparative study of the domestic domain*. Cambridge: Cambridge University Press.

Hanson, F. A. 1975. *Meaning in Culture*. London: Routledge and Kegan Paul.

Jorgensen, J. G. 1979. Cross-cultural comparisons. *Annual Review of Anthropology* 8: 309—31.

Kaplan, A. 1964. *The Conduct of Inquiry: methodology for behavioural science*. San Francisco: Chandler.

Kimball, S. and J. Watson. 1972. *Crossing Cultural Boundaries: the anthropological experience*. San Francisco: Chandler.

Köbben, A. J. F. 1952. New ways of presenting an old idea: the statistical method in social anthropology. *Journal of the Royal Anthropological Institute* 82: 129—146.

—— 1970. Comparativists and non-comparativists in anthropology. In *A Handbook of*

Method in Cultural Anthropology (eds) R. Naroll and R. Cohen. New York: Columbia University Press.

Kuhn, T. 1970. *The Structure of Scientific Revolutions*. Chicago: University of Chicago Press.

Leach, E. R. 1950. Review of G. P. Murdock: *Social Structure*. *Man* 50: 107—8 (No. 169).

—— 1965. Comment. *Current Anthropology* 5: 299.

Naroll, R. and R. Cohen (eds). 1970. *Handbook of Method in Cultural Anthropology*. New York: Columbia University Press.

Needham, R. 1962a. Notes on comparative method and prescriptive alliance. *Bijdragen tot de Taal-, Land- en Volkenkunde* 118: 160—82.

—— 1962b. *Structure and Sentiment: a test case in social anthropology*. Chicago: University of Chicago Press.

—— 1974. *Remarks and Inventions: skeptical essays about kinship*. London: Tavistock.

—— 1975. Polythetic classification: convergence and consequences. *Man* (N.S.) 10: 349—69.

Okely, J. 1975. The self and scientism. *Journal of the Anthropological Society of Oxford* 6: 171—88.

Ortner, S. B. and H. Whitehead. 1981. Accounting for sexual meanings. Introduction to *Sexual Meanings: the cultural construction of gender and sexuality*. Cambridge: Cambridge University Press.

Parkin, D. 1980. Kind bridewealth and hard cash: eventing a structure. In *The Meaning of Marriage Payments* (ed.) J. L. Comaroff. London. Academic Press.

—— (ed.). 1982. *Semantic Anthropology*. A.S.A. Monograph 22. London: Academic Press.

Phillips, D. L. 1971. *Knowledge from what?: theories and methods in social research*. Chicago: Rand McNally.

—— 1973. *Abandoning Method*. San Francisco: Jossey Bass Publishers.

Phillipson, M. 1972. Theory, methodology and conceptualization. In P. Filmer et al., *New Directions in Sociological Theory*. London: Collier-Macmillan.

Rabinow, P. 1977. *Reflections on Fieldwork in Morocco*. Berkeley: University of California Press.

Radcliffe-Brown, A. R. 1951. The comparative method in social anthropology. *Journal of the Royal Anthropological Institute* 81: 15—22.

Read, K. 1965. *The High Valley*. New York: Scribner's.

Sarana, G. 1975. *The Methodology of Anthropological Comparisons*. Tucson: University of Arizona Press.

Schapera, I. 1953. Some comments on comparative method in social anthropology. *American Anthropologist* 55: 353—62.

Schneider, D. M. 1965. American kin terms and terms for kinsmen: a critique of Goodenough's componential analysis of Yankee terminology. In *Formal Semantic Analysis* (ed.) E. A. Hammel. *American Anthropologist* 67, Part 2, Special Publication.

—— 1969. Kinship, nationality and religion in American culture: toward a definition of kinship. In *Forms of Symbolic Action* (ed.) R. F. Spencer. Proceedings of the

1969 Annual Spring Meeting of the American Ethnological Society. Seattle: University of Washington Press.

Silverman, D. 1972. Methodology and meaning. In P. Filmer et al., *New Directions in Sociological Theory*. London: Collier-Macmillan.

Spradley, J. P. 1980. *Participant observation*. New York: Holt, Rinehart and Winston.

Steiner, F. 1951. Review of G. P. Murdock: *Social Structure*. *British Journal of Sociology* 2: 366−8.

Strathern, M. 1981. Culture in a netbag: the manufacture of a subdiscipline in anthropology. *Man* (N.S.) 16: 665−88.

Stryker, S. 1980. *Symbolic Interactionism*. Menlo Park, California: Benjamin/Cummings Publishing Co.

Sturtevant, W. 1964. Studies in ethnoscience. In *Transcultural Studies in Cognition* (eds) A. K. Romney and R. G. D'Andrade. *American Anthropologist* 66, No. 3, Part 2, Special Publication.

Tyler, S. A. 1969. Introduction to *Cognitive Anthropology*. New York: Holt, Rinehart and Winston.

Wilson, B. R. (ed.). 1970. *Rationality*. Oxford: Blackwell.

2

Summer's Days and Salad Days:
The Coming of Age of
Anthropology?

Mark Hobart

Shall I compare thee to a summer's day?
Thou art more lovely and more temperate:
Rough winds do shake the darling buds of May,
And summer's lease hath all too short a date . . .
Shakespeare, Sonnet XVIII

In dingy stores in the shadier streets of Singapore, for a few dollars over the counter, one used to be able to obtain a small bottle from the Chinese pharmacopoeia. It contained a wondrous elixir which could be sniffed, smeared on, or drunk. The label guaranteed its efficacy against all manner of ills, including (as I recall) old age, typhoid, cholera, headaches, kidney failure, sexual impotence, constipation and flatulence. To obtain the intellectual equivalent fortunately one need not go to the corners of the earth — indeed this is liable to bring the panacea into disrepute — it is available at one's local department of anthropology, without prescription. If learned and inwardly digested, the comparative method claims to solve the myriad problems of man in society by mulching them into suitable pap for consumption or for the lustration of later generations.

Non-anthropologists might wonder what all the fuss is about. What is so special about comparison? Briefly, it underpins — explicitly or implicitly — almost all the ways of talking about other cultures. Whether we study agriculture or food, narrative or myth, Divinity or witches, we are comparing our popular or technical categories with other peoples'. Analysis in terms of economic 'infra-structures' or self-interest assumes the shared reality of production or the utilitarian nature of human action. Discussions of 'political systems' presuppose the generality of systems and that forms of power are comparable. 'Ritual', 'religion' and similar terms commonly imply universal

criteria of rationality by which to distinguish true knowledge from symbols or ideology.

So what is wrong with comparing? The answer is that it depends on what one understands by comparing and how one uses it. The trouble is that the comparative method is linked to claims that anthropology should be 'scientific'. Unfortunately recent debate suggests not only that science is often not scientific, but also that it is not facts we compare, but discourses, each with their own presuppositions. Exporting our models has serious and insidious implications for how we understand, talk about and treat other peoples. As a method in anthropology, comparison tends to confuse several distinct processes and overlook the degree to which comparison and translation are acts on the part of the analyst which involve culturally available alternatives. Anthropology also faces the curious problem that our categories are 'second-order', as they depend on (possibly incommensurable) native discourses. So analysis may require multiple perspectives — a sort of poetic, rather than scientific, realism — and reflection on how discourses overlap. Perhaps we are closer to the poet above who recognizes the implications of his analogies and medium, than we are to neutral scientific observers peddling panaceas.

STONE AGE SCIENCE

Anthropology by its brief is concerned with exploring and, in a sense, 'explaining' variation between societies or cultures. According to a classic view this requires the comparative method. For 'without systematic comparative studies anthropology will become only historiography and ethnography. Sociological theory must be based on, and continually tested by, systematic comparison.' (Radcliffe-Brown 1958a: 110) Comparison is viewed as the anthropological equivalent of the controlled experimentation of natural scientists.

For social anthropology the task is to formulate and validate statements about the conditions of existence of social systems (law of social statics) and the regularities that are observable in social change (laws of social dynamics). This can only be done by the systematic use of the comparative method. . . .

(Radcliffe-Brown 1958a: 128)

Social facts are held to have essences discernible independent of observers and frames of reference. Behind such an inductive approach, however, lurk far-from-empirical assumptions about the degree to which societies, systems and facts exist untainted by, or extricable from, rival interpretations, heuristic models and values.

Use of the comparative method is not just a convenience, but is closely linked to the question of whether the subject is a natural science or not, a matter over which there has been much controversy.[1] What then do its proponents understand by science? Even at the time of its proposal, Radcliffe-Brown's vision was an unlikely fossil left over from schoolboy notions of natural science (cf. Losee 1980: 145—220). So, before hailing their subject ('discipline' smacks of an order, a rigour, even a regimentation replete with boots and leather) as scientific, anthropologists might well reflect on changing understandings of what science is. The difficulties in Radcliffe-Brown's simple use of induction, for instance, have been exposed by Popper's critical rationalism; and interest has shifted to evaluating research programmes by results, or to evolving sets of logically coherent theories (Lakatos 1970), although here only the most marginal results are empirically falsifiable (Quine 1953). The wheel has nearly come full circle. Scientists themselves have begun to appear as unwitting subjects of cultural history, ripe for anthropological examination (Feyerabend 1975: 223—85) and their practice as depending on historically specific presuppositions (Collingwood 1940; Kuhn 1962) or on customary ways of solving problems (Kuhn 1977). The anthropologist hoping to play natural scientist may be like an intrepid explorer who sets off to discover new continents only to find himself in his own back garden.

Some habits still linger. Induction relies on a prior judgement as to what will count as similarity, through selecting out 'essential' features from contingent ones. The rest looks spuriously simple:

The postulate of the inductive method is that all phenomena are subject to natural law, and that consequently it is possible, by the application of certain logical methods, to discover and prove certain general laws, i.e., certain general statements or formulae, of greater or less degree of generality, each of which applies to a certain range of facts or events.

(Radcliffe-Brown 1958b: 7)

The reference to natural law begs the question of the basis of regularity, but the method yields apparent results by having already classified the 'facts' (particulars). Unfortunately, as Barnes has pointed out, in the world

there are no clearly identical, indistinguishable particulars to cluster together. For all the complexity and richness of language, experience is immeasurably more complex, and richer in information. Physical objects and events are never self-evidently identical or possessed of *identical essences*.

(B. Barnes 1982: 28, my emphasis)

The comparative method draws attention away from how the data (note these are 'given') to be compared are constituted in the first place. One may postulate a realm of ('etic') social facts independent of indigenous models, but most anthropological data are mongrel, as they involve two discourses and sets of 'learned similarity relations' (Kuhn 1977: 307−19). So it is far from straightforward to tell to what ostensible regularities are due. The passion for general laws involves an appeal to a stone age notion of natural science which in the meantime has arguably become more concerned with uniqueness and 'exciting particularities' (Ions 1977: 9).

STEAM AGE SCIENCE

These difficulties have led to a new scientism — rationalist rather than empiricist — structuralism. The certainty of fact is replaced with assumptions about how mind classifies experience by virtue of its innate structure. The relation of comparison and general laws is reversed, as ethnography reveals how mind (both as genus and species) constrains cultural possibility.

In anthropology as in linguistics, therefore, it is not comparison that supports generalization, but the other way around. If . . . the unconscious activity of the mind consists in imposing form on content, and if these forms are fundamentally the same for all minds — ancient and modern, primitive and civilized . . . it is necessary and sufficient to grasp the unconscious structure underlying each institution and each custom in order to obtain a principle of interpretation valid for other institutions. . . .

(Lévi-Strauss 1968a: 21)

There are some big 'ifs' here. The fundamental laws of culture reduce to the unconscious structuring of mind; and structure is the necessary and sufficient condition of human neural organization. Ethnographic evidence no longer underwrites generalization: rather comparative work confirms the universal working of mind.

To its detriment, the argument presupposes a classification of relevant facts; and 'mind' is treated as an entity independent of the contexts of its activity. 'Structure' also has several potentially different senses. It may be anatomically or physiologically neural (so producing 'structure' as form or as process); it may refer to ideals, rules or regularities in society (vaguely conceived); or a *pot-au-feu* of the lot known as an 'underlying structure' — an obscure, transcendental and largely unfalsifiable notion. We do not need such postulates to account for what people say and do anyway (Bourdieu 1977). As Ions put it succinctly, we are dealing with 'Positivism in the French mould'

(1977: 135).[2] The argument for comparing structures based on the universality of the human mind is circular (1977: 138—9). As the notion of structure begs the question, it may be tautologically true but uninformative.

How exhaustive and exclusive is a structural explanation of ethnography? Because it seemed to make sense of some of the perplexities of myth, kinship and symbolic dualism, it has been treated, like the Chinese medicine, as a cure-all. It cannot deal, however, with simple utterances like sentences, let alone texts (Ricoeur 1971; 1976), discourse (Foucault 1972; 1979) or style (Donoghue 1981), which depend on predication and implicit presuppositions, except by breaking these down into rudimentary units to be treated as if they were signs (the fallacy of division). If it is not exhaustive, by the same token it is not exclusive. Myth lends itself to subtler analyses (Girard 1978: 178—98; Culler 1981: 169—87); classification may be more sensitively understood (Karim 1981); and the ethnography more fully explicated by recognizing metaphysical presuppositions (Inden 1976; 1985; Overing 1985b). The human mind is more complex and subtle than structuralism can allow.

Sufficient has already been written about the epistemological problems of structuralism that they do not bear repeating.[3] At the best of times reliance on analogic reasoning is problematic (Lloyd 1966: 304—420); and not only does structuralism presuppose criteria of likeness, but things which are analogous are not identical. So comparison in invariably skewed and inaccurate *ab initio*. By admitting only two forms of association (from the 'four master tropes', themselves dubious essences of diverse figures of speech) everything is reduced by a further, and false, dichotomy so that what is not metaphor is *ipso facto* metonymy. If the former covers a multitude of sins, the latter is positively promiscuous (Levin 1977: 80—2). (One might note that metonymy has been linked to scientific reduction and metaphor to poetic realism (Burke 1969: 503—7), in which case Lévi-Strauss tries to have his cake and eat it.) By depending upon the method of division and the choice of concepts and logical operations appropriate to it, the world appears structured in a binary fashion. However, this is not a result of Mind at all, but of the categories allowed in the analysis.[4]

Structuralist analyses are more often the showcase for *virtuoso* prestidigitation than for strict method or ethnographic enlightenment. On a lighter note, one can produce delightful absurdities as easily as purported profundities. For example, Lévi-Strauss's classic analysis of the Oedipus myth (1968b: 206—19) has a 'structure' identical to the Dracula legend, as any afficionado of Hammer Horror films may attest. Briefly, the four themes in Oedipus (1968b: 214—15) are recapitulated in the story of Dracula as follows:

Overrating of	: Underrating of	: : Denial of	: Persistence
blood relations	blood relations	autochthony	of autochthony

Dracula sucks	: Dracula kills	: : Dracula	: Dracula always
victim's blood	victim by	destroyed	rises from
	draining blood	by men	grave again

There is also an interesting 'transformation' in the other classic Gothic tale of Frankenstein (both said to have been originally conceived on the same evening in 1816 beside Lac Léman). The relation of the two structures may be described as follows:

$$a \; : \; b \; : : \; c \; : \; d \qquad \text{becomes} \qquad a \; : \; b \; : : \; e \; : \; f$$

Overrating of	: Underrating of	: : Spontaneous	: Denial of
blood relations/	blood relations/	(male)	spontaneous
affinity	affinity	creation of	creation of
		life	life

Frankenstein	: Frankenstein	: : Frankenstein	: Frankenstein
mixes parts of	kills people	creates life	is himself
humans	to do so	without birth	killed

One could elaborate the details *ad nauseam*. For example, if Frankenstein is Promethean, Dracula is a superlative autochthonous being who returns to his native soil each night and may only be killed by a wooden stake moving downwards, the reversal of the natural (plant) growth of autochthony. The two stories also display the ambiguity in Lévi-Strauss's account of how myths 'resolve contradictions'. Dracula works by providing an alternative to the serious human problem of death, in the still less palatable possibility of becoming an eternal and miserable 'undead', for whom death is a merciful release ('the Asdiwal solution' where Asdiwal's fate is worse than the inconveniences of matrilocality: Lévi-Strauss 1967). Frankenstein resolves the problems of the bodily and social integrity of persons by converting the problem into a less serious and academic one, namely the possibility of exclusively male creation of life ('the Oedipus solution', where a similar problem is converted into a juxtaposition of rival ancient Greek accounts of reproduction. Without too much ingenuity multiple 'oppositions' may be discerned between the two heroes:

Dracula	:	Frankenstein
Destroying life	:	Creating life
Ascribed status	:	Achieved status
Nature carried to excess	:	Culture carried to excess
Anti-Christian as diabolic	:	Anti-Christian as Jewish

If my analysis is trivial or wrong, the onus is on structuralists to provide criteria of method; something they are loth to do, perhaps because such analyses are notoriously idiosyncratic.

INCOHERENCES

'Descriptions of indubitable facts conflict with one another.'
(Pepper 1942: 25)

When we compare, what exactly are we, or should we be, comparing to what? At this point serious problems of the comparative method become apparent. Confusion arises when we imagine we are comparing facts from different cultures instead of comparing frameworks or discourses. As M. Jourdain spoke prose all his life without realizing it, we may have been comparing unawares in a potentially informative manner. First, however, it is necessary to consider what comparison involves and why the common-sense view — that it is facts we compare — is inadequate. In the next section, I consider the dangers in applying standard anthropological discourse to the interpretation of other cultures and conclude by suggesting ways of obviating the difficulties.

The impression that we compare facts assumes that

knowing is tacitly conceived as a processing of raw material into a finished product; and an understanding of knowledge is thus supposed to require that we discover just what the raw material is.
(Goodman 1972: 26)

The corollary of this is that facts do not simply determine theory. Theories are remarkably resilient to contradictory evidence where it rears its ugly head (Quine 1953: 42 ff.) but are wreathed in verisimilitude because

observational reports, experimental results, "factual" statements, either *contain* theoretical assumptions or *assert* them by the manner in which they are used.
(Feyerabend 1975: 31)

To the extent that different theories are incommensurable, so may be their 'facts'.[5]

What then is meant by comparing? In the simplest version it connotes likening, that is 'to speak of or represent as similar', or more specifically 'to mark or point out the similarities and differences of (two or more things)' (*Oxford English Dictionary*, parentheses in the original). There are several separate issues here. Social acts or representations are not things with essences which can be simply abstracted from context. The definition is already discomfiting. Similarity is not sameness; and pointing to similarities begs the question of the criteria anyway. Representing as similar is a commentator's act and is not given in things themselves.

> In representing an object, we do not copy . . . a construal or interpretation — we *achieve* it. In other words, nothing is ever represented either shorn of or in the fullness of its properties. A picture never merely represents x, but rather represents x *as* a man or represents x *to be* a mountain, or represents *the fact that* x is a melon.
>
> (Goodman 1981: 9)

This approach allows one to ask under what conditions people represent something as something else and so bring context and power back into the study of collective representations.

Matters are just as bad if we look at how we establish what things have in common.

> The essential feature it seems would be what one might call a specific experience of comparing and of recognizing. Now it is queer that on closely looking at cases of comparing, it is very easy to see a great number of activities and states of mind, all *more or less* characteristic of the act of comparing. This is in fact so, whether we speak of comparing from memory or of comparing by means of a sample before our eyes. . . . The more such cases we observe and the closer we look at them, the more doubtful we feel about finding one particular mental experience characteristic of comparing.
>
> (Wittgenstein 1969: 86)

If this is so, as Wittgenstein argues for cloth samples, how much more intricate is the kind in which anthropologists indulge? At best we see complex forms of behaviour; more often we deal with interpretations of behaviour and statements about abstractions, like roles, institutions and values.

What then underwrites Radcliffe-Brown's, and others', assuredness that it is facts we compare? Usually it is some assumption about natural law, or the nature of human beings. The antecedents of the former view draw upon the distinction between *phusis* and *nomos*, nature and convention, where natural regularity is unmediated by culture (although 'law' itself is a metaphor from *nomos!*). As Collingwood pointed out as long ago as 1945, inconveniently the conception of these laws has changed at least twice in Western scientific thinking. A subtler version involves the further assumptions that human perception and mutual intelligibility are universal because there is (a) a psychic unity and (b) a necessarily shared rationality of mankind (see Hollis 1970; 1982). Recent variations on this theme include assertions about the generality of 'material-object language' (Horton 1979) and propositional thinking (Sperber 1975; 1982). Both arguments are open to serious criticism (see the contributions in Overing 1985a). Now what would happen if people in other cultures explained regularities or universals in different ways such that it affected their actions and so was not just an issue of interpretation? To consider these questions, we must turn to ethnography.

The explanation of order and accident is a matter of textual and popular concern in Bali. Balinese seem largely to lack a dichotomy between nature and culture: all regularity — be it the seasons, plant or human life, or the pattern of daily existence — is due to Divinity, Ida Sang Hyang Widi Wasa. *Widhi* is 'rule, law, ordering, regulation'; *kawidhi* 'to command, order'; *wasa* 'power, force, dominion'; and *widhiwasa* 'the power of fate or destiny' (Zoetmulder 1982: 2262—3, 2213—14). So this is not a mere name (as Duff-Cooper suggests, 1985: 71) but arguably Divinity *as* order, in the sense both of what orders and the power of order(s) or fate. In another aspect Divinity is the power (*sakti*) available to people to affect one another's lives. So order and power are both determinate of, and yet affected by, human actions. In place of a dichotomy we have overlapping classes, aspects or perspectives on a complex reality.

Where anthropologists are prone to focus on concomitant variation (A. Cohen 1969), Balinese stress the particularities of evolving forms. Everything in the world is changing (*matemahan*) into something else. In this Heraclitean universe regularity is a sign of potential disjuncture or disrupture. Also, concern is less with explaining the normal than the idiosyncratic or unexpected, when chance or fate (*ganti*) operates. Where we stress the regularity of the diurnal cycle, the unending succession of days and nights, Balinese are more struck by the differences between days, and between what happens by day and night. The facts are not in dispute so much as what one makes of them.

The universality of perception — and so the grounding of comparison in identical appreciation of facts — has recently been debated using Balinese materials (Bloch 1977; Bourdillon 1978; Howe 1981). Bloch raises two interesting and important questions: are perceptions of natural process, or time, universal? And how do such perceptions relate to action? There must, he argues, be a difference between culturally specific 'ideologies' and 'knowledge' of a shared reality 'available in all cultures' (1977: 285), a view confirmed by the possibility of communication and translation, and guaranteed by a felicitous conjunction of logic and nature. For a universal 'concept of time' is both logically necessary to language *and* naturally determined (1977: 283, 285). Apart from the startlingly idealist assumption that, if people do not share a cognitive model, they are incapable of registering what happens let alone responding, one does not need a concept of time to act. The assumption that 'linear, irreversible time' is universal and therefore real merely dignifies an ethnocentric spatial metaphor.[6] Far from being radical, as suggested, Bloch's argument is profoundly conservative, embracing an equally dated rationalism and positivist utilitarianism at once. With charming epistemological ingenuousness, its Marxism is fraternal rather than philosophical.

Balinese, in fact, rarely refer to time (*kala*) as the generalized essence of qualitatively different processes, preferring to stress their particular attributes. They explicitly eschew the spatial metaphors their commentators so readily impute to them. Bloch's examples of agriculture and politics serve to make the point. Rice cultivation is not spoken of in terms of cycles; for each differs and has its own entelechy. Nor can one simply treat the ritual 'cycle' as mystifying relations of production in real time because ritual and labour are inter-related in various ways (Hobart 1978). Balinese speak of labour and technology as necessary but not sufficient conditions of successful rice-growing. Cultivation is explained transformationally: labour, raw materials and technology must be controlled to produce an appropriate outcome, instantiated in one form in ritual. So the use of odd-looking things like torch batteries as fertilizer (see *sari* below) is justified by a processual paradigm, quite different from, but just as workable as, a model of material causation.

Public politics in Bali has been claimed to be a form of theatre (Geertz 1980), which contrasts with 'real' power relations (Bloch 1977: 284). This rests on a mistaken, if suggestive, importation of metaphor. Balinese ideas of the relation of theatre or performance and reality differ sharply from ours. The relation of public and private politics is often expressed in the image of puppets and shadow puppeteer, just as the style of political negotiation draws upon the tactics of royal statecraft. 'Practical' goals are as culturally mediated as are 'symbolic' ones (Durkheim 1933: 200–19; Parkin 1976: 163–74). The semblance of comparability comes from imposing alien metaphors and metaphysics on unsuspecting others.[7] Like those gentlemen who live off ladies of easy virtue in other streets in Singapore, it brings in a good living but does little more than pander to depraved, or perhaps deprived, tastes.

It should be evident how uninformative it is to talk about facts free from observers or commentators. For, frames of reference . . . seem to belong less to what is described than to systems of description. . . . If I ask about the world, you can offer to tell me how it is under one or more frames of reference; but if I insist that you tell me how it is apart from all frames, what can you say? We are confined to ways of describing whatever is described. Our universe, so to speak, consists of these ways rather than of a world or of worlds.

(Goodman 1978: 2–3)

If we are not simply comparing facts, on what does the feasibility and intellectual coherence of comparison rest?

Philosophers sometimes mistake features of discourse for features of the subject of discourse. . . . Coherence is a characteristic of descriptions, not of the world: the significant question is not whether the world is coherent, but whether our account is. . . . What we must face is the fact that even the truest description comes nowhere near faithfully reproducing the way the world is . . . (no true description) tells us *the* way the world is, but each of them tells us *a* way the world is.

(Goodman 1972: 24, 29, 31)

So we are comparing, not facts or the world, but descriptions or discourses. Does it then follow that, in comparing 'data' structured according to different frameworks, we are involved in a kind of category mistake? It is to this issue I now turn.

IMPORTANT ARSENALS

Comparing is one of several ways of relating attributes or things — preselected by some (often implicit) criterion — like contrasting, illustrating, elucidating, weighing, evaluating and representing. We also compare differences, illuminate by contrast, elucidate by analogy and so on.[8] Comparison is sometimes used of relating things which differ in degree but are of the same kind; and contrast where they differ in kind but have some similarity of degree (e.g. Crabb 1974: 178). This is inadequate, however, where neither classification into kinds nor the distinction between degree and kind can be assumed. The problem is related to the traditional difference between what is distinct — ideas, concepts, or values which are discrete and differ — and what is opposite — where categories overlap. The qualities of being just, generous or courageous are distinct; good and bad are opposites and may be related dialectically. Whether differences are of degree or of kind depends on the style of analysis being carried out (see Collingwood 1933: 26 ff.). Whatever their personal proclivities, anthropologists are not justified in jumping to assumptions about how such categories are viewed in other cultures. The relationship between the analyst's and the actors' classifications of the world in any instance should not be decided *a priori*.

Although anthropologists observe behaviour, more than is often credited depends on native statements in interpreting what constitutes significant behaviour and in defining the relevant context before such statements can be checked against the observer's constructions of the behaviour. In other words, we relate indigenous and anthropological systems of description or discourse. So much is obvious. What may be less so are the preconstraints and presuppositions of the technical arsenal we bring to bear. When we invoke the language of social structure, systems of relations, institutions, symbols, beliefs and collective representations, we must watch out for what we assume for ourselves and our informants, in so doing. Two simple questions come to mind. How do the observer's categories relate to indigenous ones? And how does our technical language affect our translations?

Society is often spoken of as 'structured'. Insofar as structure is a feature of discourse we are comparing models of the world. The potential problems emerge in discussions about the Balinese state, which is often said to have a 'feudal', or 'patrimonial' structure. The divergences from Western ideal types are held accountable in terms of economic, local political or symbolic structures (the 'Asiatic mode of production', cross-cutting ties or the 'symbology of power'; see Geertz 1980). Now it is one thing to use Western models to gain insight into Balinese politics, it is another to anticipate indigenous representations.

Some of the problems are plain. Definitions of 'the State' presuppose structure in the first place. Powers are dispersed in all sorts of ways; and the State should perhaps be seen as part of a discourse of contested political claims, as an aspect of social relations, rather than a structure in and of itself (Skillen 1985). Granted the labile and disputed nature of Balinese power relations, it is difficult, even meaningless, to isolate and compare the 'traditional' and modern structures of the State. Political argument in Bali dwells not so much on structure as on whether power flows down from Divinity through an ordered hierarchy or is competitively open to all. So our language of 'kings', 'ministers', 'priests' and 'subjects' is curiously inappropriate to a discourse where the metaphors are not static and material (the State and power as something one holds, has, wields), but are about transformation and the control of change. *Timeo Danaos et dona ferentis.*

As with 'structure', it is easy to assume 'system' — kinship systems, naming systems and so on — where this exists solely in the anthropologist's frame of reference. The rationale for the comparative study of kinship terminology and relations is partly that one can compare different indigenous models of the natural phenomena of human reproduction. So far so good, but it does not necessarily follow either that kinship constitutes 'a discriminable class of phenomena' (Needham 1971: 5), or that ideas of nature are universal. What may be important is not, for instance, the 'biological' events of parturition or the transmission of genetic characteristics, but ideas of substance and causation, of relationship and the moral or cosmological implications of order in a given culture.

Recent work on Bali has rejected attempts to delimit a domain of 'kinship' in favour of contextualizing it as a tension between principles of sociality and sameness of natural kind (Geertz and Geertz 1975: 167), or a cultural debate about the nature, kinds and implications of similarity and difference (Hobart 1980). The point is that kinship neither has, nor ethnographically appears to form, a system. Coherence may be contextual rather than systemic. Another example is the diverse ways in which Balinese name humans and species and which make more sense as a commentary on indigenous notions of social roles or ontology than as a system in itself.[9] Recourse to 'systems' easily leads to misleading imputations of coherence.

The kind of behaviour in which anthropologists are traditionally interested is, in Nadel's famous phrase, 'standardized modes of co-activity', or social institutions, which 'represent both summaries of behaviour and rules for behaviour' (1951: 108, 111).[10] The difference has sometimes been formalized into a distinction variously between jural, ideal ('mechanical') or symbolic models as against action, 'statistical' models or the real (Firth 1964: 43, 45; Lévi-Strauss 1968c: 283—9; and Bloch 1977 respectively). Apart from leaning heavily on an untenable dichotomy between fact and value, this hypostatizes one set of assertions, in a field of potentially conflicting views. Likewise, concern with 'the degree and nature of the standardization visible in the co-activity' (Nadel 1951: 111; a careful empiricist formulation) turns, in structuralism, into a tidy, homogenized and Platonic world of rules which omits indigenous ideas of action, value, rule, intention and so forth. As analysts' constructs, social institutions depend upon native statements and so are not parallel interpretations, but second-order ones. If anthropology is the study of the relations of relations, there is an epistemological disjuncture, or enfolding, of the relations of the culture under study with those of the culture doing the studying.

The vacuity of comparative definitions is illustrated by the institution of marriage (Leach 1961b: 107—8; Rivière 1971). Were it extended to Balinese practices, it would read something like 'an actual or postulated relationship, possibly initiated or recognized by one of a range of rites, involving more than one party, human, animal, plant or otherwise, living or dead in some sense, conferring some or no rights . . . etc.' This rococo phrasing is needed to cover the occasional marriage-like relation of siblings, of people to swords and pigs or slit-gongs to one another. Rather than import an essential 'marriage' and argue the endless exceptions as metaphor, it might be wiser to start with Balinese ideas of the appropriate relation between complementary opposites.[11]

Another example is witchcraft and sorcery. It is interesting how widespread these appear to be. Witchcraft is typically an inversion of the normal or moral order, often attributed to, or passed through, women who fly out at night mystically to attack their enemies; while sorcerers of either sex achieve similar ends by strange, but putatively effective, medicines. The notion of witchcraft, except as a label to be qualified, is a good instance of essentialism on the hoof. For closer inspection shows the imputed generality to be largely a product of our discourse, with its determination to see others through Victorian spectacles as different, savage or reminiscent of our own past.

It is hardly world-shattering if some people dislike, or might benefit from the misfortunes of, others. And determining aetiology and responsibility is hardly a fine art (Turner 1964). Inversion covers a plethora of logically different relations (Needham 1983: 93—120); and the normal or moral requires exceptions to flesh it out. Our complacent materialism blinds us to the problematic nature of evil and deviance (see Parkin 1985), and the degree to which many cultures recognize the importance and efficacy of mind or spirit in some form. Witchcraft needs to be seen in the context of what is held to exist and the forms of its agency; as must be the mystical power of women in the light of the powers available to men, and what (and how) each transmits influence to their children (see Leach 1961a: 18—19). Visual metaphors often link darkness with ignorance, be it practical, moral or metaphysical. If the nature of attack fits our mechanistic conception of causation, we call it 'sorcery'; if it doesn't, it is 'mystical' — a troublesome dichotomy (Needham 1976). Nor need the medicines be strange. In Bali, for instance, they are simply part of the pharmacopoeia (Weck 1937). If it all looks odd, consider the claims for phrenology in the last century.

Airy generalizations tend to float lightly over the evidence. For example, in Bali females and males may inherit or learn unusual skills, putatively or actually, from either parents or strangers. They may or may not fly, use technical aids, work by night, or attack friends and family or enemies. The powers as they possess are often shared by doctors (*balian*), princes and others and may be used to uphold as well as subvert the moral order.[12] In a sense such beings help to define normality, but are perhaps better seen as part of a cultural argument about the nature of chance, idiosyncracy and agency. Contrasting imaginations, though, is not what hard-line comparativists usually have in mind.

To avoid tedious repetition, some other bits of the anthropological arsenal, like 'symbolic beliefs' and 'collective representations', may be disposed of briefly. As Barley has remarked, 'the decision to interpret behaviour as "symbolic" is often the product of the failure of the anthropologist to comprehend something, plus a dogmatic commitment to the rationality of primitive man.' (1983: 10) Symbolism is what appears irrational to the analyst. Being defined negatively, it is a suitably amorphous category to act as an explanatory *deus ex machina*, with a generality stemming from an appeal to a dubiously universal notion of rationality. What is rational to think constitutes knowledge; what isn't makes up ideology or belief.

Charting imagined worlds is no substitute for ethnographic inquiry. One may ask the Balinese if something is symbolic by using the Indonesian *simbolis* (from the Dutch *symbolisch*), but as they do not recognize such general terms one is politely invited to ask a coherent question. The Balinese recognize instead a whole range of terms. For instance, *ciri* covers much of what strict Saussureans might call a sign; but where a sign is mnemonic, it is a *painget*. The difficult domain of exemplification, metaphor and allusion is commonly handled by contrasting *conto* and *pra(tiw)imba*, which one might gloss as 'example' and 'analogy' respectively. The distinction depends on complex criteria of verification (which include whether the connection is manifest and whether it is intrinsic or imputed). Balinese also distinguish two kinds of believing: *pracaya* and *ngega*. The former implies some kind of commitment in the absence of certain knowledge; the latter suggests a similar commitment but with grounds for knowing (*uning*) something to be so. This is not to replace vapid Western concepts with equally nebulous Oriental ones, but simply to point out that such indigenous classifications in use are part of the empirical evidence. Anthropologists rarely lose sleep, or reputations, over such issues: Clifford Geertz's study of the symbolism of the Balinese state blissfully ignored the categories Balinese actually use (see 1980: 135), or even the possibility that they might not conform to his!

Similar problems pervade even that hardiest anthropological perennial 'collective representations'. Originally a heuristic device to argue the irreducibility of social phenomena to individual, or psychological, choices, it has come to confer a spurious generality to what others say and do in their putatively 'closed' and cosy worlds. How many people, though, have to share a representation before it is collective? Sharing language, in the sense of using the same words (or 'tokens'), does not entail people extracting the same meanings from them — if indeed they extract meaning at all — any more than they represent things in the same way. 'Sharing' is a notion fraught with ambiguities. The countless ways in which people may use words, interpret, dispute and rephrase others is boiled down into a contextless essence which provides suitable grist to the comparative mill.[13]

Cultural representations have recently been resuscitated by Sperber in defending his view that true knowledge consists of propositions about the world. 'Ignoring the difficult philosophical problems this raises' (1985: 76), he postulates a *pot-pourri*, of natural and psychological universals, spiced with innate cognitive dispositions and held together by an oddly antic causal ribbon. Representations are reduced to simple correspondences between 'mental forms', brain patterns and 'concrete, physical objects' (1985: 77). Representation, however, is not a closed field — people portray things in particular ways on different occasions — and torturing it on the Procrustean bed of naive realism merely leaves one with useless appendages. What lives on as fact in monographs are the ethnographer's representations of people often long since dead or, strictly, recollections of a few of the ways a handful of people spoke about the world on a few occasions. Such realism is an unfortunate heritage of our own peculiar scientism and essentialism. If it comes as a surprise to contemporary social scientists, it did not to our literary betters and forebears. My opening quotation concludes:

> But thy eternal summer shall not fade,
> Nor lose possession of that fair thou owest;
> Nor shall Death brag thou wander'st in his shade,
> When in eternal lines to time thou growest:
> So long as men shall breathe, or eyes can see,
> So long lives this, and this gives life to thee.

ARMCHAIR ATLASES

One of the best arguments for some kind of comparison turns on the problem of translation. It is the familiar thesis that we cannot translate between languages unless there are perceptual and logical processes common to all humans: 'the inquirer must presuppose shared percepts, judgements, concepts and rules of judgement in the making of his empirical discoveries about beliefs.' (Hollis 1982: 73) This is not all. There must also be a

"massive central core of human thinking which has no history" and it has to be one which embodies the only kind of rational thinking there can be. The "massive central core" cannot be an empirical hypothesis, liable in principle to be falsified in the variety of human cultures, but luckily in fact upheld. . . . There has to be an epistemological unity of mankind.

(Hollis 1982: 83–4)

Translation presupposes both comparison and a battery of human universals. The weakness of the non-universalist stance, on this view, is that it inadvertently assumes universal rationality and order to establish a 'bridgehead' into other cultures. This is a reasonable point. But quite what does the bridgehead involve? Crucially, there must be a correspondence, or equivalence, between native and analyst's utterances (see Hollis 1970: 214). Matters are not so simple, however. Such 'equivalence structures' do not guarantee identity of mental, or logical, processes. All that is needed is for those concerned to be able to read an interpretation of actions, events or words, which does not violate their own particular standards. Wallace, with salutary scepticism about the positivist pretensions of this whole line of argument, has pointed out that it is doubtful if any but the simplest society could work without widespread miscommunication (1961: 29–44). The rationalist dream of the conditions of translation is likely to prove a practical nightmare.

One reason why the argument looks so plausible is that it rests upon the long-in-the-tooth, but popular, presupposition that either translation is possible and propositions true across languages, or we could never understand other people at all. This 'myth of perfect communication' presumes that understanding cannot be partial, even within our own culture: an odd observation from academics who so often offer quite different accounts of what happened at the seminars they attend. Behind the myth are several pernicious and related dichotomies. Either one understands people or one doesn't. Either statements are true or they are not. Either native beliefs accord with the universality of logic, perception, classification or what not, or they are culturally specific. Either native utterances are factual (propositional or rational) or they are symbolic. Like Morton's fork there are two convenient categories. If we think we understand a native statement or infer intelligible-looking motives for action, this is evidence of a shared reality. If we cannot, it must be culture-specific. The armchair analyst is always, if tautologously, right.

If realism is top-heavy with metaphysical presuppositions (some of which Hollis concedes, 1982: 84), how does one translate without a bridgehead? In trying to make sense of another culture, the use of postulated equivalences — be they perceptual, evaluative or logical — is simply a useful starting point, not a conceptual crucifix. We use all sorts of information to try to grasp what our informants tell us about what we see. Call these 'bridgeheads' if you will. Translating is not so different from interpreting and poses analogous problems of validation (Hirsch 1967). As knowledge and understanding gradually increase, previous assumptions are modified. Radical translation is not an all-or-nothing venture; it is a dialectic (the parallel in interpretation being the hermeneutic circle) between our informants' and our own varying representations.

Recognizing these problems would make anthropology a more sensitive and intellectually demanding subject than most practitioners would wish to allow. Adopting the ostrich option will not spirit them away, however, as a glance at three widely used Balinese expressions and their vocabulary of comparison shows.

Eating

Everywhere animals and people eat. Is this not a universal which underwrites translation? Now Balinese has several lexical levels with ranked terms for the same object or act. Words for ingesting include *miunan, marayunan, ngajengang, madaar, ngamah, ngaloklok, neda* and *nyasèksèk*. The first two are used of high priests and Brahmans, or when inferiors address princes. *Ngajengang* is used for most other high castes. *Madaar* is used with strangers, where status is unclear, for politeness, by some ambitious people about themselves, but also of the sick. *Ngamah* is used of lower castes and, by them, for people they know well. It may also be used loosely of animals. Different animals are distinguished by their way of feeding. So *ngaloklok* is said of beasts which gulp, like dogs and pigs (*neda* is used of dogs owned by high castes); *nyasèksèk* describes how a chicken picks at the ground, and how people pick out items from a collection. There are many others.

Is there a basic act, say *ngamah*, with synonyms? But how synonymous are these if they connote respect, or other attitudes? Or is it a matter of style? How we interpret usage, however, depends on prior assumptions. Propositionally, the words may be treated as synonymous predicates; as sentences or utterances, they are not. For they are not substitutable, both because terms are fairly fixed for certain castes and because their extensions differ. We may decide that we are dealing with an activity common to humans and animals, to be explained *prima facie* as a single phenomenon. Do the Balinese, though, regard it this way? Classically, members of different castes are different kinds of beings; and animals are quite apart in the Scale of Being. It is easy to assume low Balinese to be 'basic' and everything else 'respect vocabulary'. Regrettably, words cannot be ranged according to a single criterion: they may indicate distance, insult, hostility, power and much besides. So it is impossible to provide simple rules of use. It would in fact be more in keeping with Balinese taxonomic styles to treat each term as the appropriate habit of a specific class of beings, without recourse to essentialized generic concepts like 'eating' at all.

Nourishment

The purpose in eating in Bali is said to be in order to *ngalih merta* (*ngarereh merta* in high Balinese). *Ngalih* may be glossed as 'fetch' or 'search'. *Merta*, however, presents serious difficulties. If one asks what *merta* is, one is liable to be told that it is what has *sari* (see below). What has *sari* is what has *guna*. What has *guna* is what brings *suksema*, which is what one has (is, feels or thinks?) when one *ngalih merta*! I am not being deliberately awkward in avoiding translating these terms (one could render them as 'nourishment', 'goodness', 'use' and 'a good feeling' at the risk of giving Sanskritists apoplexy). The difficulty of mutually defined terms is that several quite different kinds of gloss make sense of some expressions and nonsense of others.

The term for cooked rice in low Balinese is *nasi*; *daar* in middle; and *ajengan* in high. It is also used more generally of food to be eaten. What is nourishing to humans, however, is *merta*; whereas *merta* for dogs includes human faeces. So the term's extension is species specific. Now *(a)merta* (also Sanskrit *amṛta, amrita*) has complex mythical and philosophical senses which include the elixir of immortality and the vital fluid of the body (Weck 1937: 40 ff.). It may be regarded as a special substance, as an attribute of certain things, or as an *ex post facto* judgement upon predispositions. Now rice may also be referred to as *merta*. In his discussion of early textual references, Bosch notes that 'we do well to remember that the conception of *amrita* originally did not imply the notion of an eternal life. . . . "Immortality to man means to live a complete life and to be happy" ' (1960: 62−3). So can Man live by rice alone?

Depending on one's preconceptions, *merta* may be simply 'food'; it may be a nourishing substance or the abstract idea of nourishment; it may apply only to humans or to animals as well; it may even be used of plants and some inanimate objects in other readings. So the Balinese may appear as simple savages who have not yet worked out a set of falsifiable propositions about energy exchange; as ingenious *bricoleurs* or early empiricists; as speculative natural philosophers; as lost in search of a mythical holy grail; or, in getting 'early' usage right, hide-bound traditionalists. It is always possible to read one's predilections about the Other into such translations.

Essence

In discussing nourishment, a key term seemed to be *sari*. Will this submit to translation more easily? In the dictionaries *sari* is often defined as 'essence' (Kersten 1978: 455; Warna 1978: 502), but also as 'flower', 'yield' and linked to the Indonesian homonym for 'core, essence, nucleus, gist . . . pollen' (Echols and Shadily 1961: 316).[14] Textually it may be traced to Old Javanese *sari*, 'quintessence, the best of something, most precious part . . . pollen, flower' (Zoetmulder 1982: 1693). Van der Tuuk is earlier, but more cautious on Balinese usage. It may refer to smell, to an egg, to the 'quintessence' of an edible offering, to the brain of shrimps, what makes the earth fertile; while its verb forms include *masari* 'to have luck' and *nyari* 'to breathe in the scent of offerings' or 'to eat sparingly' (1897, vol 3: 52—3). Its compounds are manifold. When I asked what it meant, on several occasions villagers made an analogy (*praimba*, see above) with 'vitamin'!

Of what is *sari* used? Most animate beings and inanimate things contain it. It is said to be in offerings to gods until the ritual is over. (Some people report that such offerings afterwards are less nourishing than ordinary food; others that they are more so.) All food (*sic*) has *sari*, as do humans, animals, plants, car batteries, buses and much else. The common translation as 'essence' is misleading, because it does not imply essential qualities in any of the usual Western philosophical senses. A better rendering might be 'vital force', which would at least make some sense of offerings or how plants derive *sari* from the ground. In fact, transformations may be expressed in terms of *sari*, rather as we use 'energy' or 'force'. A more sensitive gloss might be 'what something requires to keep it being what it is, or is required for its development'. It is far from clear, though, that there is much in common between different uses of *sari*. Once again, in a stroke the Balinese may be transformed from rather odd mystics, gravely mistaken philosophers or unrepentant Aristotelian entelechists, to nineteenth-century vitalists in a world full of fascinating forces (cf. Needham 1976).

These examples show some of the obvious difficulties in imagining that translation is simple or that one can compare words or propositions because they deal with a shared reality. A bridgehead does not tell us which reading is the right one (none fits all the statements made by Balinese). The retort that I have managed to translate quite well despite my disclaimers overlooks the fact that, in this case, the contents of the 'bridgehead' are so vague and flexible as to be meaningless. As Overing has remarked, the problem is what is one to put in the bridgehead anyway (1985b: 154). A more serious issue is that it may be hard to choose between versions because they are articulated in terms of indigenous ideas which are mutually defined and far from the periphery of experience. These two concerns reflect grave criticisms of naive realism and empiricism. Facts do not easily determine theory or translation (Quine 1960: 26—79). And different 'translation manuals' make equal sense. Anyway, words arguably do not come singly, but as part of complex sets which are open to falsification only in the limiting case (Quine 1953: 37—47). But how is one to falsify the link between, say, *merta* and *sari*?

Matters are not quite so desperate, though. Some cultures have their own highly developed views on such matters as language or comparison. Ignoring such sources at times looks dangerously like intellectual arrogance. Balinese vocabulary for comparison, for instance, recognizes nuanced differences of degree and kind. The nearest equivalent to 'compare' is probably *nyaihang*, from the root *saih*, 'resemble or be equal'. It tends to imply sifting or searching carefully for something amid other things, which links it to the near-homonym *nyaipang*, 'to sift or sieve'. Where we might use 'contrast', the Balinese term is *ngalènang*, from *lèn*, different, other, distinct. There are further terms, two of which are relevant here: *masib*, looking for resemblances of a weaker kind than implied by *nyaihang;* and *matetimbangan*, from *timbang*, to weigh, which is more or less explicitly evaluative. The words are used in daily life, often with more care than we show.

Balinese precision in other respects is striking. Asking if something can be compared to something else, or whether it resembles it, is not a well-formed utterance unless one specifies the attribute or term held to apply to both. I once inquired if two full brothers were alike, only to be told sharply that the question was meaningless. Was I asking about their facial or bodily form, their character traits, inherited or acquired idiosyncracies, the distance from a common origin (here mother and father), their strength or energy, or what? Different kinds of feature require different terms for similarity, according to both degree and kind. Two men with similar character traits are *masaih* (from the same root as 'compare', *nyaihang*), in other words alike in that respect. But if they look alike, they are *nampek* (seemingly a spatial metaphor) or 'near'. Kin, however, are held to resemble one another strictly only in caste and descent group membership. Here the term is *pateh*, the same or equal with respect of that criterion alone. While it is possible to speak of 'comparing' features which are not *masaih*, but say *nampek*, Balinese tended to avoid using *nyaihang* in this sense by circumlocution. So attention to indigenous discourse does suggest an interesting means of weighing the relative merits of different interpretations. Our home-grown language of comparison gets short shrift in a world as subtly differentiated as the Balinese. Armchair atlases are best left to armchair Atlases.

SCALY FORMS

Contemporary anthropologists have been described as mice gnawing on the bones of dead dinosaurs.[15] Is there a coherent alternative, though, to a Rabelaisian repast of Rationalism and Realism? For, if we follow Quine, how are we to choose between different translations, or interpretations? Are we left in relativist dreamtime where anything goes; a Romantic world where the creativity of the ethnographer is the only constraint; where ethnography is an elegant fiction or a series of more or less ingenious and informative sketches?

Or have we reduced other cultures to silence by being able to say too much about them? The alternatives are humbler, but there is something to be said for small furry mammals rather than moribund reptiles.

Relinquishing reason and reality as sufficient, if still useful, guides need not pitch us into loony relativism, nor make ethnography into the creative act of a novelist. If it did, the account of anyone who wrote about Bali without reading about it, doing fieldwork or knowing the language would be as valid as the most informed analysis. Needless to say, this has not stopped many people from trying! We are not quite dealing with the eponymous individual champing at the creative bit, because the notions of 'individual' and 'creativity' are part of available social frames of reference (which change, of course — they are not prisons). It is in this sense that I understand the contributions of Overing and Parkin in this volume.

A popular tack by malcontents with existing approaches is to embrace a perspectival metaphor, in one of two senses. One may counter-balance different views of the same events, or look at the different ways in which events present themselves. For,

it is customary to think that objective reality is dissolved by such relativity of terms as we get through the shifting of perspectives. . . . But on the contrary, it is by the approach through a variety of perspectives that we establish a character's reality. . . . Indeed, in keeping with the older theory of realism (what we might call "poetic realism", in contrast with modern "scientific realism") we could say that characters possess *degrees of being* in proportion to the variety of perspectives from which they can with justice be perceived.

(Burke 1969: 504)

Are all perspectives or translations equally valid? Clearly a reasonable fit with observable actions, utterances and indigenous exegeses is a necessary condition; while interpretations which are consistent with indigenous pre-suppositions and criteria of explanation, economy, elegance, coherence or whatever (see Hesse on the requirements for translation manuals, 1978) would deserve close attention. An account would be suspect to the extent that it incorporated alien presuppositions or pre-empted discussion by *a priori* claims about what culture, language or the world must be. If there is no such thing as a perfect translation or interpretation, there are still better, worse and idiotic ones. What, then, is one to make of misplaced metaphors like 'the theatre state' or 'linear time'? Are they illuminating or ultimately misleading? I leave the matter to the reader's judgement.

Perspectival approaches, however, have a serious drawback. They tend to ignore the overlap and broader historical changes in discursive traditions. Anthropological writings, for example, too often add to the spatial distance of those they study by displacing them in time too (see Fabian 1983), and so dismiss the extent to which Others have always impinged more or less upon us, and we on them. The Balinese had a significant impact on Western European music in the late nineteenth century; as Europeans did on them even before colonization. An alternative to such exclusive scientific classes of 'distincts' are overlapping classes of 'opposites' or, to be precise, of 'differences of a peculiar kind, which are differences at once of degree and kind' (Collingwood 1933: 73).

Not only can cultures or discourses incorporate new information about the world, but previous knowledge is continually being reworked in the light of experience. So knowledge is partly both archaeological and contextual. The resultant dialectic has been called a 'Scale of Forms' (Collingwood 1933: 54—91). This is not to suggest any necessary evolutionary progress, or internal consistency. Discourses, in this sense, are not static, exclusive or exhaustive. As the Balinese have encountered large-scale tourism, their image of Westerners has tended to change from seeing them as powerful, dangerous figures to over-sexed, extravagant and crude; while our images of Bali run the gamut from cultural museum to Pacific isle. Now something interesting happens when we reconsider 'radical translation', which rarely turns out to be as clear-cut as was implied. To the extent that discourses overlap, they affect one another. In encountering or talking about other peoples we modify our own categories. As we come to know more about the Balinese, we are also learning more about ourselves, or understand ourselves in different ways. The Balinese, of course, are doing something similar from a different starting point. The process is a kind of mutual, if partly incommensurable, critical ethnography of people in one culture on people in another.

The debate about comparison and translation is not just an esoteric academic argument. The commonest theoretical approaches dismiss much of what the rest of the world has to say. They reduce others to silence, while obscuring this behind a miasma of metaphor. Such pretensions are as Cretaceous as they are hegemonic. Peddling an outdated scientism is not just pushing a dubious panacea, but is frankly totalitarian. I hope those were for anthropologists, as one absolute ruler put it,

> My sallad days,
> When I was green in judgement: cold in blood. . . .
> *Antony and Cleopatra*, 1. v. 73—4

You will recall what happened to her after embracing a scaly form.

NOTES

1 The *loci classici* are Radcliffe-Brown 1958a [1952] and 1958b [1923] and Evans-Pritchard's reply (1950; 1961; 1965) drawing heavily, it seems, on Collingwood's detailed distinctions between natural scientific and philosophical, or historical, methods (1933 and 1942). A far more sophisticated protagonist of a scientific approach to culture is Bateson (1958; 1973). There is no need to discuss here the extensive literature on formal comparison (e.g. Murdock 1957a; 1957b; 1967), now largely rejected but implicitly revived, often under the guise of 'structure' by Lévi-Strauss (1969), despite long-standing criticisms (e.g. Schapera 1954; Goody 1956; Leach 1961a; Needham 1971; Ions 1977: 134—42). In retrospect, Evans-Pritchard emerges rather well from the debate.

2 In Anglo-Saxon usage, structure takes on a more empirical or positivist flavour (Kuper 1975), or stresses 'conscious models' (Ward 1965, exemplified by R. H. Barnes 1974: the latter's focus on indigenous categories avoids some nasty confusions of the former).

3 On a questionable understanding of dichotomy, see Lloyd 1966: 156—62; P. S. Cohen 1975; Hallpike 1979: 224—8. On confusions of differences in degree and in kind ('opposites' and 'distincts', Croce 1948), see Collingwood 1933: 64—91. On more general criticisms of structuralist assumptions and method, see Hayes and Hayes 1970; Derrida 1972; 1976; Macksey and Donato 1972; Culler 1975; Sperber 1975: 51—84; 1985: 64—93; Benoist 1978; Wilden 1980.

4 As Nagel has noted, for any sequence of events whatsoever, it is possible to construct a mathematical function, even when they are notionally random (1961). The unhappy moral for lovers of system is that it is possible to imagine and argue order where none exists: a problem which Simpson raises (1961: 5) and round which Lévi-Strauss tiptoes on highly questionable grounds (1966: 9—10). On further problems in the nature of systems, see Collingwood 1933: 176—98.

5 Hacking has pointed to a difference in Quine's and Feyerabend's theses: 'Quine urges that there is *too much* possibility for translation. The opposed doctrine maintains there is *too little*. Two human languages could be so disparate that no system of translation is possible. This is the spirit of Feyerabend's doctrine of incommensurability' (Hacking 1975: 152). For 'translation' one can also read 'comparison'. While Hacking reasonably notes some of the different stresses in the two approaches, in other ways they are less diverse than he implies. Both recognize the theory-laden nature of evidence and the underdetermination of fact by theory; but both develop different aspects of the argument.

6 Recently Bloch has asserted that a statement is metaphoric or literal depending on which a speaker indicates to his audience (1985: 632). Does it follow that, if Bloch indicates time is metaphorically linear it is so only in a manner of speaking, but if literal then it really is linear?

7 Despite their ostensible differences, Bloch and Geertz are intellectual bedfellows. Their stated commitment to ethnography disguises a massive burden of *a*

priori assumptions. Both assume, for instance, the psychic unity of mankind and the ultimate adequacy of Western reason and (positivist) ontology to explain culture and all its variations. Both assume a Cartesian dichotomy of mind and body, expressed as the centrality of the distinction between the instrumental and the expressive (as 'practical' and 'symbolic', a false dichotomy and an odd reading of Kant's strictly analytic, not substantive, distinction between 'hypothetical' and 'categorical' imperatives) and — Geertz explicitly, Bloch implicitly — the dependence of action on ideas and ideologies. They differ merely in the relative stress on the opposed dogmas of Utilitarianism and Romanticism, seeing humans epitomized in the Western metaphors of Napoleon's English shopkeeper and the self-conscious aesthete respectively. It is a domestic tiff exported to Bali.

8 Collingwood is interesting and careful on the differences between what can be compared and what measured (1942: 24); and on the role of evocation in contrasting (comparison appropriately being defined as finding out 'what contrasts with what'; 1942: 49—50).

9 It is often assumed (for example in the structuralist focus on *signifiant* and *signifié*) that the word-object relation is uncomplicated or universal. On the contrary, class terms, proper names and descriptions are a minefield for the unwary (e.g. Strawson 1950; Kripke 1977). If words or names do not have the same sense or reference in all cultures (and there is evidence that they do not), then we cannot compare what is referred to in different languages without prior investigation of use.

10 Nadel's reflections were typically more sophisticated than those of many of his successors, the statement above being hedged about with *caveats*. For example, he noted that activity implies intention, but this was made a potentially empirical matter which did not postulate inner states, as the 'purposive aspect refers only to the task-like nature of organized behaviour . . . not to any ulterior or ultimate purpose which the investigator might claim to have discovered in them' (1951: 109).

11 The expedient invocation of metaphor is a hallmark of realism *in extremis*. Apart from indulging in many of the fallacies discussed above, it exports a naive metaphysics. Even such ostensibly fundamental 'biological' relationships as, say, mother and son presuppose ideas about causation, substance or influence, continuity, similarity and personal identity. On what grounds, for instance, should we assume the cosmos, deities, and culturally important objects to be represented in terms of metaphoric extensions of family relations, rather than family relations being exemplifications of the same metaphysical principles which are held to inform the cosmos etc. (Goodman 1984: 59—60)?

12 This kind of power is generally known as *kasaktian*, and so *manusa sakti*, people with such powers. 'Witches' is a poor gloss for the richly nuanced terminology available. Much of the ostensible oddity of such figures comes from taking them out of the context of the many kinds of being and agency which the Balinese recognize.

13 H. P. Grice to J. S. Mill might be more appropriate, if ironic. For, as part of his grand programme of re-treading the footsteps of the Logical Positivists, Sperber

has, rightly, been concerned with developing a theory of context (Sperber and Wilson 1986). Unfortunately, although it starts by modifying Grice, the argument seems to owe more to Mill's inductive metaphysics than to Grice's cautious pragmatism.

14 Dictionaries illustrate unregenerate essentialism *par excellence* at work. And one might be wise not to inquire how their decontextualized 'meanings' were reached. Balinese was fortunate, though, as it was documented by Herman Neubronner van der Tuuk (1897). In one of the great works of Orientalism he gives sentences and contexts of use more often than a translation, a caution which has stood later generations in good stead. He has been followed to some extent by Zoetmulder (1982) for Old Javanese, the language of many texts, but one which has percolated into everyday Balinese speech.

15 I am grateful to Nigel Barley and Edwin Ardener for the suggestive image and retort respectively.

REFERENCES

Barley, N. F. 1983. *Symbolic Structures: an exploration of the culture of the Dowayos*. Cambridge: Cambridge University Press.

Barnes, B. 1982. *T. S. Kuhn and Social Science*. London: Macmillan.

Barnes, R. H. 1974. *Kédang: a study of the collective thought of an eastern Indonesian people*. Oxford: Clarendon.

Bateson, G. 1958. *Naven: a survey of the problems suggested by a composite picture of the culture of a New Guinea tribe drawn from three points of view*. 2nd edn. London: Oxford University Press.

___ 1973. *Steps to an Ecology of Mind: collected essays in anthropology, psychiatry, evolution and epistemology*. St Albans: Paladin.

Benoist, J.-M. 1978. *The Structural Revolution*. London: Weidenfeld.

Bloch, M. 1977. The past and the present in the present. *Man* (N.S.) 12: 278—92.

___ 1985. Almost eating the ancestors. *Man* (N.S.) 20: 631—46.

Bosch, F. D. K. 1960. *The Golden Germ*. The Hague: Mouton.

Bourdieu, P. 1977. *Outline of a Theory of Practice*. Cambridge: Cambridge University Press.

Bourdillon, M. F. C. 1978. Knowing the world or hiding it: a response to Maurice Bloch. *Man* (N.S.) 13: 591—9.

Burke, K. 1969. *A Grammar of Motives*. Berkeley: California University Press.

Cohen, A. 1969. Political anthropology: the analysis of the symbolism of power relations. *Man* (N.S.) 4: 215—35.

Cohen, P. S. 1975. Palpable nonsense in the conflict of life and death. *Man* (N.S.) 10: 620—2.

Collingwood, R. G. 1933. *An Essay on Philosophical Method*. Oxford: Clarendon.

___ 1940. *An Essay on Metaphysics*. Oxford: Clarendon.

___ 1942. *The New Leviathan, or man, society, civilization and barbarism*. Oxford: Clarendon.

—— 1945. *The Idea of Nature* (ed.) T. M. Knox. Oxford: Clarendon.

Crabb, G. 1974. *Crabb's English Synonyms*. Revised and corrected edn. London: Routledge and Kegan Paul.

Croce, B. 1948. *Ciò che è Vivo e ciò che è Morte nella Filosofia di Hegel*. Bari: Laterza.

Culler, J. 1975. *Structuralist Poetics*. London: Routledge and Kegan Paul.

—— 1981. *The Pursuit of Signs*. London: Routledge and Kegan Paul.

Derrida, J. 1972. Structure, sign and play in the discourse of the human sciences. In *The Structuralist Controversy*. Baltimore: Johns Hopkins University Press.

—— 1976. *Of Grammatology* (trans.) G. C. Spivak. Baltimore: Johns Hopkins University Press.

Donoghue, D. 1981. *Ferocious Alphabets*. London: Faber.

Duff-Cooper, A. 1985. An account of the Balinese 'person' from Western Lombok. *Bijdragen* 141: 67—85.

Durkheim, E. 1933. *The Division of Labour in Society* (trans.) G. Simpson. Illinois: The Free Press of Glencoe.

Echols, J. M. and H. Shadily. 1961. *An Indonesian-English Dictionary*. Ithaca: Cornell University Press.

Evans-Pritchard, E. E. 1950. Social anthropology: past and present. *Man* 50: 118—24; reprinted in *Essays in Social Anthropology*. 1962. London: Faber.

—— 1961. *Anthropology and History*. Manchester: Manchester University Press; reprinted in *Essays in Social Anthropology*. 1962. London: Faber.

—— 1965. The comparative method in social anthropology. In *The Position of Women in Primitive Society*. London: Faber.

Fabian, J. 1983. *Time and the Other*. New York: Columbia University Press.

Feyerabend, P. 1975. *Against Method*. London: Verso.

Firth, R. 1964. Social organization and social change. In *Essays on Social Organization and Values*. London: Athlone.

Foucault, M. 1972. *The Archaeology of Knowledge* (trans.) A. M. Sheridan. London: Tavistock.

—— 1979. What is an author. In *Textual Strategies* (ed) J. Harari. London: Methuen.

Geertz, C. 1980. *Negara: the theatre state in nineteenth-century Bali*. Princeton: Princeton University Press.

Geertz, H. and C. Geertz. 1975. *Kinship in Bali*. London: Chicago University Press.

Girard, R. 1978. *To Double Business Bound*. Baltimore: Johns Hopkins University Press.

Goodman, N. 1972. The way the world is. In *Problems and Projects*. New York: Bobbs-Merrill.

—— 1978. *Ways of Worldmaking*. Brighton: Harvester.

—— 1981. *Languages of Art*. Brighton: Harvester.

—— 1984. *Of Mind and other Matters*. Cambridge, Mass: Harvard University Press.

Goody, J. 1956. A comparative approach to incest and adultery. *British Journal of Sociology* 7: 286—305.

Hacking, I. 1975. *Why Does Language Matter to Philosophy?* Cambridge: Cambridge University Press.

Hallpike, C. R. 1979. *The Foundations of Primitive Thought*. Oxford: Clarendon.

Hayes, E. N. and T. A. Hayes (eds). 1970. *Claude Lévi-Strauss: the anthropologist as hero*. London: M.I.T. Press.

Hesse, M. 1978. Theory and value in the social sciences. In *Action and Interpretation* (eds) C. Hookway and P. Pettit. Cambridge: Cambridge University Press.

Hirsch, E. R. 1967. *Validity in Interpretation*. New Haven: Yale University Press.

Hobart, M. 1978. Padi, puns and the attribution of responsibility. In *Natural Symbols in South East Asia* (ed) G. Milner. London: School of Oriental and African Studies.

—— 1980. *Ideas of Identity: the interpretation of kinship in Bali*. Denpasar: Universitas Udayana.

Hollis, M. 1970. The limits of irrationality. In *Rationality* (ed.) B. Wilson. Oxford: Blackwell.

—— 1982. The social destruction of reality. In *Rationality and Relativism* (eds) M. Hollis and S. Lukes. Oxford: Blackwell.

Horton, R. 1979. Material-object language and theoretical language. In *Philosophical Disputes in the Social Sciences* (ed.) S. C. Brown. Brighton: Harvester.

Howe, L. E. A. 1981. The social determination of knowledge: Maurice Bloch and Balinese time. *Man* (N.S.) 16: 220—34.

Inden, R. 1976. *Marriage and Rank in Bengali Culture: a history of caste and clan in middle period Bengal*. Berkeley and London: California University Press.

—— 1985. Hindu evil as unconquered lower self. In *The Anthropology of Evil* (ed.) D. J. Parkin. Oxford: Blackwell.

Ions, E. 1977. *Against Behaviouralism*. Oxford: Blackwell.

Karim, W.-J. B. 1981. *Ma'Betisék Concepts of Living Things*. London: Athlone.

Kersten, J. 1978. *Kamus Kecil Bahasa Bali*. Singaraja: Privately published.

Kripke, S. 1977. Identity and necessity. In *Naming, Necessity, and Natural Kinds* (ed.) S. P. Schwartz. Ithaca and London: Cornell University Press.

Kuhn, T. S. 1962. *The Structure of Scientific Revolutions* (2nd edn enlarged, 1970). Chicago and London: University of Chicago Press.

—— 1977. *The Essential Tension*. Chicago and London: University of Chicago Press.

Kuper, A. 1975. The social structure of the Sotho-speaking peoples of Southern Africa. *Africa* 45: 67—81, 139—49.

Lakatos, I. 1970. Falsification and the methodology of scientific research programmes. In *Criticism and the Growth of Knowledge: proceedings of the international colloquium in the philosophy of science, London, 1965, Volume 4* (eds) I. Lakatos and A. Musgrave. London: Cambridge University Press.

Leach, E. R. 1961a. Rethinking anthropology. In *Rethinking Anthropology*. London: Athlone.

—— 1961b. Polyandry, inheritance and the definition of marriage: with particular reference to Sinhalese customary law. In *Rethinking Anthropology*. London: Athlone.

Levin, S. R. 1977. *The Semantics of Metaphor*. Baltimore and London: Johns Hopkins University Press.

Lévi-Strauss, C. 1966. *The Savage Mind*. London: Weidenfeld and Nicolson.

—— 1967. The story of Asdiwal (trans.) N. Mann. In *The Structural Study of Myth and Totemism* (ed.) E. R. Leach. London: Tavistock.

___ 1968a. Introduction: history and anthropology. In *Structural Anthropology* (trans.) C. Jakobson and B. F. Schoepf. London: Allen Lane.

___ 1968b. The structural study of myth. In *Structural Anthropology* (trans.) C. Jakobson and B. F. Schoepf. London: Allen Lane.

___ 1968c. Social structure. In *Structural Anthropology* (trans.) C. Jakobson and B. F. Schoepf. London: Allen Lane.

___ 1969. *The Elementary Structures of Kinship* (trans.) J. H. Bell, J. R. von Sturmer and (ed.) R. Needham. London: Eyre and Spottiswoode.

Lloyd, G. E. R. 1966. *Polarity and Analogy: two types of argumentation in early Greek thought*. Cambridge: Cambridge University Press.

Losee, J. 1980. *A Historical Introduction to the Philosophy of Science*. Oxford: Oxford University Press.

Macksey, R. and Donato, E. (eds) 1972. *The Structuralist controversy: the languages of criticism and the sciences of man*. Baltimore: Johns Hopkins University Press.

Murdock, G. P. 1957a. World ethnographic sample. *American Anthropologist* 59: 664—87.

___ 1957b. Anthropology as a comparative science. *Behavioral Science* 2: 249—54.

___ 1967. *Ethnographic Atlas*. Pittsburg: University of Pittsburg Press.

Nadel, S. F. 1951. *The Foundations of Social Anthropology*. London: Cohen and West.

Nagel, E. 1961. *The Structure of Science*. New York: Harcourt Brace.

Needham, R. 1971. Remarks on the analysis of kinship and marriage. In *Rethinking Kinship and Marriage*. London: Tavistock.

___ 1976. Skulls and causality. *Man* (N.S.) 11: 71—88.

___ 1983. Reversals. In *Against the Tranquility of Axioms*. Berkeley and London: University of California Press.

Overing, J. (ed.) 1985a. *Reason and Morality*. London: Tavistock.

___ 1985b. Today I shall call him 'Mummy'; multiple worlds and classificatory confusion. In *Reason and Morality* (ed.) J. Overing. London: Tavistock.

Parkin, D. J. 1976. Exchanging words. In *Transaction and Meaning: directions in the anthropology of exchange and symbolic behaviour* (ed.) B. Kapferer. Philadelphia: Institute for the Study of Human Issues.

___ ed. 1985. *The Anthropology of Evil*. Oxford: Blackwell.

Pepper, S. C. 1942. *World Hypotheses: a study in evidence*. Berkeley and London: University of California Press.

Quine, W. V. O. 1953. Two dogmas of empiricism. In *From a Logical Point of View*. Cambridge, Mass. and London: Harvard University Press.

___ 1960. *Word and Object*. Cambridge, Mass.: Harvard University Press.

Radcliffe-Brown, A. R. 1958a. The comparative method in social anthropology. In *Method in Social Anthropology: selected essays by A. R. Radcliffe-Brown* (ed.) M. N. Srinivas. Chicago and London: Chicago University Press; originally published 1952 *Journal of the Royal Anthropological Institute* 81: 15—22.

___ 1958b. The methods of ethnology and social anthropology. In *Method in Social Anthropology: selected essays by A. R. Radcliffe-Brown* (ed.) M. N. Srinivas. Chicago and London: Chicago University Press; originally published 1923 *South African Journal of Science* 20: 124—47.

Ricoeur, P. 1971. The model of the text: meaningful action considered as a text. *Social Research* 38: 529—62.

____ 1976. *Interpretation Theory*. Texas: Texas Christian University Press.

Rivière, P. 1971. Marriage: a reassessment. In *Rethinking Kinship and Marriage* (ed.) R. Needham. London: Tavistock.

Schapera, I. 1954. Some comments on the comparative method in social anthropology. *American Anthropologist* 55: 353—62.

Simpson, G. G. 1961. *Principles of Animal Taxonomy*. New York: Columbia University Press.

Skillen, A. 1985. Politics re-entered: the state in its place. *Radical Philosophy* 41, Autumn: 23—7.

Sperber, D. 1975. *Rethinking Symbolism*. Cambridge: Cambridge University Press.

____ 1982. Apparently irrational beliefs. In *Rationality and Relativism* (eds) M. Hollis and S. Lukes. Oxford: Blackwell.

____ 1985. Anthropology and psychology: towards an epidemiology of representations. *Man* (N.S.) 20: 73—89.

Sperber, D. and D. Wilson. 1986. *Relevance: communication and cognition*. Oxford: Blackwell.

Strawson, P. 1950. On referring. *Mind* 59: 320—44; reprinted in *Logico-Linguistic Papers*. 1971. London: Methuen.

Turner, V. 1964. Witchcraft and sorcery: taxonomy versus dynamics. *Africa* 34: 314—24.

Tuuk, H. N. van der. 1897. *Kawi-Balineesch-Nederlandsch Woordenboek*. Batavia: Landsdrukkerij.

Wallace, A. F. C. 1961. *Culture and Personality*. New York: Random House.

Ward, B. E. 1965. Varieties of the conscious model: the fishermen of South China. In *The Relevance of Models for Social Anthropology* (eds) M. Gluckman and F. Eggan. London: Tavistock.

Warna, W. (ed.) 1978. *Kamus Bali-Indonesia*. Bali: Dinas Pengajaran.

Weck, W. 1937. *Heilkunde und Volkstum auf Bali*. Stuttgart: Enke; reprinted 1976, Jakarta: P. T. Bap Bali and P. T. Intermasa.

Wilden, A. 1980. *System and Structure: essays in communication and exchange*. 2nd edn. London: Tavistock.

Wittgenstein, L. 1969. *The Blue and Brown Books* (trans.) G. E. M. Anscombe. 1st edn 1958. Oxford: Blackwell.

Zoetmulder, P. J. 1982. *Old Javanese-English Dictionary*. 2 vols, with S. Robson. The Hague: Nijhoff.

3

Comparison as the Search
for Continuity

David Parkin

It is often supposed that when anthropologists compare, they do so by treating societies and institutions as distinct 'things'. In looking at the language they use, however, we find that they rely heavily on key metaphors to make sense of likeness and difference. The result of such metaphorical linking is that they tend to see continuity in phenomena, a kind of chain-of-being. The so-called comparative method is here often closer to the illuminations of poetry and art than to objectively existing science.

Evans-Pritchard's scepticism concerning the possibilities of a comparative method in social anthropology was joined by that of other scholars. Lévi-Strauss withdrew from totemism its claim to be the origin of the religious life and indeed to be regarded necessarily as a religion at all. Religion itself was no more nor less a system of classification than the Hindu caste hierarchy (1963). Needham rejected the idea of kinship as having a distinct and concrete identity. So many phenomena were subsumed under the term, which had therefore the status of an 'odd-job' word, that we were best advised to conclude that kinship did not exist (1971: 5). Rivière likewise dissolved marriage in the more accessible generality of male-female relations (1971: 70). Crick converted the anthropological category of 'witch' and 'witchcraft' into just one of many possible ways in which human conduct could be morally evaluated (1976: 109—29). Returning to religion and to Needham's approach, Southwold urged that religions be definable in terms of overlapping resemblances, no one of which, not even belief in a God, need obtain throughout all religions (1979).

At the same time, the various metaphors of society by which anthropologists have shaped their analytical conclusions, have changed from the unambiguously demarcatory to the inter-relational. That is to say, we have moved from the idea of society as body or machine, neatly made up of separable working parts, to that of language, which while formed from distinctive phonemes and other

-emes, at least presupposed ultimate universal communicability, to that of text which did not stress inner distinctiveness or divisibility but instead promised globally infinite interpretation (Geertz 1973), and more recently to that of discourse which sees the unequal dialogues (or absence of dialogue) between people as defining who they are and what society they constitute (Parkin 1982: xlv—xlviii). One could go on extending the list. Why not society as a quark, given the current scientific predilection for emphasizing the randomness of particles? Or society as a painting, in which relations between foreground and background figures, and the use of shape, colour, tone, and line, variously depict the pattern of social life that many of us must feel both as people and as anthropologists.

Any of these metaphors including the last two can be taken quite seriously, not in the sense that they can be said completely or truly to represent the reality of society but simply because they each inform some of the ways in which we make ordinary, everyday judgements about society. They are each perspectives on the way we make judgements, as well as being possible ways in which, in our anthropology, we identify and then compare institutions, beliefs, and societies.

What the sceptics and the creators of new social metaphors have in common is their wish to dissolve existing epistemological language, and to replace it with new. Insofar as theoretical language is metaphorical, and metaphors become inappropriate over time, this seems to me an admirable way of breathing new life into our jargon. But we can make use of the growing list of dead metaphors and their new successors. As the list extends, and bearing in mind that each metaphor refers to a particular perspective in use at a given time in history, we see an unfolding of comparisons. Thus, society as body was found wanting (for who could determine the head and limbs of society?)[1] and that of machine was seen as a better depiction. But machines leave out the mind, and so structuralism and its stress on language and communication replaced that metaphor. The determinism in structuralism was still too strong, and so society as infinitely interpretable text was substituted. Finally, because a text is graphically fixed, however widely it may be interpreted, discourse emerges as more likely to reflect the dynamic paradox of human dialogue, in which the possibility of totally free speech is constrained in ways largely hidden from us, and in which differences of power result from the extent to which actors accept the fiction of free speech.

This succession of metaphors of society (or institution or whatever) is no mere sequence of words. As Salmond has demonstrated (1982), a central metaphor in theory articulates a range of related metaphors, so that the very way we perceive our subject matter is subtly shaped by that core metaphor. As the list expands over time, however, the range of perspectives on society widens. For this reason, it is epistemologically wasteful simply to jettison the insights gained from previous theoretical paradigms. There has certainly been a tendency in anthropology, as in other humanities, to assume that the paradigmatic revolution requires a complete and utter mental clearing operation. Natural scientists may have to do this, but not ourselves.

Why should this be so? I think the difference is that theory in anthropology and other humanities offers the possibility not of testable truths but of an ever-widening horizon of nonverifiable understandings, none or all of which will ever be sufficient. That said, I believe that society seen as discourse is the most comprehensive metaphor so far. It encompasses the rest. Thus, in many situations it is our informants themselves who liken society or a custom to a body or machine and who may even speak of, say, the ancestors or creation gods as being in some ways the authors of society, or of, say, a sacred text determining the nature and purpose of institutions. Discourse is more than conversation. It shapes argument which may yet be sufficiently reflexive to lay bare these different metaphors of which it is composed.

It follows from this that discourse is itself implicitly and sometimes explicitly comparative. One speaker may liken a rite to a machine in its pragmatic effects on society ('by this funeral we shall please the ancestors who will then bring us good fortune'.) Another speaker may respond simply by reverently naming specific ancestors once known to him, with whom he would like to communicate, not in order to solicit or appease but for communication's sake or for personal reassurance that life continues in death. Speakers may not distinguish statements such as these as functional and expressive respectively, but they are aware of the difference, which is used to compare and contrast events (e.g. a functionally explicit curative ritual as against a spirit seance conducted ostensibly only for communion with the dead). Most importantly, it is only through discourse that questions can be distinguished from answers, commands from exhortations, assertions from ambivalences and contradictions, and so on. It is these features, in a conjoined metaphorical and essential sense, that shape, distinguish, and link social events as variously presupposing each other.

While the idea of discourse captures best the rule-governed, creative flux by which we see ourselves and others as socially constituted, it is also the language of everyday judgements. It is made up of all the conceptual jumps, switches, and unevenness by which we decide whether to take a taxi or go by train, to regard someone as friend or foe, or contradict an earlier claim. Discourse entails judgements, decisions, and therefore comparison. We recognize this in our everyday speech, and in our metaphor of society as discourse, and yet we, or at least some of us, still have difficulty in regarding anthropology as based on a comparative method. Folk thinking contradicts professional epistemology.

If we continue the parallel further, we can see how this happened. The comparisons underlying everyday judgements are specific to isolated situations (catching a train, rather than a taxi, writing rather than phoning), which need never be brought together and ranged alongside each other for further comparison. If they were, we would be amazed at how much less consistent than the Azande we are. Comparative judgements sheltered from each other do no harm. But in comparing whole societies, institutions, or customs, the curtains dividing different empirical situations are removed, the inconsistencies are exposed, and a way has to be found to reduce them to the few factors they may be judged to have in common. We reduce by imposing native rules of, say, the funeral on the diversity of different funerals, using also what observations we can make of apparently recurrent features.

This creation of similarity out of diversity, even when it is acknowledged as such and as a particular chosen level of abstraction, is where the problems of comparison start. Rather like the flawed initial premise of an elaborate scientific formula, it can be used without further question as one of the cornerstones of higher level comparison.

With considerable insight, Southall saw a way of reconciling Lévi-Strauss's ideal structures and ethnographers' empirical findings in the suggestion that we look at the differences arising from (institutional) similarities (1965). This made for one of the most sensible 'models' to appear in anthropology. Nevertheless even Southall saw the model as feasible only if applied to cognate and neighbouring peoples, among whom initial similarities could be observed by the one scholar and more legitimately be assumed than if they were totally separate from each other. *Human Relations Area Files* global and non-regional similarities have been regarded as comprising too many variations along too many different axes to warrant much higher-level comparison. This is not simply to castigate their authors and exonerate Southall. It is only to point out that moving from (a) the creation of similarity out of inexplicable diversity to (b) explicable differences arising from similarities to (c) a comparative statement of relational effect will yield acceptable results only when placed within a cultural region. Thus, Leach's topographical metaphor of a rubber sheet told us much of the variations of Kachin marriage, descent, and alliance (1961: 7, 90—104). It could indeed have been applied by the criticized Audrey Richards herself to the material on peoples of the central African matrilineal belt. But in what sense would we have obtained a comparable picture? At this higher level of global comparison, it is unlikely that we would have learned more than that in many parts of Africa descent really does tend to have conceptual, organizational, and even metaphysical (Leach 1961: 21–7) priority over alliance, and that the latter is more often found in other parts of the world. Such a conclusion might be worth having, except that in the light of the work of Héritier and other Africanist colleagues (1981) it already seems too broad. We seem to be left with the view that the main usefulness of such detailed models is in understanding variations within a cultural region.

At this point, then, it seems worth distinguishing, very simply, two types of comparison in social anthropology: global and regional. In fact, this is a misnomer. I want to show that, though they may both be called comparative, they in fact pursue different objectives. Global comparison assumes or searches for universals in human society, while regional comparison is rather like the judgements of everyday life, to which I referred: it records isolated clusters of relationship possibilities, whose conversion into non-regional generalities becomes the quite different task of global comparison. To jump from assumptions of particularities to assumptions of universals, and vice versa, seems like trying to cram the accumulated information of all the world's recorded history into the mind of one person. This would indeed be impossible. But is it really like this?

I shall try to answer by looking at the way regional comparisons may or may not be generalizable beyond the region. Regional comparison has a respectable history, and its conclusions, if inevitably limited, expand the general body of anthropological ideas. Ideas that arise from the regional comparison almost certainly originate in language used by informants themselves. Thus, Africans appear to talk a lot about descent, while certain peoples of South-East Asia seem to talk much about alliance or about marriage exchanges. It is when these general ideas (e.g. the priority of descent or of alliance) come to be regarded as universally applicable hypotheses that there is the danger that ethnographic data may be fitted and shaped, so to speak, to the requirements of the hypothesis.

I do not wish to give the impression that regional comparison gives us no problems. There is the obvious difficulty of translating the native terms in a way that does not deviate too much from the sense of the original. No one expects this to be isomorphic, for the feel for an alien language and culture can only ever be a matter of degree: even among members of a so-called single culture, the extent to which mutually held understandings cluster does vary. Nevertheless, I do think that some examples of regional comparison show that this is the most immediately fruitful source of perspectives on society. Recent attempts at regional comparison seek to show that a range of recognizably cognate institutions in neighbouring societies appear different but are in fact ordered around a 'core', even proto-typical, form. They are also referred to as variations on a theme, transformational set, etc. Lévi-Strauss dealt with this for myth in both a regional and global manner, but there are a number of studies which deliberately confine themselves to a region in the way I have described, and I shall select a few including my own.

What is immediately interesting is the tenacity of the comparative approach through the study of regional transformations. If anything, interest in it is increasing, possibly as a partial compromise between global comparisons and single-society studies, which is itself a contrast between a broad cultural universalism and extreme cultural relativism. The most recently published study is that by Rivière (1984), whose comparison of Lowland South American societies sees each as a variant logical possibility of a basic structure. A less recent study is that by de Heusch (1982, but in French in 1972) whose study of many Central African Bantu myths and rituals reveals several basics of Bantu thought, using myths which, by themselves, suggest little, but which have added significance when compared with other 'incomplete' myths. De Heusch (1981) is also in company with such Francophone scholars as Dupire (1970) and Muller (1981), who have carried out comparative regional analyses of African marriage systems, and whose interests find additional theoretical expression in Héritier's development (1981) of Lévi-Strauss's structuralist methods. Burnham (1987) and Fardon (1984) applaud the emphasis on regional comparison but doubt that the structuralist concept of transformation, with its stress on logical principles, can adequately depict historical process, especially the role of human agents in initiating change. This question of whether history and human agency can be accommodated within the study of cognate societies seen as transformational sets promises to be one of the most interesting problems facing comparative analysis.

While this transformational, regional approach will continue to develop, it is instructive to go back to one of the earlier empirical applications, that by Nur Yalman in 1967, whose debt to Lévi-Strauss is made explicitly and unreservedly. Yalman titled part of his book, 'Variations on a theme' and 'The transformation of models' (1967: 332 ff.). In this study he describes how in South India and Sri Lanka the rule of cross-cousin marriage may have contrasting implications for the composition of a caste, depending on whether marriage is patrilocal, matrilocal or bilocal. The various possibilities that this contrast may take are seen as emanating from a single logic. As with Lévi-Strauss's work, there is something in Yalman's use of the terms 'logic' and 'principles' of the idea of an underlying generative grammar. Leach's rubber sheet analogy is also used earlier in the book to illustrate the general line of argument.[2] Throughout there is the assumption of an intellectual design behind both the thinking and behaviour that make up these variations, which, because they are rooted in the emotions that make up the family unit, do not become detached from that basic design. Yalman is aware of, but does not propose to answer, the question of at what point does a variation take on a life of its own, so to speak. If we can answer this question, then we may provide a useful key to solving the problem of how to reconcile regional with global comparison.

Structuralist logic is, of course, based on a fundamental binary opposition or set of oppositions, as is clear from Yalman's own study. In a recent study of the Mijikenda and Swahili of coastal Kenya, I show how an initial semantic distinction or opposition within a marriage payment between the payment for the wife and the payment for any children produced by her may account for variations in marriage and separation patterns between neighbouring peoples. I show also how it may culminate as a dual marriage system, where one marriage type provides a man with a wife's sexual and domestic services only, and the other more expensive and prestigious marriage type additionally provides him with her children (1980). While there is the idea of a logic or grammar, i.e. the basic opposition between the two types of payment, as generating the variations, the distinction is also seen as a yardstick by which a father, son, and husband, or mother, daughter, and wife, might assess their personal worthwhileness and the value of other parties to the marriage. The study is regionally defined, and so, though the existence of dual marriage systems elsewhere in Africa and, importantly, in Sumatra, was noted it would have been difficult to extend the analysis through the incorporation of such examples, at least that of Sumatra. This would have required a thorough exploration of Sumatran native categories and distinctions, and there is no *a priori* reason to assume that it was an initial semantic opposition between wife- and child-payments that gave rise to the dual marriage system in Sumatra. If, however, that proved to be the case, then it would suggest the existence, if not of a universal disposition to articulate the relative values of men, women, and children in predictable ways, then at least of its occurrence elsewhere than in Africa. Only intensive regional comparison in Sumatra could reveal how far this is so. Even so, the conclusion, though helpful, would immediately beg two further questions: e.g. in what ontological sense are Sumatran men, women, and children differently valued from each other and how far does this show similarity with Africa? At this point, our global comparison of regional comparisons of marriage payments throws us back into a search for particulars, i.e. Sumatran ontology. Such a delicate craft requires not rules of method but a sensitive interpretive balance between the regional and global, with the global never given the status of a conclusion but more of relational possibilities.

Converting a regional logic of oppositions (e.g. marriage payments) into a problem of ontology is one way in which we may carry out the to-and-fro comparison of first the regional and then the global and then the regional again, and so on. That is to say, we convert a problem ostensibly identified as variable marriage payments into one of how such payments are viewed as part of the way in which persons are given existence and agency. Is a woman who co-habits with another man but for whom no payment has been made a 'full' woman at all, or simply a different 'kind' of woman, and what power does she then have? Similar questions can be asked of men and children. The range of possible questions and answers is enormous. With these different ontological answers, drawn from different regions, we expand our understanding of how payments or transactions are related to theories of personal existence.

The alternative to this procedure is to go no further than state that the regional comparison of cognate cultures is based on some underlying logic. This is to admit that the logic is not necessarily humanly universal but is of value in showing the interrelationship of different regionally specific variables. Among the Sotho peoples of southern Africa, Adam Kuper has likened the interplay of such variables as rules of succession, kinship terms, rules of exogamy, and residence, to the operation of a game (1975: 146). He avoids equating such a game with any 'universal logic', preferring rather to see it as more like a 'situational logic' (p. 146). He also raises the question, to which I referred earlier in discussing Yalman, of where one draws the boundaries of the regional game. The boundaries are that, in different ways and to different extents, agnatic and matrilateral marriage is permitted among the Sotho peoples. By contrast, among the Nguni peoples, also of southern Africa, neither marriage nor sexual relations of any kind is allowed with people related through any of the four grandparents. The Nguni may be expected to be playing a quite different game. Similarly in my comparison of Mijikenda marriage payments the boundary of the game occurred when a people did *not* semantically distinguish child- and wife-payments.

More recently, Kuper has turned his attention to the structure of Bantu homesteads, principally among Nguni but also among Sotho peoples (1980), relating this to a number of other South African transformations (1982). Among both these large groups of South African peoples he finds the 'same underlying structures' in the circular or semi-circular spatial organization of homesteads: an opposition between the 'right' and 'left' of the homestead and one between its centre and its sides. The first orders wives by seniority and the second contrasts kin and wives. 'Right' and 'left' may also, of course, be contrasted in some cases with East and West respectively. The Balinese also add to the centre/periphery opposition that of high and low respectively and, through such 'natural' examples of directional thinking, are able to legitimatize the purity of 'high' castes and the 'impurity' of low ones (Hobart 1978). Other examples throughout the world show different cultural elaborations of a basic opposition between diametric and concentric spatial opposition, to say nothing of the many re-workings of rectangular and triangular modes of spatial organization.

We appear to be dealing with features of spatial thinking which exist independently in different parts of the world. But their precise cultural expression and the way in which they are combined is not easily reducible, it seems, beyond the conclusion that diametric, concentric, and other geometrical oppositions and spatial forms are humanly widespread.

Even in southern Africa, the boundaries of any transformational set may conflict with that of another. Thus, Kuper felt able to distinguish the Sotho and Nguni as different sets concerning marriage choices, but he saw them as part of one set regarding the spatial thinking underlying homestead lay-outs. What are we to do with global comparisons if, within a single relatively small region of the world, we find 'underlying structures' which do not fit comfortably one on top of the other? A good ethnographer can, possibly, find as many 'underlying structures' as his data and ingenuity allow him. I certainly think that we should investigate apparent points of divergence as well as convergence which link and divide cognate peoples, though I would prefer to see them as the shifting boundaries by means of which such people define their humanity (or lack of it). To see such differences and similarities as amenable only to structuralist comparison, however, is to drive towards an infinite regress of more and more structures. Whereas an earlier anthropology was accused of regional-to-global butterfly-collecting, regional structuralist comparison may be capable of inventing extraordinarily attractive species of the order Lepidoptera composed of features which cross-cut, overlap, and stand or fly in conflict with, or on different planes in relation to, each other. Structures are, also, without end.

While regional structuralist comparison is a decided advance on its predecessor, it will only survive as a method if we re-cast the concepts making up 'underlying structures' in terms of what they *mean* to the peoples who actually use them. What, in other words is their ontological and metaphysical status? We would need to know, for example, how a people's ideas of direction or space link with ideas of being and becoming, and of effect and causation. Why should it matter to a person that a hut door faces in one rather than another direction? This can be done for individual societies which an ethnographer has studied personally (e.g. Littlejohn 1967; Cunningham 1973; Hobart 1978; Turton 1978), but it is by definition difficult to extend empathetic interpretation much beyond this. De Heusch's detailed survey of African sacrificial rites and beliefs does adopt a semantic approach much more than in his other work, though it continues to be called 'structuralist' (1985).

My own approach has been through language: to explore the untranslatable 'shadows' of meaning (Ardener 1978: 108) in the indigenous terms or phrases which make up what we please ourselves to call an underlying structure of oppositions. One example actually concerns the alleged opposition between male and female. Thus, we often share our informants' characterization of women as persons who are expected to move at marriage. We speak of the exchange of women, and both folk and analytical assumptions are of mobile women and static men. Men stay on the land and women move between descent groups or villages. This contrast is extended in other ways which reinforce assumptions of male authority, strength, a dominant role in perpetuating the society, and female subordination, weakness, and an ancillary role in reproducing society. Yet, when we look etymologically at some of the Bantu terms in Africa for woman, wife, co-wife, etc. we in fact often find a reference to women as the fixed and constant reproducers of society. Thus, the Giriama term for wife of so-and-so is *mu-kaza*. *Mu-kakazi* means co-wife, while *mu-kazi* means an unmarried girl who looks after children. The use of the suffix -*kazi*, or a similar form, to denote a woman or female roles, is in fact widespread in Bantu languages. It often has further semantic associations of female reproductive fertility and of female-induced fertility of the soil (reinforced by the notion that women's work is focused on the land rather than on cattle-herding and fishing). The terms derive from *ku-kala* to reside, stay in one place, endure, and more specifically from the causative and repetitive form of this verb, *ku-kaza*. In Giriama, this means to persist, carry on, increase. In the closely related Swahili language, *ku-kaza* means to make fast, tighten, with the derived term, *Mkazi*, also referring to God as the upholder (of the world). The underlying notion of fixity, persistence, continuity, and surely, strength, and the linking of this to womanhood, seems to me persuasively archetypal over large Bantu areas at least. It is in secret talk, jocular asides, and special songs that women are most likely to explore, so to speak, this semantic reversal of their official status. As speaking subjects they can develop the knowledge of subversion even if they lack the power, and it is by no means the case that an 'underlying structure' constrains them. Further semantic analysis of other parts of the world might indicate whether such ideas are more extensive (see Parkin 1979a: 329—35).

To take another example of this approach through the regional analysis of ontological concepts, I have elsewhere suggested that a group of terms used to refer to the act of crossing (over) and of straightening is each likely to figure in a number of associated expressions ('metaphors') denoting or connoting 'ritual' danger and safety respectively. Thus the Bantu root term -*kida** (from Guthrie) exists in actual languages as, for example, -*kira, chira, kila, chila,* etc., which means to cross over or traverse, and may be the basis of ideas concerning afflictions resulting from the breach of various prohibitions (Parkin 1978: 327—30; 1979b; and, more recently, Epstein 1981). Given the prevalence of this association in other quite unrelated languages in the world, we have something of a semantic archetype which need not be posited as a universal but simply as a recognizable feature of human languages, all of which, if not easily nor directly translatable, do at least mutually communicate sense and perspective.

At this point, then, it is clear that we are back with discourse. I am arguing that ethnographers can re-define the familiar Western concepts by which we measure and compare other cognate societies through a kind of cross-cultural etymology. The point of this etymology is to show areas of semantic overlap. A superb example is provided by Southall in a paper on 'cross-cultural semantics', in which it is shown that linking two otherwise linguistically and culturally distinct neighbouring peoples, there are terms and concepts which derive from common sources (1971).

Discourse comprises but involves more than etymology. It consists of constraints and directives arising from 'regularized' accidents of history, so to speak, rather than from any plan or predictable logic. The metaphor also reminds us that, however brilliant the comparison of social formations, we are in the end concerned with how people speak and think about them. In speaking about variations on what appears to us to be a common pattern, people are in fact giving themselves and us a range of perspectives. Different speakers may be aware of the common pattern, as when nearby ethnic sub-groups reverse their customs and openly talk about such reversals. Where there is no such apparent consciousness, then we are entitled only to claim that it is we, the outside ethnographers, who see them as perspectives on a theme. This illustrates the point that we educate ourselves in tracing differences among the 'other'.

Needham's suggestion that polythetic classification better denotes the reality of how institutions may be compared with each other has been very influential, both in exercises in comparative definition and in our thinking generally (1975). But we can go further with it than see it as proceeding only from the tabulation of successively overlapping but not wholly shared formal criteria. Polythetic classification can be seen also as the chain of perspectives which link the speech of peoples within and between so-called discrete cultures. What I, as a Nuer, call descent, may be akin, through what it lacks as well as shares, to what you, as a Dinka, call descent, and so on between neighbours. The sense of comparability comes from what is absent as much as present, and the different utterances add to the patterns which we, as ethnographers, may capture and add to our own store of perspectives. The term descent, and its translated equivalents, are then part of what Derrida (1972) has called an 'endless signification', in which surplus meaning always flows from the use of a term in its infinitely varying contexts.

This surplus meaning need not be seen as existing at different levels: the one higher or more fundamental than the other. Descent fulfilling all designated criteria is not purer than descent fulfilling only one. They are equally relevant alternative perspectives whose relevance is decided by whatever value a people places on them. Nor should a concept, like descent, which refers metaphorically to another concept, like right-handedness, be regarded as somehow more central. In comparing the Luo and Kikuyu of Kenya, I described the Luo as debating the relative values of two male-headed family types: the compound polygnous and the monogamous. I also described the Kikuyu as comparing two types: the male-headed monogamous and the female-headed matricentric (1978: 295—6).

The comparisons could be given as follows:

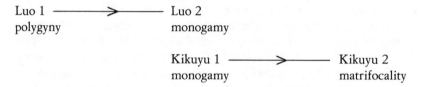

Luo 1 ——————> ———— Luo 2
polygyny   monogamy

Kikuyu 1 ————> ———— Kikuyu 2
monogamy   matrifocality

For both peoples, questions of ontological re-definition were raised. For many Luo the shift from polygyny to monogamy was tantamount to their resembling the rival Kikuyu, and therefore to be resisted. For many Kikuyu, the shift from monogamy to matrifocality was seen as an acceleration of the war between the sexes. The place of men and women in the world was being re-defined.

The common element shared by the two peoples was monogamy. But it was placed by each people within a different framework. For conservative Luo it was the route to polygyny, and therefore the proper means of reaching full manhood and lineal perpetuity. For 'radical' Luo men and women, as for Kikuyu men, it was a desirable end in itself. For these people monogamy should not be followed by polygyny. Polygyny was regarded as a waste of resources that could be better spent on educating few children to a high standard, rather than many to limited levels. In all cases key words were used to describe these different human states.

There is no value in distinguishing these as different *levels* of comparison. The comparisons are all part and parcel of each other and are the surplus meaning which results when people focus on a limited number of key words to refer to a range of experiences. Such speakers create more and more perspectives from the use of these few words which we, as outside listeners, apply to our experiences. Hence my use, in the comparison, of the phrase, 'war between the sexes', which is, of course, a perspective which any Westerner will recognize, and which therefore becomes added, as 'our' reflection, to those of the Luo and Kikuyu.

From this view that distinguishing levels of comparative relevance and meaning falsely distorts the way speakers themselves talk about experiences, we move to what I think is a key problem in structuralist comparison, whether of the regional or global kind. It is a problem which was not, curiously, anywhere as great in the typology-making of previous years. The problem is the tendency which all of us, perhaps, have in imbuing central significance to the expression 'underlying structure' or some such phrase.

The structuralism of, say, Lévi-Strauss or Piaget has the idea either of a generative structure and its surface products, or of a structure of hidden potentialities which are realized as the manifestations (cultural or whatever) which we can see. In both cases the underlying structure is the privileged one: it is the essence, powerhouse, black box, mind, or creative field, to which the appearance of phenomena are forever indebted. Durkheim saw society as being privileged over and above the individual, regarding the latter as little more than the product of the former, and in linguistics Saussure made explicit the controlling power of *langue* over *parole*, investing *langue* with the rules, and *parole* with rule-governed creativity which was too varied, random, and elusive for us ever to capture in analysis. This is too well-known to require elaboration, except to insist that, for all the current post-structuralist criticism, an unambiguous structuralism made possible an anthropology that could dispense at one stroke with history, psychology, and sociology, as these are conventionally understood. I was once asked to imagine what anthropology would now be like if Lévi-Strauss or one like him had not existed. This is a disarmingly simple question with, however, mind-boggling implications. No doubt it may be argued, in parody of comments from elsewhere, that if Lévi-Strauss had not existed, we would have had to invent him. However, I would like to speculate that an alternative course may have been open to us which, because it originates from outside the entrenched disciplines of academe, was less consciously concerned to advance, launch, or break with a distinctive self-disciplinary view.

Impressionism has been called an approach in art that is concerned with depicting 'variations on a theme'. Since, as I mentioned above in my reference to Yalman, this is one of a number of phrases by which structuralism has been identified, we should expect to find the 'theme' in impressionist art as being equivalent to an idea of a generative, underlying structure or logic, and the 'variations' as little more than surface manifestations of that logic. But, in looking at, say, the work and views of Cézanne, we find no such equation, even during his more theoretically reflective final decade. The six variations of, for example, *Still Life with Apples and Oranges*, can suggest a sense of completeness and unity, or a development, if looked at in the order in which they were probably painted (see Reff 1977: 29—30), of the artist's conception of colour; and other aspects of his work. Yet these variations cannot ever be regarded as complete, nor as a full development of the artist's explorations into colour. Had he wanted to, he could have painted a seventh, eighth, or n-th number of variants, and the sense of completeness and overall unity would still be evident to us. It is the way we regard the sum of the variants, however many there are, as interlocking yet independent perspectives that gives us the overall unity. It is we as observers who construct the unity and impute artistic development.

The crucial issue here is understanding the idea of variation. Is each painting a variation of another variation or of some idea resting in nature? It is in fact neither. Now it is perfectly true that Cézanne's stated objective was to 'read nature and to realize it' (the model being painted being the aspect of nature in question) (Gowing 1977: 61—2). But this separation of nature and its many realizations did not privilege one over the other. The two had equal status. They were complementary. He is reported as having said 'There are two things in the painter, the eye and the mind; each of them should aid the other. It is necessary to work at their mutual development, in the eye by looking at nature, in the mind by the logic of organized sensations, which provides the means of expression' (cited by Gowing 1977: 61—2). Each variation, then, is one of a potentially endless creation of complementary perspectives. Again, this view is not unlike Derrida's (1972) concept of endless signification. Even though Cézanne would speak of 'laws', they were not those that generate less worthy products. The 'law of harmony' was simply the sequence of colours making up the spectrum. It was perfectly visible there in nature itself and also available to us for our creative use, to divide the spectrum up into as many hues as we wish. If there are constraints of colour and, indeed, of form, they are as irrelevant to our creative endeavours as the question of whether time, space, and the universe are or are not bounded.

In the structuralism that came to dominate both linguistics and anthropology, the idea of a controlling logic absorbed phenomena: it caused structuralists to regard appearances as governed and limited by an essence. Instead of endless but illuminating perspectives, we had the countless elaborations of culture converted back into a limited set of principles.

The humanities have responded to this privileging of underlying structures by attempts at deconstruction. Yet, we need only go back in art to cubism at the beginning of this century to realize that a very explicit deconstructionism was already at work. Since the later Cézanne was also effectively the founder of cubism, we have a nice line of continuity from his artistic perspectivism to deconstruction, during which the idea that a controlling essence determined all else was never allowed to develop.

I find it remarkable that, at roughly the same time, the Cartesian heritage should culminate in Saussure, while the artistic pragmatism of impressionism and cubism should become, say, dadaism, which openly mocked the possibility of even thinking in terms of fixed structures and certainties. Given that both the cubists and dadaists were doing what post-structuralists want to do today, we can only conclude that the artists were a couple of generations ahead of the philosophers, linguists, and anthropologists. The experimentation of illustrative form preceded that of the word. Remembering the power of prehistoric rock paintings to move us today both emotionally and intellectually, this priority is perhaps to be expected.

It does, however, mean that we should imagine ourselves back with Cézanne and ask ourselves what kind of a comparative anthropology his work might have inspired.

First, we might have conceded that no culture is in any sense original, however remote it might be. Any so-called discrete culture is a re-working of a myriad of other previous cultures, just as an object of art or a text are the laboured products of many predecessors.

Second, this idea of culture as a constantly re-worked product would not have led us into the blind alleys of relativism and universalism. The re-workings would have neither beginning nor end, nor be subject to underlying rules. They would simply be the most harmonious bringing together of diverse and ever-accumulating perspectives.

Third, our encounter with Saussure might have taken a different turn. Having satisfied ourselves that endless *visual* perspectives are our reality, we could have used the metaphor of language to the same end: society and culture consists of limitless *discursive* perspectives.

Fourth, through this self-conscious use of metaphor we might have seen much earlier how the language of comparison is itself metaphorical: indeed that metaphor is comparison is metaphor.

Finally, we might then have arrived at a conclusion, which I think is central to this whole argument: that the human drive to compare is really the search for continuity in phenomena.

This final point in fact makes two claims. The first is that humans everywhere are driven by this quest for continuity, even though they may vary in the value they place on what and how they see things and/or people linked. This is clearly an ontological claim that people everywhere have theories about how they exist, become other people or other things, and how these differences arise. We can see the continuity as descent, property, collective solidarity, reciprocal exchange, the alternation of generations, scholarship, and so on. Secondly, however, comparison ultimately seeks identity in diverse cases. For Peirce, this is the description of continuity (1968). Even when we compare ethnographic cases and conclude that they contrast with or are the inverse of each other, as in Nadel's famous study of witchcraft in four societies (1952), we really describe them together as a larger realm of possibilities. The Mesakin are the obverse of the Korongo only because each lacks what the other has. They are linked in the comparison by a pattern of presences and absences. They are part of an extending range of overlapping perspectives, each incomplete in itself. The incompleteness is what inspires us to search for more.

I would conclude, then, by saying that anthropologists need only to realize that what is really at issue is not comparison but how to represent continuity in the diversity we call cultures. We have long learned not to expect to find original causes, permanent structures, and independent natural laws in the discourse we call culture. Next we may learn that our endless perspectives on those of others, which we call their culture, are the creative quest that is both means and end.

Visually, though inartistically, the argument is:

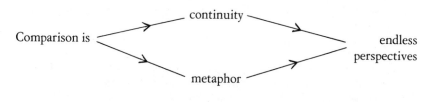

NOTES

1 The legacy of Comte's equation of bodily element, tissue, organ and species with family, authority, community and humanity is less in these parallels than in the functionalist atomism characteristic of organic metaphors.

2 Here it should be noted that Leach's own earlier work on the alteration of *gumsa* and *gumlao* systems was unlikely, by itself, to have led him to coin his rubber sheet metaphor. He needed Lévi-Strauss's structuralism for that. For the *gumsa* and *gumlao* systems were *not* variations on a theme. They *were* both manifestation and essence, both variation and theme. There was no underlying generative grammar.

REFERENCES

Ardener, E. 1978. Some outstanding problems in the analysis of events. In *The Year-book of Symbolic Anthropology* (ed.) E. Schwimmer. London: C. Hurst.

Burnham, P. 1987. Changing themes in the analysis of African marriage. In *Transformations of African Marriage* (eds) D. Parkin and D. Nyamwaya. Manchester: Manchester University Press; Bloomington: Indiana University Press.

Crick, M. 1976. *Explorations in Language and Meaning.* London: Malaby.

Cunningham, C. 1973 [1964]. Order in the Atoni house. In *Right and Left: essays in dual symbolic classification* (ed.) R. Needham. Chicago: Chicago University Press.

Derrida, J. 1972. Structure, sign and play in the discourse of the human sciences. In *The Structuralist Controversy.* Baltimore: Johns Hopkins University Press.

Dupire, M. 1970. *Organisation Sociale des Peul.* Paris: Plon.

Epstein, A. L. 1981. *Urbanization and Kinship.* London: Academic Press.

Fardon, R. 1984. Review of L. de Heusch *The Drunken King, or the Origin of the State.* 1982. *Africa* 53: 102—4.

Geertz, C. 1973. *The Interpretation of Cultures.* London: Hutchinson.

Gowing, L. 1977. The logic of organized sensations. In *Cézanne: the late work* (ed.) W. Rubin. London: Thames and Hudson.

Héritier, F. 1981. *L'exercise de la Parenté.* Paris: Gallimard.

Heusch, L. de 1981. *Why Marry Her?* Cambridge: Cambridge University Press.

——1982 [1972]. *The Drunken King, or the Origin of the State.* Bloomington: Indiana University Press.

——1985. *Sacrifice in Africa: a structuralist approach.* Manchester: Manchester University Press.

Hobart, M. 1978. The path from the soul: the legitimacy of nature in Balinese conceptions of space. In *Natural Symbols in South East Asia* (ed.) G. Milner. London: School of Oriental and African Studies.

Kuper, A. 1975. The social structure of the Sotho-speaking peoples of southern Africa (Parts I and II). *Africa* 45: 67—81, 139—49.

——1980. Symbolism and the Bantu homestead. *Africa* 50: 8—23.

——1982. *Wives for Cattle.* London: Routledge and Kegan Paul.

Leach, E. R. 1961. *Rethinking Anthropology.* London: Athlone.

Lévi-Strauss, C. 1963. The bear and the barber. *Journal of the Royal Anthropological Institute* 93: 1—11.

Littlejohn, J. 1967. The Temne house. In *Myth and Cosmos* (ed.) J. Middleton. Austin: University of Texas Press.

Muller, J. C. 1981. *Du Bon Usage du Sexe et du Mariage.* Quebec: Serge-Fleury.

Murdock, G. P. 1949. *Social Structure.* New York: Macmillan.

Nadel, S. F. 1952. Witchcraft in four African societies. *American Anthropologist* 54: 18—29.

Needham, R. 1971. Remarks on the analysis of kinship and marriage. In *Rethinking Kinship and Marriage* (ed.) R. Needham. ASA Monographs 11. London: Tavistock.

____ 1975. Polythetic classification: convergence and consequence. *Man* (N.S.) 10: 347–69.

Parkin, D. 1978. *The Cultural Definition of Political Response*. London: Academic Press.

____ 1979a. The categorization of work. In *The Social Anthropology of work*. ASA Monographs 19. London: Academic Press.

____ 1979b. Straightening the paths from wilderness. *Journal of the Anthropological Society of Oxford* 10: 147–60.

____ 1980. Kind bridewealth and hard cash: eventing a structure. In *The Meaning of Marriage Payments* (ed.) J. Comaroff. London: Academic Press.

____ 1982. Introduction to *Semantic Anthropology* (ed.) D. Parkin. ASA Monographs 22. London: Academic Press.

Peirce, C. S. 1968 [1923]. *Chance, Love and Logic: philosophical essays*. New York: Barnes and Noble.

Reff, T. 1977. Painting and theory in the final decade. In *Cézanne: the late work* (ed.) W. Rubin. London: Thames and Hudson.

Rivière, P. 1971. Marriage: a reassessment. In *Rethinking Kinship and Marriage* (ed.) R. Needham. ASA Monographs 11. London: Tavistock.

____ 1984. *Individual and Society in Guiana*. Cambridge: Cambridge University Press.

Salmond, A. 1982. Theoretical landscapes: on a cross-cultural conception of knowledge. In *Semantic Anthropology* (ed.) D. Parkin. ASA Monographs 22. London: Academic Press.

Southall, A. W. 1965. A critique of the typology of states and political systems. In *Political Systems and the Distribution of Power* (ed.) M. Banton. ASA Monographs 2. London: Tavistock.

____ 1971. Cross-cultural meaning and multilingualism. In *Language Use and Social Change* (ed.) W. I. Whiteley. London: Oxford University Press.

Southwold, M. 1979. Religious belief. *Man* (N.S.) 14: 628–44.

Turton, A. 1978. Architectural and political space in Thailand. In *Natural Symbols in South East Asia* (ed.) G. Milner. London: School of Oriental and African Studies.

Yalman, N. 1967. *Under the Bo Tree*. Berkeley: University of California Press.

4

Translation as a Creative Process: The Power of the Name

Joanna Overing

My discussion will centre upon the creative process of translation. It will be a plea for that creativity which assumes from the start the value of an anthropology which is based upon a dadaist methodology. Feyerabend in *Against Method* (1975) argues such a case for science, and states that progress in science has been achieved to the extent that its practitioners have indulged in such an anarchistic methodology and in so doing ignored its 'law and order' alternatives. In a footnote (1975: 21, n. 12), he comments that upon reflection he would prefer the term 'dadaism' to 'anarchism', since political anarchism in practice 'contains precisely the kind of Puritanical dedication and seriousness' that he detests. The dadaist, in contrast to the anarchist, Feyerabend says,

is utterly unimpressed by any serious enterprise and he smells a rat whenever people stop smiling and assume that attitude and those facial expressions which indicate that something important is about to be said. A dadaist is convinced that worthwhile life will arise only . . . when we remove from our speech the profound but already putrid meanings it has accumulated over the centuries ('search for truth', . . . 'passionate concern').

(1975: 21, n. 12)

In advocating an anarchist/dadaist methodology for science, Feyerabend (1975: chapter 17) unravels what he sees as fictions of 'scientific methodology'; those prescribed by such philosophers of science as Popper, Hempel, and even by his late friend and fellow-renegade Lakatos. The fictions he finds most harmful are those created by the logicians with their illiterate demand for a single and simplified objective language for analysis, their preaching of the virtues of clarity, consistency and tightness of argument, their demand for definitional clarity, and their insistence that the success of any given investigation is dependent upon the application of a particular set of 'laws of logic' (see also Barnes and Bloor 1982: 35). All such demands, Feyerabend argues, lead to a conceptual totalitarianism which is directly forthcoming from a modern Western metaphysics which posits the existence of one 'true world', an external, objective, unchanging 'reality' (compare with Hawkes 1977: 103; Goodman 1978; and Barnes and Bloor 1982). What should be both interesting and highly puzzling to us is that the model for Feyerabend's anarchist/dadaist methodology which would serve to combat the strait-jacket of traditional scientific methodology is that of anthropology (1975: 252).

Since anthropology is Feyerabend's model for a future of hope in science, we need to look respectfully (if not dedicatedly) at those aspects of anthropological methodology upon which he pins such hope; for it is clear that much in science of which Feyerabend despairs is also part and parcel of most anthropology as we know it to be practised. The same fictions underlie our own discipline: we too believe our discoveries are due to an approach which, when followed, actually hinders the possibility of discovery. Only some anthropology, the best of it, is a result of an anarchist/dadaist methodology which Feyerabend sees as being the great strength of successful anthropology and, in his view, successful science in general.

What fascinates Feyerabend about anthropology is its recognized involvement with incommensurable systems. 'Incommensurability' is a notion about which one must attempt to be clear in discussion; for its meaning is almost as varied as the number of scholars who, in argument, use the term. Analytic philosophers in the on-going 'rationality' debate usually define commensurability in terms of a prescriptive or formal view of logic. It is in their knowledge interests to assume the universality of this view, and upon it depends their own paradigm of science (see Overing 1985b; Hobart 1985). In their view, if such a rationality does not fit, then incommensurability follows. The issue of incommensurability is thereby reduced to academic question and never to practice, since its occurrence by their own definition of it (the negation or omission of a rationality which they state to be a universal) is impossible. For many analytic philosophers, human nature is known and charted, and incommensurability would at the least be a daft act against it (see Hollis 1982).

There is no need, however, to discuss incommensurability in terms of a specific cognitive process and a specific human nature, i.e. the Western one. Feyerabend takes the more anthropological road by defining incommensurability (1975: chapter 17) as two world views based upon totally different universal premises. Thus, as he uses the term, and I shall mean no more by it in the following discussion, incommensurability refers to difference in metaphysical ideas. Despite the dogma of certain philosophers, the critical question of effect of premises upon 'styles of reasoning' still must be investigated. But the focus comes to be shifted to knowledge and away from the hoary question of 'mind' and 'rationality'. As an aside, the anthropologist should give a sigh of relief to realize that the successful description of alternative worlds, which may well make a travesty of the philosopher's possible ones, carries with it no implications which might offend the 'liberal' sensibility. My argument below is basically that the anthropological focus is rightly upon 'products of the mind', and not mind *per se.*

The aspect of the problem of incommensurability that interests Feyerabend in anthropology is the requirement that 'alien' ontologies (or cosmologies, in his terms) must be expressed by the anthropologist in his own language. Unlike Winch who despairs (1970a, 1970b) when faced with the task of translating, Feyerabend sees the communication of systems or statements incommensurable to our own (or to the one at hand, e.g. the language of a particular theory) as a challenge and as an art of the possible. In the first place, no language is magically set forever. As Feyerabend (1975: 251) notes, languages can be *bent* in many directions and 'every language contains within itself the means of restructuring large parts of its conceptual apparatus' (1975: 273). Otherwise, neither science fiction nor science would be possible — nor would anthropology. It is this aspect of comparison, that of the *description* of systems more or less incommensurable to our own, on which I am focusing in this discussion.

The view that all language is metaphorical or that a large number of important scientific concepts are metaphorical — and vague — is becoming an increasingly acceptable position among philosophers of science (see the volume edited by Ortony, 1979; see also Ricoeur 1978; Lakoff and Johnson 1980; Hesse 1985). Feyerabend is not alone among philosophers of science in his argument that vagueness and lack of clarity in major analytical concepts are critical aspects of scientific methodology. The strain toward definitional clarity is increasingly seen to be one of the more stultifying dogmas of logical positivism (see Overing 1985c). Wittgenstein (1953) talked about the 'blurred' edges of concepts and also argued for vagueness: he said that we want to say there cannot be any vagueness in logic and we expect clear rules of the logical structure of propositions; but on the contrary we need to overcome such preconceived ideas of crystalline purity and accept the fact that the criteria of membership for most natural kind terms *cannot* be fixed by definitional convention (see Wittgenstein's (1953: 34 ff.) discussion of 'family res- semblance'). Wittgenstein (1953: 34) raises the same question about concepts in aesthetics and ethics, and this is of obvious relevance to social anthropology where the description of moral universes is a basic project of the discipline.

Kuhn (1979) on the same topic, observes that a defining description of any natural kind term is an arbitrary one. He gives the example of 'electric charge' which is a concept that has a number of ambiguous referents and for which the actual establishment of a particular referent requires a good deal of knowledge, a process that is not particularly enhanced by definitional criteria. Like the anthropologist in a foreign land who knows too little and labels a relationship as one between father and son when he should have labelled it as one between brothers-in-law, the young scientist often makes a mistake about the referents to 'electric charge'. His knowledge of language and definitional criteria are not at stake; but his knowledge of the world is. I shall return to the problem of knowledge and anthropology below.

Aside from the difficulty of 'adequately' defining any powerful abstract concept, it is the *creative* power of the simplified observational language constructed in accordance with certain laws of logic and with rigid definitional criteria that is especially being called into question and which the above authors are characterizing as the great myth of the natural sciences. It is, in particular, the transitional stages in theory building, as one moves from the old to the creation of the new, that must be accompanied by 'irrationality' (with respect to the old): creativity can only occur through a determined production of nonsense and the allowance for such production. As Feyerabend rather whimsically asks:

let us study the language of new theoríes not in the definition-factories of the double-language model, but in the company of those metaphysicians, physicists, playwrights, courtesans, who have constructed new world views!

(1975: 282)

Madness must be allowed before the sanity of the new world view can emerge. To remain within the bounds of the established observational language and its logic restricts discussion to what is already 'known' and 'understood'.

THE FUTURE OF AN ILLUSION:
DEFINITIONS AND THE POWER OF LABELLING

It cannot be denied that much of our argument in anthropology is directly centred upon the problem of 'correct' definition, rather than upon the elucidation of worlds alien to us and our own terminology. We spend an inordinate amount of time in our teaching — to the dismay of our students — upon our jargon, upon the definition of this or that, of marriage, descent, alliance, culture, society, ethnicity, kinship-based society, or — to their even greater despair — on the deconstruction of these terms. We may willingly accept the impossibility of universal definitions, but we do not at the same time spin out for our students the implications for anthropology of our deconstruction because we ourselves have only partial insight: we see that the definitions do not work, but we are uncertain and frustrated by their failure. We feel inadequate in the face of 'blurred edges' and vagueness. We have been indoctrinated both subtly and not so subtly with the wisdom of the myth of science.

If we look at the *structure* of successful deconstruction[1] in anthropology, we can begin to observe where the real problem lies, and this is in the definitional process itself, the great illusory quest of scientific methodology. If such a quest is an illusion for the natural sciences, how much more is it so for anthropology where we are not merely dealing with concepts, but with concepts of concepts and human agency. What we discover is that each of our labels carries along with it a good deal of baggage. Lévi-Strauss (1963) in his attack on the analytical value of the construct 'totemism' showed us that the term had been used not only to label a particular mode of classification, but to 'identify' a cluster of institutions that scattered out into the domains of marriage, religion, and politics, a clustering which was more a figment of the anthropological imagination than the case in fact. Likewise, Leach (1961) in his deconstruction of 'marriage', Needham (1971) in his both of 'kinship' and of 'prescriptive alliance', and Scheffler (1966) in his of 'descent' illustrated that each of these concepts as anthropologists used them carried in their application unwarranted assumptions about a necessary combination of particular rules, behaviour, and group formation. In brief, each term that we use seems to carry with it, as Hacking (1982) coins the phrase, its own 'style of reasoning' about the world. Each label we apply is the centre of numerous lines or relational ties that connect it to other words, behaviours, and propositions about the world or about particular worlds. Our definitions are, necessarily, always stuck to specific understandings either of the world or of worlds of particular kinds. Think of the baggage associated with such labels as the following: tribal, pre-State, hunting and gathering, capitalist, African, South American. The very use of such a term conjures up in the mind of the reader a number of other terms and a very specific kind of existence in the world, a process of decoding which is but a statement of both the power and the danger of our labelling, especially when it is taken too seriously, i.e. thought to define the facts of the matter.

The various translations of the tenth-century epic of *Beowulf*[2] when sequentially laid out are striking evidence of the power of labels in the conjuring up of new worlds, or old ones. In the nineteenth-century translations, which we can call 'the pre-Raphaelite' version of *Beowulf*, the romantic world of medieval feudalism colours the material. Rulers who are kings and soldiers who are retainers of knights must face battle with the dreaded monster. Kings and knights dwell in castles with their ladies; kings are rulers of nations, and their peoples are the kings' subjects. Adding further force to this nineteenth-century encodement of the epic as a genre of medieval romance is the stylistic use of metre and rhyme. A second version of *Beowulf*, a modern translation, is one that we can call 'the African' model, for in it, with what is nowadays a typical attempt to capture the 'ethnographic reality' of the tenth-century Anglo-Saxon world, there are chiefs and warriors who belong to encampments, clans and tribes. Women appear in this version, and not damsels and ladies. In keeping with 'ethnographic correctness', the modern style is one of alliterative prose, and not metre and rhyme. Finally, there is a translation from Chicago which we can refer to as 'the Gangland' model. In it bosses and their henchmen gather at their headquarters to fret about the danger of the dragon, and at night they go back home to their molls. This, I suppose is also an effort to capture, albeit in idiosyncratic manner, the 'reality' of early Anglo-Saxon lifeways.

The three worlds presented in these various translations, the 'Pre-Raphaelite' version, the 'African' and the 'Gangland' models, are totally incommensurable with one another. What is more, there is no logical terminology to explain or *judge* the shift from the one to the next: through the use of a particular *set* of related concepts each translation creates a transformation of the *Beowulf* material that is both closed and totalizing. To comprehend the 'Gangland' model the universal principles (in the terms of Feyerabend 1975: 269) both of the 'pre-Raphaelite' and of the 'African' versions must be suspended. Each version is *irrational* when viewed through the labels of the other two, and it is impossible to judge the superiority of one translation through the concepts used to construct the others. The implications of the totalizing effect of the use of a set of related concepts for the quest of an objective common language of analysis or for a common stock of primary theory (as, for instance, postulated by Hollis and Lukes (1982: 9)) are obvious. As Feyerabend comments:

a change of universal principles brings about a change of the entire world. Speaking in this manner we no longer assume an objective world that remains unaffected by our epistemic activities when moving within the confines of a particular point of view.

(1978: 70)

The argument of Barnes and Bloor (1982) on the impossibility of direct translation is similar to that given by Feyerabend. In questioning the promotion by Hollis and Lukes (1982) of the existence of a 'rational bridgehead', a common core of belief and logic shared by all cultures, they too stress the incommensurability of belief systems as one moves from culture to culture.

They characterize concepts as 'arrays of judgements of sameness' and note that 'every such array, being the product of a unique sequence of judgements, is itself unique': 'no array in one culture can be unproblematically set into an identity with an array from another culture' (Barnes and Bloor, 1982: 39). In short, a shared natural rationality by no means guarantees one unique logical system, and the authority of any given system of logic is both moral and social — not natural (see Barnes and Bloor 1982: 44). Thus, any translation for practical purposes is acceptable as judged by contingent and *local* (theirs or ours) standards. I wish to explore the possibility that such an argument of relativism need not cause the social anthropologist to despair.

We worry about the 'proper' and the 'exact' translation of words; we worry whether we have used terms in accordance with the received knowledge of them, as 'properly' defined. These are two separate worries, but underlying each is the same misconception both about what translation is to do and about what we are 'properly' capable of doing as a science. To seek for 'exact' translation and 'exact' definition is not only wrongheadedness, but also leads to muddled analyses and muddled arguments (see Overing Kaplan 1975). No word, and certainly no major concept, can ever be exactly translated from one language into the next. Quine (1960) has argued well on the problem of radical translation, but in doing so he has created a major philosophical 'problem', which, on the contrary, should be viewed as a triviality or as an obvious fact of life, e.g. there are no 'perfect' translations (see Feyerabend 1975: 287). The 'problem' of translation (and of 'definition') is not a problem of translation, but one of relevant emphasis and, more importantly, of knowledge, experience and creativity. It is on these issues, the relation of translation to emphasis, creativity and knowledge that I shall dwell in the remainder of the paper.

THE PROBLEM OF TRANSLATION: ANOTHER ILLUSION

It is not the 'word' that we must translate, but another way of understanding things about the world that we must comprehend and *learn*. Words do not exist in a vacuum; rather they fit into a particular 'style of reasoning' (Hacking 1982) that gives the word meaning as it sits within a network of other words, concepts, and thoughts. It is not the 'word' about which we should be anxious; we should be concerned, instead, about an 'alien' framework of thought which is based upon an 'alien' set of universal principles about the world (Overing 1985c).

Often, the word itself in all its complexity (its incommensurability) is not important to an analysis, and a 'simple' translation is adequate. For instance, with no guilty conscience I (Overing Kaplan 1973; 1975) have translated the Piaroa word *itso'de* in ethnographic descriptions of Piaroa settlement patterns as 'house' or as 'communal house': it refers to the building in which the local group resides, and it is the word which the Piaroa, Amerindians of the Venezuelan Rain Forest, normally use in referring to it. They also can subdivide the world of residences according to the shape or material of the house: *uchuo'de* is the traditional conically shaped house; *hare'baho'de* is the more modest (and easier to build) round construction; and the *redak'a itso'de* is a subsidiary house constructed of earth rather than thatch. Such refinements in ethnographic reporting would be appropriate to a discussion of status and authority in Piaroa land; for it is only a powerful man who has a following of sufficient size, the labour power, to build the large and complex structure of the *uchuo'de*.

Another contrast would be between the *itso'de* and the *ruo'de*, which are respectively the house of residence and the ceremonial house. The 'literal' translation of *ruo'de* is 'the house of the *ruwang* (leader)'. However, one must be a *ruwang* to own either the *ruo'de* or the *itso'de*, and therefore the *itso'de* is also 'the house of the *ruwang*', owned by him and so designated: he is the *ruwang itso'de*. Thus, when describing the physical layout of a plaza it is wiser not to translate 'literally' but 'appropriately', i.e., to distinguish between the ceremonial and the residential. It is the *ruwang* (leader) as the ritual leader of the settlement who is being focused upon in the labelling of the *ruo'de*, or ceremonial house; and it is therefore relevant in a discussion of ceremonial to point out the 'literal' meaning of the term, as it is equally appropriate to speak of the ritual aspect of *ruwang*ship (leadership) in such a context.

Nevertheless, if one were to attempt a *radical* translation of *itso'de*, shades of the Quinean problem of translating 'rabbit' (Quine, 1960) quickly emerge. *O'de*, as the reader might have observed from the above discussion of types of houses, is the root for 'house' while the prefix *uchu*, for instance, states the type of house. *Itsa* (*itso'de*) is a complicated prefix. If one asked a Piaroa its meaning out of the context of its use, the answer would be insect, the plural of which is *itso'tu*, a swarm of insects. However, *itsa* is also used more generally to refer to any one item, animate or inanimate, and likewise *itso'tu* is used to refer to a congregation or plurality of identical items. In myth, the Piaroa creator god and members of his family travelling with him are introduced as *itso'tu*; one must listen for a time and endure ambiguity before the personal names of the characters are given. The term for woman is *itsa'hu*, a word comprised of the singularity prefix and a feminizing suffix.

There are, then, many strands through which one could analyse the word 'house', *itso'de*. If the etymology is taken into account, the term conjures up the large communal house sitting alone — as one of its kind — in the centre of a plaza, i.e., the traditional settlement spatial organization of the Piaroa. In another analytical endeavour, one could focus upon the intricacies of Piaroa classification schemes in which the trope, synechdoche, consistently plays a large part. And, in yet further analysis, one could dwell upon the philosophical implications of a classificatory scheme that plays upon the distinction between one of a kind and a plurality of those of a kind, and the lack of marking in such distinctions between the animate and the inanimate, the human and the non-human. One could dwell upon the relationship of a multiple world cosmology and the elegant use of affixes by the Piaroa in expressing such an ontology. In short, *itsa* as a word has many aspects, or strands, which when followed through lead us to particular classifications and to abstract thinking involving universal principles quite alien to us. No single English word (e.g., 'thing') could possibly do for a radical translation, and any given discussion of the term could only deal with certain aspects of its use. 'Totality', or 'total meaning', is not what we wish to achieve in our descriptions, and it is at any rate an impossible task, just as in the natural sciences it is impossible to describe within one paradigm *all* aspects of something in the material or biological world (see D. Kaplan 1965; also see Feyerabend 1975: 279; and Evans-Pritchard 1962: 45 on realism). The achievement of appropriateness, or appropriate knowledge, for the problem at hand is our chore, just as it is in the natural sciences. Thus, in agreement with Barnes and Bloor (1982: 36) and with Feyerabend (see especially his objections to dictionaries, which he views as a 'lousy' way of introducing the concepts of a language that is not closely related to our own; 1975: 272), I stand on the side that views radical translation as a 'red herring', a false problem that if taken too seriously impedes investigations into the diversity of systems of thought and knowledge (see Overing 1985c; contrast Hollis and Lukes 1982).

The question may well be raised whether in our 'partial' translations we are not doing an injustice both to the way in which our informants 'view the world' and to their use of language. To a large extent this can be empirically established. When the Piaroa use the term *itsa'hu* ('woman') in a contrast frame with *u'bo* ('man'), I would argue that they are thinking of and referring to a female human — 'woman' — in exactly the same way as we think when we apply our word 'woman'. Context determines whether one is speaking of a child ('girl') or adult, or, indeed of a female animal (which is anyway a 'human' in two of the worlds of the Piaroa cosmos: in its home beneath the earth and in the world of the mythic past). In normal use, the Piaroa consider the word, *itsa'hu*, as a unit; they do not think of its agglutinative construction (when we use the word 'radiator', do we break the word down and think of 'an object that radiates'?). This is not to say that the Piaroa are unaware of etymology; on the contrary, word play, punning, is a frequent occurrence in everyday speech, and forms the esoteric element of chant language which is predicated upon the masterful use of affixes (Overing 1982). *Itsa'hu* most certainly does not bring to mind an 'insect', and it would only be through their own linguistic analysis that a Piaroa would note the connection, as in linguistic play or when 'pushed' by the questioning of the anthropologist.

The most important point is that communication about other frameworks of thought does not entail comparability in the meaning of words. Such communication is a matter of knowledge and experience of use, not of translation as we normally understand it to be. Too often we superimpose a particular logic on our data, distorting it, before we have sufficient knowledge to communicate appropriately. Too dutiful an acceptance of a powerful paradigm in vogue continues the 'truth' of that paradigm, but does not necessarily affirm the 'truth' of the 'facts' being structured by that paradigm. The structural analysis of kinship terminologies was (and is) a particularly obvious case of a paradigm so powerful that it rather quickly killed the possibility of further advances being made in kinship theory, the very area where anthropology was once so rich and where creative investigation was allowed.

The radical nature of the initial success of ethnosemantics, through componential analysis and through the development of transformational 'grammars' of terminologies, accounts to some extent for its power. These methods also held the lure of a promise, that of making anthropology a 'true science', one based upon a rigour of analysis and a definitional clarity never before attained. Modern lingusitics and anthropology could both be on a par with the natural sciences, and the dream of the logical positivists appeared to be fulfilled. Through the work of Lounsbury, we saw that we had been naive in our earlier understanding of the structure of terminologies (see especially Lounsbury 1964; 1968). But method became a world view: the logic of the method through sleight of hand became the logic of terminological use, and we arrived once more at the 'universal', the genealogical meaning of kinship terms. Unfortunately it was not only an uninteresting conclusion, which in itself drove many away from kinship analysis, but the method itself allowed for no other interpretation: the meanings of terms were made to fit with the domain of logic and (Western) common sense upon which the method was premised. In other words, the course of kinship investigations was deflected into the narrow channel of that which has already been discovered through structural analysis, and the possibility of fundamental conceptual discoveries in the domain of kinship has thereby been considerably reduced. 'Truth' emerges through the sophistication of the investigator's technique, and not through his acquisition of another's knowledge.

Elsewhere I have argued (Overing 1984; 1985b; 1985c) that the formal semantic analysis of kinship domains in its method and assumptions about the world can be an impediment to knowledge and to the outsider's comprehension of the use of kinship terms in most 'traditional' cultures. While formal analysis can impose an order with only minimal knowledge of a domain, it can also preclude the possibility of learning the metaphysics of others (Overing 1985b). Piaroa kinship terms, which I have relabelled 'personal kind terms' (1985c), have heavy metaphysical and related moral loading which allows for their powerful use in the highly flexible areas of the social structuring of emotions and the playing out of political battles. In application, Piaroa personal kind classification appears whimsical and is highly irrational when judged by any canons of Western logic and cognitive rationality. Nevertheless, it is perfectly understandable as a classificatory process that is used, among other things, to express moral judgement on qualities of relationship. The predication of Piaroa personal kind terms takes one to an alien world of explanation and abstract theory construction about difference and similarity in society and the cosmos (Overing 1984; 1985c). Once these principles of explanation are understood, so then can the predication be. Neither the predication nor the alien world of explanation could be learned or expressed through formal analysis, a method which reduces such worlds to a cognitive process, that of analogic thought made manifest through classification.

In part, the present-day disdain of cultural relativism comes in the wake of structuralist dogma. And, of necessity it must do so; for the stress of structuralism, its priority, is upon certain universals of human thought. It is a totalizing cosmology, just as are functionalism and any other powerful paradigm, that when used as the sole means of understanding the world precludes the development of new ways of understanding it. As Feyerabend stresses (1975: 267 ff.), and as I hope my example of the *Beowulf* models well illustrates, one cannot develop a new way of understanding through the concepts of an old way of organizing reality: cosmology A dissolves the entire universe of thought of cosmology B. Diffusionism has no room for the facts of structuralism, just as the Homeric cosmology with its emphasis upon appearances cannot be understood through the post-Homeric cosmology where the emphasis is placed upon essences, and appearance is viewed as illusory. We are dealing with totally different understandings of the relationship between entities in the world.

When a new 'cosmology' or paradigm is being invented, its successful completion is often dependent upon purging itself of chunks of old theories which are lurking within it. Alliance theory is a case in point. Although the battle was with the descent theorists, the cosmology of Radcliffe-Brown remained firmly embedded within the alliance cosmology until sufficient *knowledge* of the variety of possibilities of 'alliance systems' was accumulated. The incommensurability of descent and alliance theory was not yet fully appreciated, and for some time the latter was viewed through some of the concepts of the former (see Overing Kaplan 1973). However, a new observational language and its related concepts cannot be tacked on to an old observational language, a process that Feyerabend refers to (1975: 266 ff.) as the 'hole theory' of cosmology. The old carries as baggage the set of concepts related to it.

KNOWLEDGE AND CREATIVITY: A METHODOLOGY OF REVOLT

Evans-Pritchard in *Social Anthropology and other Essays* (1962) said in a different manner much of what I have been arguing above: he was sceptical of the search for 'universal laws' and the treatment of society as 'a natural system'; he saw (1962: 62) the aim of anthropology instead to be the treatment of societies as moral, or symbolic, systems where the main chore of the investigator should be the understanding of systems — and especially systems of thought — incommensurable to his own (Evans-Pritchard 1962: 35). To do so, he said, is a process of learning, and not one of logical reconstruction. As Feyerabend (1975: 250) observes, *'this process must be kept free from external interference'* (his italics). One must not turn to paradigms at hand in order to rush the process of learning: the old theory quickly applied to key words and concepts would prevent the investigator from collecting the material needed to understand these concepts. Again, vagueness must be tolerated until enough information comes along.

Feyerabend and Evans-Pritchard are in agreement about the correct methodology for anthropology; where they differ is in their understanding of the relationship of such a methodology to the natural sciences. Evans-Pritchard (1962: 85) places anthropology firmly within the realm of the Humanities and the Arts,[3] while Feyerabend argues that the anthropological methodology as Evans-Pritchard describes it is exactly the one which *allows for creative success in the natural sciences*: scientific progress is much more dependent upon imagination and knowledge than upon definitional clarity and logical rigour. Clarity and logic do not lead to, but rather are the *end result* of, successful investigation.

So perhaps we underestimate the power of our own methodology. We might argue that each successful description of another society is equivalent to a *major advance* in the development of the natural sciences, and it is therefore small wonder that Feyerabend is impressed with our methodology or with its aims. In so far as we view our major task to be that of communicating incommensurability, we *cannot* have a single observational language; for the communication of each new insight is dependent upon the highly creative use of language. This is the second stage of investigation, the first being that of learning, attaining the knowledge of, a framework of thought and action based upon an entirely different set of universal principles than any previously known by us. *We are in the business of revolution*, and this is why Feyerabend turned to anthropology — and especially to Evans-Pritchard — for support of his understanding of revolutions in the natural sciences.

The most creative aspect of our discipline is that of communication and the play of complex language games to do so. As discussed above, learning key concepts of a language very different from our own tends to shatter the classification of both our own and other worlds as we already know them. This is especially the case with terms, such as *itsa* described above, whose nature consists of complex relational properties which link it to various aspects of a strange ontology. The unfolding of the strange ontology cannot be achieved by relying on the *standardized* terminology and definitions that have been developed for the purpose of describing other societies, especially those of regions distant from the society in question.

We tend to think that a set of terms is cross-culturally appropriate for societies of similar technological 'achievement', an unquestioned assumption which is a part of our heritage of evolutionary theory from the nineteenth century. We think that X type of technology requires X type of labels: headman, elder, big man, chief, shaman, priest, and king. We might have tossed out the theory, but the nineteenth-century prejudices remain with us, well-hidden, embedded in, and expressed through most of our technical vocabulary (see also Overing 1985a; 1985b). If one thinks about it, most of our jargon designates 'primitiveness' and therefore 'lesser'. We wish to capture the difference of 'the other'; yet in so doing we often (unwittingly) denigrate 'the other' through the very process of labelling him/her as different. I think it certainly true of such labels as 'kinship-based society', 'magical rites', 'mythology', 'shaman', and so on. None of *these labels* have anything to do with levels of technological 'advancement', but rather they refer to social roles, frameworks of thought, symbols, systems of morality, axioms, values and sentiments — all areas of life and related theory that may well be more sophisticated than the same areas of life and related theory in our own society. Moreover, the fact that two societies use the same agricultural techniques does not entail commensurability in other realms of living: this is a matter for empirical investigation, and not one that can be taken *a priori*. I am making an obvious point, but it is nevertheless one that should be emphasized repeatedly. We could probably do without most of this vocabulary, and, if only as an ethical stance, we should perhaps practise an exercise of purging. It is only by *not* using these terms, all coloured by a nineteenth-century morality and understanding of both human nature and human progress, that we might understand the power of the terms themselves in creating very specific worlds. Such creation imposes a constraint upon analysis and blinds us from seeing and attaining what could well be more interesting insights into areas of sophistication or complexity in other ontologies and epistemologies that the labels themselves prevent us from learning. Attempts to use more 'uplifting' labels might well have surprising results, as I (1985a) recently discovered in using the Western terms 'sin', 'guilt' and 'salvation' in discussing moral thought among the Piaroa. Such labels are not usually applied to the thought systems of tropical forest Amerindians; but except for convention, and I was able to show this to be so, there was no 'technical' reason for not using these labels. The words oriented the reader — and played as I wished on the reader's (unconscious) prejudice. It was this orientation that allowed for an easier communication of the 'stranger' elements of Piaroa ethics and ontology than otherwise would have been the case.

By giving a name to something, we create a world; by changing the name for something, we transform its impact, both emotionally and intellectually. Thus, we must often make moral decisions about the *aim* of each communicational endeavour. The label 'magic' is probably one of the more intellectually interesting words we use; but it is, as well, one of the most emotionally loaded terms in our technical vocabulary. Magic is a phenomenon that we modern Westerners do not understand, for it imputes a 'mystical' relationship between elements in the universe. A belief in the mystical entails a belief in forces imperceptible to the senses, which are real for the 'tribal' but not for us (see the discussion by Evans-Pritchard (1965: 82—4) on rationality and the mystical). We know better than they; for our technology is superior to theirs. To point to certain ritual as 'magic', no matter how well we might understand this magical action to be part of a coherent system of thought, tends therefore to denigrate.

What would happen if when we come upon a strange, 'unreasonable' ritual or a statement that ignores our empirical judgements about the world we used the term 'ontology' (what is considered real in the world or cosmos) or 'epistemology' (theories of knowledge about understanding the reality of that world or cosmos), rather than 'magic' or 'symbol' to lead to questioning about the 'unreasonable'? The labels 'ontology' and 'epistemology' are easily interchangeable for 'magic' and 'religion': all are terms referring to the realities of the world as a person (philosopher or priest) or as peoples (Western or African) know, believe, or understand them to be.

In my own work on the Piaroa (1975), I have talked about the role of the *ruwang*, his mastery over mystical forces and his knowledge of the world of the supernatural. In fact, I made an ethnographic mistake: from the Piaroa point of view the wisdom of the *ruwang* (a wizard, a shaman, a priest, or chief — whatever you will) is empirically based; for his ritual creates ontological changes *that can be seen by him*. Much of the everyday world is the *ruwang*'s own creation: it is one in constant transformation as he daily conjoins elements from other worlds, as he chases forces out of the social world, as he brings past worlds into the present and unites present worlds with the past (Overing 1982; Overing and Kaplan 1987). The comprehension of other worlds and the creation of new ones go on together as a single process (compare Goodman (1978) on scientific understanding). The *ruwang* is able to do both through his powers of sight and movement. The *ruwang*'s *ta'kwa ruwang*, his 'master of thoughts', an homunculus who dwells in his eye, flies to worlds beneath the earth and beyond it. Through the flights of his 'master of thoughts' the shaman *sees* these worlds and thereby knows their reality. Through the power of the hallucinogens that the *ruwang* takes nightly, he *sees* the protective monsters who leave their home within the armadillo shell that he taps against the floor of his house. It is his ability *to see* other realities and worlds that gives the *ruwang* his credibility as 'a man of knowledge' and thus a man of power. The Piaroa define truth in accordance with the empirical principle that truth depends upon the evidence of the senses, sight taking precedent over all else (Overing 1982). While 'magic' might be an appropriate label for the ritual of the *ruwang* within the cosmology of our own culture and discipline, it is not magic for the Piaroa: the power of their ritual does not entail forces imperceptible to the senses of the ritual leader.

I did not understand Piaroa statements about the world as they did until I changed the labels through which I was looking at their statements, i.e., when I dropped 'magic', 'religion', and 'shamanism' to look instead at 'ontology', 'cosmology', 'epistemology' and 'power'. The important lesson we can learn from the effect of this change of labels is that we must remember that the terms we use do not give us magical access into another's world; they can only aid us in, or deter us from, doing so because of the intellectual loading they carry within our own minds.[4] In construing unfamiliar statements, what must give is knowledge about the world; it is not the word itself that is critical, either ours or theirs (Overing 1985c). When there is an incompatibility between the utterance and the world as we view it, it is creativity, experimentation, and the suspension of belief that we need: once the alien world is understood, we can then make final decisions, moral or otherwise, about the appropriateness of labels, those that would enable us to communicate best about that world.

NOTES

1 I am using the term 'deconstruction' loosely. In the main, I refer to the aim of deconstruction to make obvious ideological reduction and to illustrate the instability of classifications so as to reveal the multiple aspects of elements and their inter-connectedness (see Culler 1983: 134 ff.).

2 For a summary of the various translations of Beowolf, see Chambers 1959, section 6.

3 I personally agree with Firth (1985) who has recently argued that it is irrelevant whether social anthropology is classed as an Art or a Science.

4 In the spirit of Feyerabend, the main gain in knowledge in such a case is achieved through experimentation. For me, a non-philosopher, terms such as 'ontology' and 'epistemology' were less loaded than the labels 'magic' and 'symbol'. Thus the former set allowed for easier access to a strange (for me) way of thinking.

REFERENCES

Barnes, B. and D. Bloor. 1982. Relativism, rationalism and the sociology of knowledge. In *Rationality and Relativism* (eds) M. Hollis and S. Lukes. Oxford: Blackwell.

Chambers, R. W. 1959. *Beowolf*. 3rd edn. Cambridge: Cambridge University Press.

Culler, J. 1983. *On Deconstruction*. London: Routledge and Kegan Paul.

Evans-Pritchard, E. E. 1962. *Social Anthropology and other Essays*. Glencoe, Ill.: The Free Press.

—— 1965. *Theories of Primitive Religion*. Oxford: Clarendon.

Feyerabend, P. 1975. *Against Method*. London: New Left Books.

—— 1978. *Science in a Free Society*. London: New Left Books.

Firth, R. 1985. On intelligibility. In *Reason and Morality* (ed.) J. Overing. ASA Monographs 24. London: Tavistock.

Goodman, N. 1978. *Ways of Worldmaking*. Brighton: Harvester.

Hacking, I. 1982. Language, truth and reason. In *Rationality and Relativism* (eds) M. Hollis and S. Lukes. Oxford: Blackwell.

Hawkes, T. 1977. *Structuralism and Semiotics*. London: Methuen.

Hesse, M. 1985. Metaphor, symbol and meaning. Seminar presented to the Department of Anthropology, School of Oriental and African Studies, 5 November, 1985.

Hobart, M. 1985. Anthropos through the looking glass. In *Reason and Morality* (ed.) J. Overing. ASA Monographs 24. London: Tavistock.

Hollis, M. 1982. The social destruction of reality. In *Rationality and Relativism* (eds) M. Hollis and S. Lukes. Oxford: Blackwell.

Hollis, M. and S. Lukes. 1982. Introduction to *Rationality and Relativism* (eds) M. Hollis and S. Lukes. Oxford: Blackwell.

Kaplan, D. 1965. The superorganic: science or metaphysics? *American Anthropologist* 67: 958—76.

Kuhn, T. 1979. Metaphor in science. In *Metaphor and Thought* (ed.) A. Ortony. Cambridge: Cambridge University Press.

Lakoff, G. and M. Johnson. 1980. *Metaphors We Live By*. Chicago: The University of Chicago Press.

Leach, E. 1961. Polyandry, inheritance and the definition of marriage: with particular reference to Sinhalese customary law. In *Rethinking Anthropology*. London: Athlone.

Lévi-Strauss, C. 1963. *Totemism*. Boston: Beacon Press.

—— 1969. *The Elementary Structures of Kinship*. Boston: Beacon Press.

Lounsbury, F. 1964. The formal analysis of Crow-and-Omaha type kinship terminologies. In *Explorations in Cultural Anthropology: essays in honor of G. P. Murdock* (ed.) W. H. Goodenough. New York: McGraw Hill.

—— 1968. The structural analysis of kinship semantics. In *Kinship and Social Organization* (ed.) P. Bohannan and J. Middleton. Garden City, NY: The Natural History Press.

Needham, R. 1971. Introduction to *Rethinking Kinship and Marriage* (ed.) R. Needham. ASA Monographs 11. London: Tavistock.

Ortony, A. (ed.) 1979. *Metaphor and Thought*. Cambridge: Cambridge University Press.

Overing Kaplan, J. 1973. Endogamy and the marriage alliance: a note on continuity in kindred-based groups. *Man* (N.S.) 8: 555—70.

—— 1975. *The Piaroa*. Oxford: Clarendon.

—— 1984. Dualisms as an expression of difference and danger: marriage exchange and reciprocity among the Piaroa of Venezuela. In *Marriage Practices in Lowland South American Societies* (ed.) K. Kensinger. Urbana: University of Illinois Press.

Overing, J. 1982. The paths of sacred words: shamanism and the domestication of the asocial in Piaroa society. Paper presented in symposium on Shamanism in Lowland South American societies. 44th International Congress of Americanists, Manchester.

—— 1985a. There is no end of evil: the guilty innocents and their fallible god. In *The Anthropology of Evil* (ed.) D. Parkin. Oxford: Blackwell.

—— 1985b. Introduction to *Reason and Morality* (ed.) J. Overing. ASA Monographs 24. London: Tavistock.

—— 1985c. Today I shall call him 'Mummy': multiple worlds and classificatory confusion. In *Reason and Morality* (ed.) J. Overing. ASA Monographs 24. London: Tavistock.

Overing, J. and M. R. Kaplan. 1987. Los Wo Tuha. In *Los Aborigines de Venezuela*, vol. 3. Caracas: Fundacion La Salle.

Quine, W. V. O. 1960. *Word and Object*. Cambridge, Mass.: M.I.T. Press.

Ricoeur, P. 1978. *The Rule of Metaphor* (trans.) R. Czerny. London: Routledge and Kegan Paul.

Scheffler, H. 1966. Ancestor worship in anthropology. *Current Anthropology* 1966: 541—51.

Winch, P. 1970a. The idea of a social science. In *Rationality* (ed.) B. Wilson. Oxford: Blackwell.

——1970b. Understanding a primitive society. In *Rationality* (ed.) B. Wilson. Oxford: Blackwell.

Wittgenstein, L. 1953. *Philosophical Investigations* (trans.) G. E. M. Anscombe. New York: Macmillan.

5

History, Culture and the
Comparative Method:
A West African Puzzle

J. D. Y. Peel

This paper began from an empirical puzzle: why has the course of religious change in the twentieth century been so different between two very comparable peoples of West Africa, the Akan of southern Ghana and the Yoruba of south-western Nigeria? The Akan were very much slower to adopt the world religions, and there have been striking qualitative differences in their religious practice.[1] These differences become especially problematic in the light of the most elegant and cogent general theory of African conversion (Horton 1971; 1975). For in terms of the factors which that theory specifies as relevant to conversion ('opening of relations to the wider world'), Akan society yields nothing to the Yoruba: earlier direct relations with Europe, a richer export-oriented colonial economy, earlier development of modern education, and so on. Why then was its religious development markedly slower and more uneven?

This empirical puzzle is only to be solved, I shall argue, by means of a properly historical comparison of the two societies, that is by relating the twentieth-century differences not only to other twentieth-century features but to their overall trajectories of change over several centuries. This implies a critique of the tradition of comparative study of West African societies within which the puzzle was first posed, and raises some general problems about the comparative method. In most of its forms, and particularly those practised within social anthropology, the comparative method has been adopted as a means to a natural science of society, in opposition to history as the study of unique sequences of events. So it has employed quite general sociological categories (e.g. 'prescriptive alliance systems', 'house property complex') and ethnographic descriptions of little temporal specificity (e.g. 'Bemba society'), and has sought explanation in synchronic patterns of relationships.

Yet such ahistorical modes of the comparative method leave large areas of indeterminacy. Horton's theory of African conversion is a particularly sophisticated example of it. Characteristically, the residuum which is left unexplained by 'hard' or social-structural factors, is loosely attributed either to culture or to history. This association of culture and history is appropriate because, as Sahlins has put it, 'culture is precisely the organization of the current situation in terms of a past' (1985: 155). Yet culture need not be left as a residuum, if it is considered, not as a mere precipitate of the past, but a process of reflection on it. In other words, we must fully recognize the historicity of our ethnographic data. In African societies culture assumes its most coherent and distinctive form in the idiom we call religion; so it is, in van Binsbergen's words, that 'religion seems to be a means for people to expose themselves to their collective history in a coded . . . form' (1981: 74). How true this seems to be for the Akan and the Yoruba will emerge in due course.

FIVE MODES OF THE COMPARATIVE METHOD

At the most general level, comparison is not a special method, or in any way unique to anthropology. Comparison is implicit in any method of deriving understanding through *explanation*, i.e. by determining the sufficient and necessary conditions for the existence or occurrence of any phenomenon or action. To say *why* an object or outcome is so, is to indicate particular obtaining conditions which may be interrelated, and it follows that where these conditions obtain otherwise, so also must the object of explanation. If it does not, the adequacy of the alleged explanatory conditions and/or the description of the explanandum are called into question. Comparison's key role, then, is as a test on explanations, in the manner classically set out in J. S. Mill's *System of Logic*, the 'Method of Difference' providing a more powerful test than the 'Method of Agreement' (Mill 1843: Book 6; see also Runciman 1983: 193—8). This is as true in principle for explanations of occurrences in anyone's daily life as it is for those sought in science, as true for explanation of socio-cultural as of natural phenomena. The fact that in supposedly 'idiographic' fields like history or textual criticism there is little attempt to codify the relations between classes of conditions and classes of effects in the form of theories does not affect the issue. All explanations lie open to the challenge of comparison; there is no field of empirical enquiry which does not use comparative analysis.

What, then, of 'the comparative method', sometimes argued to be *the* method of social anthropology (cf. Hammel 1980) and often discussed as if it were one single thing (e.g. Ginsberg 1961; Evans-Pritchard 1963). In fact we should distinguish between at least five distinct modes of comparative method, which differ in the ways they handle history:

1 a single, universal, ideal history or 'natural history of society';
2 a branching, concrete history, on the model of comparative philology;
3 where history is denied or ignored, as comparison is used to derive sociological universals or general laws;
4 where a degree of common history is presumed, as in regional comparative studies;
5 where it is histories, not societies, that are compared.

These modes tend to be products of particular historic moments, but at the same time they have a perennial appeal, since they represent distinct logical options for the analysis of social phenomena.

MODE I: AN IDEAL, UNIVERSAL HISTORY

Mode I began as the 'natural history of society' or *'histoire raisonnée',* and involved the search for a single logically appropriate (and hence also normative) sequence of stages. The comparative method was to provide the confirming evidence. This mode existed fully fledged by the 1760s and 1770s in the 'four stage theory' of Smith, Turgot and Millar (cf. Meek 1976). The presents of backward societies were the equivalent of the pasts of advanced societies, so that comparative evidence from contemporary non-European societies could be used to fill in or corroborate evidence for stages of Europe's past. 'It is [the American Indians'] present condition we are to behold, as in a mirror, the features of our own progenitors' (Ferguson 1966 [1767]: 80). Thinkers varied in terms of how far they used empirical or rational methods to derive the sequence of stages, and few were as candid as Adam Smith in recognizing the possibility of major divergence between rationally appropriate and empirically existing sequences (A. Smith 1964 [1776]: 340). The nineteenth century produced much fresh data, more complicated stage-models and several special applications (e.g. to marriage-types, forms of religion), as well as the authoritative paradigm of comparative anatomy and physiology, worked through most thoroughly in Spencer's theory of social evolution; but the basic components were the same.

Though social evolution had ceased to be the absolutely paramount form of social thought by 1914, Mode I comparative method continued to be practised in anthropology for some time. Indeed one could hardly find better instances of it than in such late works as Hobhouse, Wheeler and Ginsberg (1915) or Hocart (1936). Neo-evolutionism apart, some of its devices continue to find valid heuristic employment within projects of a quite different overall character. For example, the device of using an undeveloped community as a model to reconstruct the baseline form from which a culturally related but developed community has grown, has been used by M. G. Smith (1960: contemporary Abuja ≏ pre-Fulani Zaria) and Horton (1969: contemporary Niger Delta fishing villages ≏ New Calabar before the Atlantic trade).

MODE II: A BRANCHING, CONCRETE HISTORY

Mode II of the comparative method had emerged by the mid-nineteenth century, its paradigm being comparative philology. The achievement of Jones and Bopp was to explain the affinities between Greek, Sanskrit and other languages in terms of their descent from a putative common ancestor, Indo-European, and to work out rules governing the sound-shifts that lay between them. The essential point of comparison here is to reconstruct a particular *ur*-form, the actual histories of the languages being paths of divergence from it. Compared with Mode I, Mode II deals with several actual histories rather than with one ideal or normative 'history'; and its focus is the point of origin or departure, rather than the path of development from it. Moreover, whereas Mode I depends on a unity grounded *in nature* ('the psychic unity of mankind'), Mode II points us to a limited and *cultural* unity, that of the Indo-European (or Ural-Altaic or Semitic . . .) stock. A linguistic version of Mode I is found in a theory like von Humboldt's, which held that *all* languages, by virtue of their common human nature, pass through the same sequence of developmental stages.

In modern anthropology, too, there are instances of Mode II, most notably Luc de Heusch's study of Bantu mythologies (de Heusch 1982). Besides Lévi-Strauss, the major influence on de Heusch has been the corpus of work by Georges Dumézil on the transformations of mythical archetypes in Indo-European cultures (cf. Littleton 1982). Both Dumézil and de Heusch, characteristically, are more concerned to demonstrate the existence of an *ur*-form which serves to bring out the resemblances between diverse myths, than to map the historical path of that form's transformations. Nonetheless this modern revival of Mode II, if linked to a regional analysis, might in turn lead to something like a regeneration of 'culture history' (cf. Zwernemann 1983).

COMPARISON: FOR OR AGAINST HISTORY?

All use of the comparative method in the nineteenth century, and especially in its dominant Mode I, was informed by two profound inclinations. The first was to reduce a vast and perplexing variety by postulating an underlying unity of some kind: in the terms of Mill's _Logic_ the 'Method of Agreement' gets vastly more attention than the 'Method of Difference'. Consequently, the manifest variations or differences are less often explained than set aside or treated as superficial: comparative analysis thus pointed away from history.

Secondly, there was the impulse to make sense of things in terms of how they had come to be, in terms of origins, sources or paths. Thus it was to Comte that the comparative method (Mode I) was a _méthode historique_, which for him also had the appeal of providing scientific grounds for the correct path into the future. But this can only be called a 'historical' approach with considerable reservations: in the sense of dealing with time and change, but not in the sense of dealing with the unique totalities or conjunctures, the action and the contingencies, out of which concrete instances of social change are formed. It was Spencer who saw that the nineteenth-century project of a science of society was opposed to any notion of a humanistic history and, with his usual candour and clarity, set forth the grounds of his opposition: science vs. history, process vs. events, structure vs. individuals, necessity vs. contingency (examples in Spencer 1972: chapter 10). The comparative method, Mode I, was deeply bound in with such ahistoricism, as Hocart's _Kings and Councillors_ shows repeatedly. For example, discussing occupational castes in ancient Egypt, he asks rhetorically 'why dispute about ancient texts when there are living descendants of the disputed facts to study?' (Hocart 1970 [1936]: 119); while in a chapter on the rise of ethical movements in religion, that topic which engaged so much of Weber's best work and in fact had a large historical literature, he both insists that the 'causes of these ethical movements are not known' and even that it lay 'outside the scope of this work to discuss the causes' (p. 72).

Hocart must be considered an acute case of cultural lag, for Maitland had already succinctly stated comparative anthropology's dilemma: 'by and by anthropology will have the choice of being history or being nothing' (Maitland 1936 [1899]: 249). Rarely has a clear statement been so misunderstood by being read out of historical context (e.g. Lewis 1968: xv). Maitland was _not_ telling a functionalist anthropology that it should study social change. His essay, 'The Body Politic' was directed at the whole organicist metaphor in which the comparative method (Mode I) sought laws of development, Spencer being taken as the great exemplar. Instead, Maitland urged that processes of change must be seen in terms of contingencies and specific conditions, not as the working out of immanent laws of organic development. The great irony was that, whereas Maitland wanted the time perspective without organicism, what British anthropology eventually produced after the structural-functionalist revolution was organicism without the time perspective.

The fundamental methodological issues here were posed most sharply in Germany, where a strong attraction to evolutionary and organicist models of society (Haeckel, Schaeffle, etc.) coexisted with the greatest contemporary school of historical scholarship and an antipathy to Anglo-French universalism and utilitarianism in such fields as law and economics. The famous *Methodenstreit* concerned the antithesis of history and science, of *Geist* and *Natur* as objects of study, and of the placement of any so-called social sciences in this academic scheme. 'Sociology' was precisely what Max Weber called his attempt to transcend the distinction, to meet scientific standards in the definition and analysis of historical problems without denying the meaningful character of their subject matter (Weber 1968: 4—24). But for all Weber's enormous influence on the later history of sociology, social anthropology was shaped instead by the rather different response to this dilemma proposed by Franz Boas, the main conduit by which German historical idealism was transmitted (in the concept 'culture') to American anthropology. Boas polarized 'the historical method', concerned with the development of unique cultural wholes, and 'the comparative method' (Boas 1896; cf. too Eggan 1954 and Stocking 1968). The latter sought to establish synchronic links between discrete variables expressed in the terms of a general theory.

This distinction of history and comparison was already implicit in what has come to be called 'Galton's Problem' (Naroll 1973; Hammel 1980: 146—7). At the first presentation of Tylor's famous essay in the comparative method (Mode I) on the evolution of systems of marriage and descent, Francis Galton had drawn attention to a major difficulty with Tylor's research design (Tylor 1889). How could one tell whether the 'adhesions' or correlations between variables were independent cases of the postulated causal relationships between traits, thus serving to confirm the theory, or were the result of societies borrowing traits at some particular stage in their history? The problem indicates the tension which must exist between the search for a theory specifying causal relations which hold irrespective of time and place, and the evident fact that social variables may be rather 'loosely fitting' and combine in unique configurations (cultures) under contingent circumstances (history). In that sense, as Boas saw, both culture and history presented refractory materials for the comparative method.

MODE III: HISTORY IGNORED

Mode III of the comparative method is when it is detached entirely from considerations of time and change. This was only decisively achieved after the structural-functionalist revolution, but some of the groundwork was already laid. Even when, as with Mode I, the ultimate object of the comparative method was to construct a 'natural history' of society, the temporal sequence was essentially something added to the correlations from outside. The sequence itself usually followed from some naturally ordered feature such as population size or density, degree of social differentiation or level of technology. The comparative method was to determine the corresponding sequence of religious beliefs, kinship systems, ethical values, etc; and it could obviously continue to be used apart from any social evolutionary project.

Moreover, there is an ambiguity in the very notion of explaining a thing by reference to its source or origins. This may be interpreted 'phylogenetically', in which case an institutional history (as with a language's descent from an *ur*-form) is required; or 'ontogenetically', in which case the genesis in an individual of an instance of the thing is required. These two interpretations can be combined, as in Freud's theory of religion, where a historical myth about its supposed origins is taken up in an account of the origin of individual neuroses which reach out to religious solutions. We find the same thing in Frazer. For besides the evolutionary progression from magic to science, he also seeks explanation by looking for a link between some need or habit of thought which is inherent in human individuals, and some type of magico-religious action. The intellectual tedium of *The Golden Bough* is largely due to the fact that the vast range of comparative materials is used to provide repeated illustration of such linkages between source and effect according to Mill's Method of Agreement.

We are here only a very short step from Mode III, which was described by Radcliffe-Brown as a means 'to pass from the particular to the general . . . to arrive at the universal, at characteristics which can be found in different forms in many societies' (Radcliffe-Brown 1951: 15—22). This is the Method of Agreement exclusively and *à l'outrance*. In the next generation this universalist ambition was sustained above all by Fortes. In *Oedipus and Job* Fortes (albeit a little ungraciously) acknowledged the lead of Frazer in the great project 'to bring home to us the unity behind the diversity of human customs', and where he refers to the beliefs of other West African peoples it is only to point out the similarities, not to use the differences to get a better explanatory purchase on the specifics of the Tallensi situation (Fortes 1959:

10 and chapter 3).[2] Again, in 'Pietas in Ancestor Worship' (Fortes, 1970) he gives far more attention to parallel cases which fit his theory that ancestor worship is a ritualization of lineage authority, and even to extensions of it to such spheres as the 'pietas' displayed by Russian cosmonauts and Cambridge college fellows, than to problematic counter cases (such as the Tiv; cf. Edwards 1984) which might sharpen up the explanation.

The conditions for finding generalizations applying to 'all human societies, past, present and future' (Radcliffe-Brown, introduction to Fortes and Evans-Pritchard 1940: xi) were better met when Lévi-Strauss displaced the subject-matter of anthropology upwards, from social relations to 'superstructure', and explanation was sought in terms of laws of the mind, not of society. Needham's recent book *Exemplars*, written very consciously as a 'comparativist', shows the clear outcome of Mode III. Though Needham considers a historical sequence of writers, neither their pastness, nor the temporal relations between them nor their historically specific circumstances are of essential concern to him; for through comparison he is looking for 'fundamental inclinations of the psyche' or 'natural proclivities of thought and imagination', (Needham 1985: 72–4, 146, 150, 151, 184). Such things point to 'cerebral vectors' as where explanation must ultimately lie; and at that point the 'natural science of society' teeters on the edge of physiology.

MODE IV: REGIONAL COMPARATIVE STUDIES

The trajectory of Mode III, from Radcliffe-Brown to Needham, was not however the most typical development of the comparative method in the hands of social anthropologists from the 1950s onwards. This was Mode IV, where more limited comparisons are essayed, usually dealing with particular social institutions and often within a particular ethnographic area. For Africanist anthropology, it arrived in the classic volumes on *African Political Systems* (Fortes and Evans-Pritchard 1940) and *African Systems of Kinship and Marriage* (Radcliffe-Brown and Forde 1950), albeit prefaced with Mode III manifestos from Radcliffe-Brown. This mode of the comparative method did not just make use of ethnographies but, more than any of the preceding ones, really arose out of ethnography and remained close to it. Consequently much more use is made of the Method of Difference, in two principal ways: explanation and exploration.

Two essays by Nadel — who had a better idea of what he was about, methodologically speaking, than any of his contemporaries (e.g. Nadel 1951: especially chapters 8–9) — indicate the difference in emphasis. Explanation is predominant in the tightly organized argument of 'Witchcraft in four

African Societies' (Nadel 1952): two pairs of closely related societies, a single definite question about each (female or male witches? presence or absence of witchcraft beliefs?) and a clear guiding hypothesis (that witchcraft beliefs answer to frustrations and anxieties arising from the pattern of social relations). The essay 'Two Nuba religions' (Nadel 1955), on the other hand, is more exploratory, seeking to clarify a rather diffuse difference between the religions of two further Nuba peoples, one of which has a more anxious, ritually obsessive outlook, and the other a more serene and submissive attitude towards the gods. No definite explanatory hypotheses are evident here, beyond an assumption that one should look for 'more significant, because more far-reaching, causal relations connecting religion with acts of an altogether different order, that is with conditions which are functionally autonomous and hence represent "independent" variables . . .' (Nadel 1955: 676). So Nadel proceeds to look at a number of variables, most of which are germane to his interest in social psychology: the regulation of adolescence, the jural status of wives, sexual morality, even attitudes to homosexuality. Thus ethnography reaches, through the comparative method, to yet further, better ethnography.

Mode IV comparative method achieves the best results when it limits itself to a particular ethnographic region. In the early 1950s, a time when the surge of new structural-functionalist ethnography had encouraged several reviews of the comparative method (e.g. Schapera 1953; Eggan 1954), Schapera had strongly urged the methodological advantages of this, in contrast with sweeping cross-cultural studies such as those based on the *Human Relations Area Files*. At the very least, where structural relations are being investigated, comparison within an ethnographic region enables culture to be held much more securely constant. Its further potential is that it allows variations genuinely to be analysed as variants or transformations of locally given basic forms. This is a far-from-exhausted seam, as recent fine studies show (e.g. Kuper 1982a, on Southern Bantu marriage systems; Fardon 1984—5 on social organization around the Nigeria-Cameroon border). One original aim of Mode IV was to avoid being bothered by culture through setting up situations where it could be set aside as a constant, yet the regional focus also opens the way back to historical questions. Mode IV tends to converge with Mode II, as with de Heusch's work.

THE ASSUMPTIONS OF MODE IV

A full view of all the achievements and limitations of work within Mode IV is not intended here. But before turning to issues that bear directly on my initial puzzle, it is necessary to examine two closely related features of British social anthropology as practised in the 1940s and 1950s (which are yet far from extinct). They infused most exercises in the comparative method (Mode IV) without being strictly entailed by it. These are (a) holistic presentism, and (b) sociological reductionism. Together they utterly inhibit an adequate analysis of the role of culture in social transformation.

Holistic presentism followed from the practical rejection of historical explanation by the founders of structural-functionalism. The histories of pre-literate societies were unknowable; 'conjectural history', using Mode I comparative method, was worthless; apparent history or oral tradition made better sense when interpreted as charters for present social arrangements. So all social phenomena had to be explained in terms of other social phenomena with which they cohered in whole systems, or of the external conditions of such systems. With this doctrine, social anthropology acquired a wonderful self-sufficiency as a discipline, since ethnographic fieldwork, if sufficiently thorough, could provide all the material needed for explanation.

What holistic presentism does *not* provide is guidance as to what explains things. In principle, it might be environment, race, technology, even cultural values or, as Malinowski preferred, biological needs. But after Radcliffe-Brown, it was social structure: social anthropology for a while became more sociological than sociology. Now, while this still leaves open many questions about the relations between such social institutions as politics, law, kinship, the economic division of labour, it does propose a definite answer, or rather two somewhat inconsistent answers, to the interpretation of culture. The essential message is: culture does not matter much in social analysis.

On the one hand, culture is a kind of clutter, which has a certain obscuring tendency, so needs to be cleared away if valid comparisons are to be made. Because there might be 'the same kind of political structures . . . in societies of totally different culture', comparison should be 'on an abstract plane where social processes are stripped of their cultural idiom and reduced to functional terms' (Fortes and Evans-Pritchard 1940: 3). Over thirty years later Lewis, in *Ecstatic Religion*, was to propose just the same thing. He urges 'the crucial importance of distinguishing between the unique cultural forms of particular institutions and their actual social significance in any society'. Only if anthropologists do this will they 'develop useful typologies which cut across cultural *forms* and which facilitate meaningful comparison'. Thus will comparative anthropology be able to storm 'the last bastion of the unique', religion (Lewis 1971: 12).

Alternatively, instead of varying randomly, culture is argued to co-vary exactly, as a dependent variable, with the forms of social structure. If the Tallensi have a cult of their ancestors, it is not (as Frazer would have argued)

because of a fear of the dead, 'but because their social structure demands it'
(Fortes 1959: 66). And it was precisely with those forms of religion —
ancestor-worship and witchcraft/sorcery beliefs — that seem *in fact* to reflect
social structure most closely that the comparative analysis of religion was
attempted to best effect: Wilson (1951), Nadel (1952), the various essays
collected in Middleton and Winter (1963), Douglas (1967), McKnight (1967),
Kopytoff (1971). As Bradbury put it in a sensitive study of the sociological
aspects of the Edo cult of the dead, where 'relations with the objects of
worship derive very directly from the typical experiences of individuals in
their relations with certain categories of deceased persons . . . severe limits
are set upon the imaginative capacities of the religious thinker' (Bradbury
1973: 230).

Bradbury clearly recognized that this need not be equally true of all forms
of religion, but any great exploration of cultural autonomy was long impeded
by a strong methodological resistance from social anthropologists. Middleton
and Winter, for example, counterposed two ways to explain the content of
witchcraft beliefs: 'cultural analysis' and 'sociology'. Only by 'sociological
analysis' (i.e. sociological reductionism), they argued, can we develop
explanations that subsume the facts from more than one society; and cultural
explanations are in any case untestable (Middleton and Winter 1963: 5—6).
Now *any* explanatory hypothesis may be impossible to test in some particular
contexts, but cultural explanations are no less testable in principle than
'sociological' ones. The contention that a social fact A in society X is due to
its being Muslim (a cultural fact) can indeed be supported by showing that it
is also present in other Muslim societies Y and Z (the Method of Agreement),
especially if it is absent from otherwise comparable but non-Muslim societies,
P, Q and R (the Method of Difference). But there has to be a theoretical
interest in finding explanations of this kind; and mostly, in the comparative
analysis of the 1950s and 1960s, this interest was excluded by satisfaction at
the power of social-structural determinism to explain at least some of the
empirical variation of African religions.

But what became clear even from the best comparative studies is that
substantial amounts of variation were left unexplained, and that these often
pointed to culture. Two examples suffice to make the point.

Gluckman's extended comparison of domestic systems among two
centralized Bantu societies, Zulu and Lozi (Gluckman 1950), is a good
example of synchronic, social-structural Mode IV comparative method. He
explains the presence or absence of the 'house property complex' and related
phenomena in terms of the presence or absence of strong agnatic lineages.
Compelled thus to extend the range of comparison, he finds his explanation
supported by the same correlations among a cluster of peoples in north-

eastern Africa. Things start to get untidy when a group of patrilineal peoples in West Africa — Tallensi, Fon, Igbo — provide a negative case — no house property complex — but this he is able to handle in a theoretically plausible, but also *ad hoc*, way, by introducing an additional negative condition — their having brother-to-brother succession.[3] But what is then the import of a case like the Yoruba, another patrilineal West African people, who manage to combine some major features of the house property complex characteristic of the Zulu, with other features more characteristic of the Lozi who lack it? Clearly it does not simply invalidate Gluckman's detailed and subtle explication/ explanation of the Zulu/Lozi differences, but it does negate any idea of a necessary link between the two variables. There is just more 'free play' between social-structural variables than Radcliffe-Brown's programme supposed, so that where variables do cohere, it is within a complex of other conditions which is the product of a particular local history. Any 'necessity' of things is the rolling product of determinations accumulating over time — a subject-matter which social anthropology, for a time, forswore to touch.

Mary Douglas's classic paper, 'Lele economy compared with the Bushong' (Douglas 1962), brings us more expressly to a similar conclusion. She asks why the Bushong are so much more productive than their neighbours, the Lele, despite identical levels of technology and a similar natural environment. Her convincing answer is that it is due to different patterns of labour use, which in turn depend on contrasting evaluations of what activities are appropriate to particular age/sex categories. In other words, the key factor is specific cultural patterns, which exist in the present simply as a precipitate of the past, and are themselves only to be explained historically.

By the same stroke, we are forced to take culture/ideas/religion seriously and to open social explanation to history. Holistic presentism had excluded historical explanations, but not explanation by reference to culture, the form in which the past exists in the present. There were some good grounds for this suspicion of historical explanations. But only its companion dogma, socio-logical reductionism, really closed the door, by refusing to acknowledge the effectiveness of any constituent of present reality besides the social relations themselves or, for those of an even harder turn of mind, their ecological and physical conditions of existence.

HISTORY REVIVED IN ANTHROPOLOGY?

For all that these were *idées maîtresses* of British social anthropology at its acme, they never won universal practical assent. Opposition to them was most forcefully expressed by Evans-Pritchard. Yet this opposition was both shifting and equivocal, and did not lead to a resolution of the problems of an ahistorical anthropology. This was because Evans-Pritchard was unable to transcend Radcliffe-Brown's terms of debate, which themselves had been set in the Montesquieu/Spencer/Durkheim tradition of science-*v*.-history; he merely opted for the other alternative. Despite his own remarkable analysis of structural transformation (*The Sanusi of Cyrenaica*, 1949), Evans-Pritchard's case for 'anthropology as history' had less to do with the treatment of time or change than with insistence on the uniqueness of what the anthropologist studies: individual cultures. History acknowledged this uniqueness, which a 'natural science of society' would deny (Evans-Pritchard 1961). The kind of 'explanation' he wanted has nothing to do with causes: it is 'exact description which bears its own interpretation' (Evans-Pritchard 1973). He was consequently unenthusiastic about the comparative method, that handmaid of science (Evans-Pritchard 1963). Some 'comparative religion' he was prepared to countenance but, insofar as it goes beyond hermeneutics, he only allowed it the very weak causal aspirations of 'relational study' (Evans-Pritchard 1965: 119–20).

But the anthropologists who most seriously re-engaged with history did *not* take their cue from the later writings of Evans-Pritchard. The new concern arose among those who had done fieldwork in some of the larger-scale African societies, typically societies which had acquired some depth of literary tradition and whose 'ethnic' traditions had the most direct relevance to the newly emergent states, peoples like the Tswana, Yoruba, Somali, Ganda and Hausa-Fulani. Methodological essays (e.g. Schapera 1962; M. G. Smith 1962), led on both to monographs (e.g. M. G. Smith 1960; Jones 1963; Lloyd 1971) and to collaborative volumes (e.g. Forde and Kaberry 1967; Lewis 1968). Though the forms of the anthropological engagement with history varied considerably,[4] the typical position was in fact diametrically opposed to Evans-Pritchard's. Rather than adopt the supposed traits of history ('idiographic', hermeneutic etc.) in order to be adequate to its subject matter, anthropology should preserve its own disciplinary identity, which was as some sort of science, and bring it to bear on questions of change. Anthropologists might interact closely with historians, but they would do distinctive things with historical data.

A full account of the contrasting styles of history and anthropology is not needed here (but see Cohn 1980; 1981). Suffice it to note briefly three characteristic ways in which anthropologists tackled historical questions.

Firstly, potted histories or ethnographies might be used to test general theories of social processes, or else theoretical models used to shed light on historical questions (e.g. Lloyd's 'conflict model' applied to Yoruba kingdoms: 1968; 1971). Implicit here is a throwback to Spencer's view (quoted in Peel

1971: 159) of the division of labour between historians ('making bricks') and sociologists ('building houses').

Secondly, anthropologists opposed the supposed historian's interest in unique sequences of events to their own search for 'structural regularities' or 'sociological time' (Morton-Williams 1968: 4). Here the most telling voice is M. G. Smith's, since no anthropologist of West Africa has collected more extensive oral-historical data or pursued such a consistent theoretical project. From *Zazzau* (1960) to *Daura* (1978) his ('parahistorical') objective has been to establish 'relations of logical necessity', holding through time (Smith 1978: 12—13). He does not shrink from the implication that the elements to be so temporally ordered require abstraction from the total historical process and that 'causal analysis', *qua* determination of the conditions of concrete historical reality, is not what he's about.

Finally, of course, there was again the comparative method. Thus Mode IV, though still marked by some ahistorical tendencies that run back a long way in the history of the social sciences, was brought directly to bear on historical questions. How it fared in relation to substantive issues in the history of West African societies, I now turn to consider.

ANTHROPOLOGY AND STATE FORMATION IN WEST AFRICA

Since the 1950s the dominant theme which has brought anthropologists and historians together has been state formation. It has been of pressing concern to West Africans themselves, and the local schools of academic historiography have made states and elites their central topic (on 'Ibadan history', see Peel 1983: 11—13). Social anthropology was able to respond effectively because it had, in its own tradition, already addressed some cognate issues. Fortes and Evans-Pritchard in *African Political Systems* (1940) provided the conceptual groundwork for Forde and Kaberry's *West African Kingdoms in the Nineteenth Century* (1967), and even the latest collection, 'Systèmes étatiques africains' (*Cahiers d'études africaines* 1982) frankly looks back to it. Moreover, behind the presentist ethnography of structural-functionalism stll lurked the evolutionary schemes, based on Mode I comparative method, of Morgan and Maine.[5] The dichotomy between segmentary lineage systems and states which was used as a static typology in *African Political Systems* was turned again into a description of process, in the studies of political centralization. State formation, or political centralization, was thus conceived as a process in which the decline of lineages is the essential condition of the state's advance.

Discussion about the causes of political centralization in pre-colonial West Africa faces a considerable initial difficulty. How do we distinguish a state of relatively greater, from one of lesser, centralization? The most appropriate sort of evidence would seem to be historically concrete actions indicative of the centre's political capacity: a king able to tax his subjects heavily, to raise armies and use them to ends determined by himself, to effect his will in distant provinces and to maintain public works, to place his own nominees in influential positions and to remove them at will. . . . On these sorts of grounds Asante and Dahomey are reasonably considered centralized kingdoms. Elsewhere, adequate historical evidence of *actions* being lacking, inferences are often made from *institutions*, typically observed in the twentieth century but presumed traditional, which are considered appropriate indicators or proxies of relative centralization. The typology contained within *African Political Systems* gives clear guidance as to what those institutions might be. The baseline for development would be a 'segmentary' state, in which titled offices belong to lineages and the king is selected by non-royal title holders from the segments of a royal lineage (e.g. Lloyd 1965; 1971: 1—8). Of the four forest kingdoms which are at the centre of discussion — Asante, Benin, Dahomey and Oyo (Yoruba) — the Yoruba approximate most closely to this model, and, in true Mode I fashion, their present condition is taken as analogous to the condition from which the others are presumed to have developed (Bradbury 1964, comparing Oyo/Benin; Morton-Williams 1969, Asante/Oyo).

There are several difficulties with this procedure. The first is logical. The argument becomes circular when the same thing, e.g. 'the decline of descent groups' is *both* used to define centralization, *and* treated as a 'factor of change' itself (cf. Lloyd 1965: 98—9). In a diachronic analysis, of course, the same institution may at one moment be treated as a cause or condition, at another as an effect. But here the comparisons are essentially static, between one generalized societal description and another, exactly in the manner of Gluckman's Zulu/Lozi comparison, albeit with the aim of isolating historically significant variables; so circularity is hard to avoid. Hence, I suspect, the perennial appeal of technological determinism, which offers a way to break the circle. Thus the argument, first put forward by Morton-Williams (1969) to explain Asante/Oyo differences, and elaborated by Goody (1971) for West Africa more widely, that military technology, specifically the horse or the gun, was the main factor determining the allegedly greater centralization of the forest kingdoms. Behind military technology lay geography (savannah/ forest) since rulers near the coast would get the guns which they could store and use to take power from lineage representatives into their own hands. But empirically, as Law (1976) has shown, Goody's geography/technology/sociology hierarchy of causes just doesn't work. To give just one example, the introduction of guns into nineteenth century Yorubaland, one of the latest areas to receive them, merely served to accentuate political fragmentation and conflict, not just between states but within them.

But centralization cannot be *plausibly* defined in this question-begging way, with a theory of the process built into the definition. The case of Asante shows this most clearly. Lloyd (1965) expressed a once common view when he grouped the Asante *with* most of the Yoruba in one category ('open representative government'), while Benin and Dahomey were placed in another ('government by political association'). In the first of these, chiefs are selected as lineage representatives, an arrangement which expresses the coherence and importance of the lineages in society at large. The latter category, indicated by non-lineage titles, close succession in the royal house etc., is more centralized. The same linking of Asante and Yoruba occurs in Fortes's essay 'Strangers' (Fortes 1975), where he argued that in both societies, because lineages are the 'building-blocks' of the community, strangers can only become members of the community through assimilation to them.[6] Mostly by the 1970s, however, the Asante and the Yoruba are placed in contrasting categories (e.g. Morton-Williams 1969), the Asante being grouped with Dahomey and Benin as relatively centralized states (gun-using, with non-lineage titled offices), in contrast to less centralized states (cavalry-using, with lineage titles), such as Oyo, Gonja or Mossi (Goody 1971). The shift in the classification of Asante resulted from Wilks's demonstration (1967) of the bureaucratic aspects of the Asante state in the late eighteenth and nineteenth centuries, which had eluded the attention of an anthropology too rooted in the colonial period (e.g. Rattray 1923; Fortes 1950).[7]

Wilks's work forces a reconsideration, not just of Asante, but of the whole comparative framework derived from *African Political Systems*. What had seemed to justify its model of centralization was that, linked to the declining significance of lineages, there should be a number of other socially significant features, including such 'common-sense' criteria of centralization as royal executive capacity (in more detail, Wilks 1975: 127). All this now collapses in the light of Wilks's account of Asante. Certainly the late eighteenth-century 'Kwadwoan revolution in government' (Wilks 1967; 1975: 446 ff.) involved the establishment of new bureaucratic offices, which were detached from the matrilineages to which titles of general community leadership belonged. But matrilineages remained of great social consequence in domestic organization, access to land and other local functions, so to be represented in the colonial ethnographies after the structures of the expansionist Asante state had fallen away. The advance of the state did *not* entail the withering away of the lineage.

Does the model fare better with the other kingdoms?

Dahomey, like Asante, combined a powerful royal system of control with the continued existence of corporate, land-holding (patri)lineages, which Herskovits (1938: I, 194) called 'the pivot of Dahomean social organization'.

Until recently, the Yoruba would not have seemed to present much of a problem. The ethnographic consensus represented their town structures as 'federations of lineages' (Llod 1960; Law 1977: 62) which failed in diverse ways to become centralized (Lloyd 1971); but this consensus is now severely questioned (Peel 1980, on Ilesha; since taken up by Law 1982: 395—6, on Oyo). Great difficulties arise from the regional variety of Yorubaland, but in general it can be said that the importance of lineage as *the* basis of social organization has been much exaggerated. Title systems don't just reflect lineage structure; in many instances residential groupings, such as quarters, are as important a principle of cooperation as descent (Eades 1980: 50—1); the so-called 'ancestral' cult or *egungun* shows a much less decisive recognition of the importance of corporate descent than do the ancestor cults in Dahomey or Asante. It is curious that corporate lineages, this supposed token of the baseline of political development, should have been more strongly emphasized in accounts of the north-western Yoruba, none of whose communities in its present form predates the wholesale upheavals of the last century, than in the centuries-old communities of the south-eastern forests, such as Ondo and Ilesha. Indeed Lloyd ends by admitting of Ibadan — the new military master of Yorubaland in the nineteenth century, which chronically failed to create a stable political centre — that its strongly corporate lineages were 'a product of the development of the political structure in response to new opportunities in the sphere of trade and war' (Lloyd 1971: 50).[8] It is true that at Ilesha the importance of non-lineage titles and non-lineal social units (such as the quarters), grew as an aspect of the town's successful expansion; but they did not bring (and cannot be used as an indicator of) any marked centralization (Peel 1980).

The last case to be considered is Benin. Its contrast with the Yoruba now looks less sharp, though the evidence of its relative centralization is not to be denied: the periodically impressive executive outreach of its kings, the extraordinary role of the palace associations in the integration of the kingdom, the stem dynasty. But is there a plausible trajectory of development? Bradbury (1973), from the evidence of the ritual opposition between the *Oba* (from a dynasty of Ife, i.e. Yoruba, descent) and the kingmaker *Uzama* chiefs (representing the elders of Benin), argued for a convergence of Yoruba and Edo (Benin) political cultures. Divergences from the Yoruba pattern were put down to *ur*-Edo cultural elements (e.g. primogeniture, lineages shallow and non-land-holding). But should we equate what seems distinctively Edo to a twentieth-century ethnographer with a putative *ur*-Edo baseline? Some things count against this: some less centralized peoples of the Edo-speaking periphery in fact have land-holding patrilineages more like the Yoruba than Benin (e.g. Otite 1973: 14—18, on Urhobo); and the *Uzama* titles at Benin, those supposed tokens of *ur*-Edo culture, are widespread as very ancient titles among the forest Yoruba (Peel 1980: 249, taking further what Bradbury 1973: 11, recognized in a footnote). In sum, it strongly looks as if at least some of those institutions distinctive of Benin were the product of its political development, rather than drawn from an *ur*-Edo baseline. If, moreover, the reduction in the significance of lineages in the heartland of the Benin kingdom was part of this process, it seems that Benin's development squares with the lineages-to-state model suggested by *African Political Systems* better than Asante or Dahomey do.

POLITICAL 'CENTRALIZATION': THE REAL PROBLEM

So what can we conclude from this debate about the conditions of political centralization in pre-colonial West Africa?

Firstly, the notion of 'centralization' is thoroughly confused. In fact, at least three distinct criteria seem to be involved. (a) All forms of political development appear to have entailed some 'concentration', an essentially spatial process by which the population and disposable resources of a region come to be concentrated at a power centre. Such concentration appears to be a necessary, but not a sufficient condition of (b) the sort of power transfer between institutions within the emergent centre that the lineages-to-state concept of 'centralization' is mostly about. Then there is (c) a growth in the capacity of a state executive to extract and direct to its own ends the labour and resources of its subjects. Criteria (b) and (c) need not coincide. Take, for example, the nineteenth-century state of Masina, on the middle Niger (Johnson 1976). This was a cavalry-based state with a mass dynasty, so belongs to Goody's group of the less centralized, by criterion (b). But its Fulani ruling estate maintained their cavalry army by extremely heavy taxation of the Bambara subject population; the land was expected to produce at least double the subsistence of its cultivators, a very high level of exploitation by West African standards. Masina was highly centralized, by criterion (c). Process (c) is surely the one which, from a general viewpoint, has the greatest historical significance. It refers to an increase in societal capacity, achieved through rulers finding ways of controlling their subjects more, making more continuous calls on their labour and resources and thus being able to take political and military initiatives not open to the rulers of less 'geared-up' societies. The large armies they raised, the vast size of their palace establishments, the accumulation of resources at their annual Customs, the road networks they maintained, all indicate that states like Dahomey and Asante took a definite developmental step. The question then is: how did they manage to do it?

It is evident that neither anthropologists nor historians have produced very satisfactory answers. The leading anthropological idea, that the advance of the state is linked to the decline of the lineage, has proved to have very little in it; process (b) is only contingently connected to process (c). Technological determinism, military or otherwise, is hardly more helpful; and even the presence of trade routes (for there is plenty of 'trade without rulers' in West Africa: Northrup 1978) does not sufficiently explain why states come into being or, in a handful of cases, succeeded in gearing themselves up to higher levels of societal performance. Can we do no more than agree with Law when he writes, after a careful review of the comparative literature, that 'ultimately, perhaps, explanations are to be sought in specific historical circumstances [for the failure of Oyo to become more centralized]'? (1977: 312). Law raises questions here about the specific factors of change, and about the value of the comparative method in general.

RELIGION, IDEOLOGY AND THE STATE

One large area of thought and activity has, by and large, been neglected by both anthropologists and historians in their attempts to explain the differences between these societies: religion. For the social anthropologists this neglect is hardly surprising in the light of the sociological reductionism which has been the main key to their interpretation of religion. Even Goody's essay 'Polity and ritual: the opposition of horse and earth' (1971: 57−72), which is almost the only treatment of religion in relation to the debate about political centralization, seems to assume that, while religion may have some real effect on the behaviour of individuals, it has no significant role in the creation of social forms. Historians too have tended in practice to deny significant historical agency to religion. The two major studies of the forest kingdoms, Wilks (1975) on Asante and Law (1977) on Oyo, have little to say about religion. It is only with Islam that a role for religion as a force of social change seems readily conceded — e.g. Johnson's argument that 'Islam, military force and taxation are connected in a complex way' in Masina's development (1976: 490 ff.)

Available evidence suggests that it was not utterly different for the 'pagan' religions, that they served as 'models for' as well as 'models of' social relations (Geertz 1966). For all that they have been little investigated, it is clear that religious innovation and controversy were integral aspects of the growth of state power in eighteenth-century West Africa. In Asante, one king provoked effective resistance from his divisional chiefs when he started to adopt Islam (Wilks 1967: 227); and in Dahomey, the great king Agaja (1708—32) introduced the Ifa cult of divination from the Yoruba (Herskovits 1938: II, 104 ff.; Maupoil 1943: chapter 2; Mercier 1954: 210). *The* central occasion for the exercise of the state's mastery over the resources and activities of its subjects was the great annual religious celebrations known as the 'Customs', preparation for which structured the activities of the entire population of the kingdom for a large portion of the year (cf. Burton 1966 [1864], on Dahomey; Rattray 1927: chapter 12, on the Asante *Odwira*). In Asante a key role in this regulation of subjects' activities was the *Adaduanan*, or 42-day calendrical cycle, which McCaskie (1980) calls a veritable *Grundnorm* of Asante life, a rooting of social activity in a cosmic pattern.

Here at last we can start to return to the initial puzzle: Akan resistance to adoption of the world religions, compared with Yaruba openness to them. For what that comparison of twentieth-century patterns of action showed is that even after the British had dismantled the structures of Asante state control, the Asante long retained a lively sense that the integrity of their society depended on the sanctions of the traditional religion. A most significant instance of this was the petition of Christian clergy, both missionary and local Akan, to the *Asantehene* in 1944, arguing that Akan Christians were loyal subjects of their chiefs, even though their religious scruples prevented them from treating Thursdays, sacred to the Earth goddess, as rest-days within the *Adaduanan* cycle (appendix to Busia 1951). It is inconceivable that Yoruba Christians (though also subject to some persecution in the early days) should have to make such a protestation as late as the 1940s. The same Akan attitude was evident in other ways too; for example, in the much greater and longer-enduring sense that chiefship and church membership were flatly incompatible, or the much commoner practice of requiring Christian converts to withdraw from the town to a quarter outside it.[9]

So my argument about religious change in twentieth-century West Africa leads back to an argument about political change, and the role of religion in it, in eighteenth-century West African kingdoms. Common to both is an insistence on an aspect of religious change which finds little cognizance in Horton's theory of African conversion. That theory is essentially cognitive or 'cool': change is explained as occurring insofar as people's new experience renders their old explanatory frameworks inadequate. The present argument, however, is that religious change is a much more affective or 'hot' process, because religion (in addition to having explanatory functions, as Horton says) also serves to define the membership of social groups and to underpin authority in them — and especially so in highly 'geared-up' societies such as Asante.[10]

It is important, when we recognize that religion serves as an ideology, to stress that it *must* be more than that. There is a danger here of another form of sociological determinism, that 'left functionalism' which embodies a teleology: the ruling class needs an ideology to justify its position, so religion must somehow be on hand to provide one. These teleologies often paper over crucial gaps in the explanation. So Wilks tells that in late eighteenth-century Asante, 'government *had* to be extended in range . . . in scope . . . and in proficiency' (1975: 127. My italics). He tells us *how* it was, but not how it *could* be so. The 'need' does not suffice to produce the effect; the crucial cultural conditions had to be met. If it 'had' to be ideology to work the trick because purely material conditions fall short — and we should never forget that in West Africa the most segmentary peoples and the most centralized states share the same technological, ecological and physical conditions of existence — there had to be some independent strength in the religious ideas drawn upon. Religion had this power because it was already the shared idiom in which both chiefs and people confronted the pains and anxieties of the human situation. *Asantehenes* really feared witchcraft (McCaskie 1981); kings of Dahomey, two of whom died of smallpox, respected its cult for all that they disliked it (Herskovits 1938: II, 132 ff.). If this was the bottom line of their reality, on what else could rulers better seek to build structures of higher obligation and control — but themselves remain constrained by its premises?

MODE V: HISTORIES COMPARED

It is now clear that some of the failure of the comparative method to explain West African centralization is to be attributed to the neglect of culture or ideology as a causal agency. But the problem goes deeper. The comparative method, as employed by social anthropologists on these questions, is really a combination of two modes: it is Mode I in its view of the process of centralization, and Mode IV in its views as to causes. Now both these modes proceed by abstracting their data from history, even when their aim is an idealized, general history or the determination of real historical causes. For what they compare are either 'societies' described in the detemporalized ethnographic present or a cross-section from a society in history, a frozen moment taken as some kind of whole, and they aim to establish relationships between variables which hold apart from historical time. But it is inconsistent with a realistic concept of what society is, and human experience within it, thus to base comparison on a procedure that eliminates change, incompleteness and potentiality, memories and intentions — in a word, historicity (Touraine 1977: 16). It is small gain to rectify the omission of culture from explanations by introducing it as yet another factor in a *presentist* scheme of comparison. For it is then reified, rather than viewed as the hinge between the past of which it is the precipitate and the future which it aims to prefigure.

What we need is a Mode V of the comparative method, where it is histories, or 'societies-in-change' rather than just 'societies', which are compared.[11] Originating with the great historical sociologists or comparative historians such as Maitland, Weber or Bloch (1967 [1928]), it has continued down to such works as Bendix (1956), Moore (1966), Anderson (1974), and Skocpol (1979). Other modes of the comparative method (except Mode II) pose questions about general sociological categories, aggregates of things taken from their several historical contexts. Underlying this is the antithesis of science and history, and the assumption that if the data are to be treated scientifically, their historicity must be purged from them. Mode V differs in several related ways. Its aim is to explain historical particulars through applying to them general statements, which are theories or models, rather than to move from particulars to empirical generalizations or 'laws'. This is to hold to the universal logic of scientific explanation as to the use of comparison, but to refuse to distort the data by dehistoricizing it, that is by taking it out of its placement in a time sequence. For their place in a time sequence is an *essential* feature of social facts, constituted as these all are by individual actions. Natural science, whose example has done so much to inspire the comparative method, need have no concern with historicity, since it deals with entities that have fixed properties and hence highly determinate relationships with one another. Social anthropology's attempts to develop such generalizations about the variables of its own subject matter have been extremely disappointing. Virtually all its generalizations turn out to be spurious, or only tendencies, or true only be definition, or holding only under particular historical or cultural conditions, or only able to state the very minimum conditions under which social facts exist. Between its variables there seems to be much 'free play': we are forced to conclude that the linkage of variables in particular cases often results less from their inherent properties than from *how they have come to be combined*, through human action in a succession of contexts. By comparing histories or societies-in-change, Mode V offers a clear path to the explanation of social phenomena without misrepresenting the general way in which they are brought about.

Two features are salient in the treatment of culture in Mode V comparative method, properly done. Firstly, its focus on historically specific action as the immediate thing-to-be-explained means that actors' beliefs and values must figure appropriately in any explanation, and *that* in such a way that culture is not *over*-objectified. It is notable that those who essay Mode V comparative method from a Marxist perspective (e.g. Barrington Moore, Anderson) tend to become substantively rather Weberian.[12] Secondly, insofar as we do need to see cultures as ordered *systems* of symbols, beliefs etc., Mode V also forces us to see these systems for what they really are, precipitates of a particular past which are liable to constant revision.

CULTURE AS REFLEXION ON HISTORY

A final recourse to the Yoruba/Akan comparison illustrates how culture serves as the pivot of social change. I have already argued that the relative reluctance of the Akan, particularly Asante, to embrace the world religions had much to do with their sense that the integrity of their society, as they had known it, depended on sanctions bound in with the old religion. Asante society was not religiously static; but the world religions could not be subjected to local chiefly control as other imported cults were. The Asante knew their political community as founded by human agreement, though also given spiritual sanction by the Golden Stool. McCaskie brilliantly conveys the Asante sense of the fragility of their achievement, speaking of their 'abiding fear that without unremitting application and effort, the fragile defensible space called culture would simply be overwhelmed or reclaimed by an irruptive and anarchic nature' (1983: 28).

The Yoruba perception of themselves and their situation was rather different. Again it is instructive to look back from their response to the world religions. Though conversion brought both conflict and persecution (cf. Iliffe 1984), the fact remains that the Yoruba were much more open to religious change. It was, of course, a less highly geared-up society, which could perhaps allow more religious toleration — already within Yoruba paganism there was both cultic diversity and religious choice — and whose rulers were perhaps less able to stop religious novelty. Whereas, after *Asantehene* Osei Kwame's flirtation with Islam in the late eighteenth century, the Asante authorities quarantined Islam and effectively prevented its further spread, in the Oyo empire at the same time Islam made such strides that Muslims became a key component in its overthrow; and Islam grew steadily in the successor states in the nineteenth century. (Today around 50 per cent of Yoruba are Muslim; less than 5 per cent of Asante are). The most distinctive component of Yoruba traditional religion is, without doubt, the oracular cult called Ifa, whose priest-diviners (*babalawo*) have great prestige as religious professionals. Through consultation with Ifa an individual may be directed to the worship of a particular deity. But most remarkably, *babalawo* could, and on occasion did, advise clients to become Muslims or Christians (Gbadamosi 1977). Why could Ifa, a key element in the 'traditional' religion, thus sponsor major religious change?

The Yoruba are organized in a congeries of kingdoms, large and small, and never enjoyed political unity or a common ethnic designation till the twentieth century; but they recognized their affinity through the claim of all their kings to descent from Oduduwa, a god who had reigned at Ile-Ife. Ife had been the first great kingdom of the West African forest (*fl.* 1100—1450; Shaw 1978: chapter 8) and, even after it had declined to a town of modest political importance, the Yoruba always looked to it not only as a supreme cultic centre but as the very site of the creation of the human race. Ife's sacred prestige in later centuries was especially conveyed in the cult of Ifa. This was not just because Ife is especially prestigious as a centre for the training of *babalawo*, but because of the way that Ife is represented in Ifa.

Ifa comprises a vast number of poems (*ẹsẹ*), organized under the 256 figures (*odu*) which the *babalawo* can cast (Bascom 1969; Abimbola 1976). The *babalawo* then recites the *ẹsẹ* appropriate to the figure cast, one of which will give the key to the client's problem. Each *ẹsẹ* takes the form of a mythical precedent; such-and-such a diviner or diviners (named by praise-names which often encapsulate the problem) is consulted by some archetypal figure (such as one of the gods, a king or chief named by his title, or even personifications from fables like Python, White Cloth or Cactus); the client does or does not do what he's told, usually to make a specified sacrifice; and the outcome is told, usually in the form of an extended aetiological myth, parable or fable; finally the precedent is applied to the case in hand. Ifa is, therefore, a vast corpus of coded messages about the past. More important than the fragments of specific 'historical' information it may contain (which are typically fragmentary and hard to use) is its overall vision of the meaning of the past.

The Ifa corpus bears a certain comparison with the 42-day calendrical cycle or *Adaduanan* of the Akan — as central elements of their respective cultures and so, as we have seen, factors in the reception of the world religions. Both are to do with the ordering of social life through the assertion that things do, and should, repeat themselves. The *Adaduanan*, with its lucky and unlucky days, is much more to do with time as such, structuring human activity in short cycles, nicely expressive of the perpetual anxiety of that hard-won and humanly constructed political order. Ifa, by contrast, is less concerned with time than with the past, specifically with 'the Glory that was Ife'. For the mythical precedents which prefigure all possible later contingencies are stated or presumed to have taken place in Ife, '*un état autrefois florissant, et dont la capitale fut une ville sainte . . . une patrie mystique*', as a *babalawo* working in

Dahomey in the 1930s put it (Maupoil 1943: 34). Ifa presents to its adherents the refracted image of a past great civilization, and it is *here* that for the Yoruba the essential order lies, an ideal order. It is moreover a divinely given, not a humanly constructed order; for Ife (unlike Kumasi, Abomey or Benin) was also the site of a cosmogony. While the *Adaduanan* actually creates definite patterns of activity, Ifa does not stipulate, but rather sanctions, in the name of this past, those actions which the client is deeply disposed to take. The flexibility of Yoruba society, its openness to change, is thus conditioned by the belief that the ultimate order is eternally guaranteed by how things began.

What our comparison most importantly teaches is that culture is less a reflection of society, than a reflexion on history.

NOTES

1 In 1960, according to the *Population Census of Ghana*, just over 60 per cent of all the Akan speakers were adherents of world religions, the vast majority of them Christians. Already by 1952 well over 80 per cent of Yoruba were, though the proportion varied considerably by Division (Peel 1967). By 1960 the difference between the two peoples was over 30 per cent. Since the mid-1960s the gap has closed, with the further growth of Christianity among the Akan. The most striking concomitant of this difference has been the ways in which the two societies have responded to the strains of high colonialism: the Yoruba by a Christian prophet movement (Aladura), the Akan by a wave of 'pagan' anti-witchcraft shrines (Field 1960; McCaskie 1981). Significantly, the Akan area which most resembles the Yoruba as regards conversion rates over time — the Nzima/Axim region of the south-west — was also most open to a Christian prophet movement (Harrism). Elsewhere, independent churches stand in a quite different place in the overall religious trajectory (e.g. Wyllie 1980, on Winneba, though he does not emphasize the contrast with the Yoruba).

2 This task is undertaken in Robin Horton's essay 'Social psychologies: African and Western', published alongside the re-issue of *Oedipus and Job* (1983), which compares Tallensi, Asante, Yoruba and Kalabari.

3 A similar 'synchronic' strategy is adopted by Lewis (1976: 255—9) in the face of the Somali combination of *high* divorce rates with strongly corporate patrilineages. Here the additional factor is how completely the wife is absorbed in her husband's lineage and severed from ties with her father's.

4 See, for example, the four West Africanist contributions (Lloyd, Morton-Williams, Ardener, and Bradbury) to Lewis (1968).

5 Kuper (1982b) makes a similar point.

6 This, in fact, is not true of the Yoruba, where lineages often recognize their descent from an immigrant to the community from elsewhere, and preserve the

memory of his original home. It is the existence of the great matriclans, *abusua kese*, spread over many towns, which make possible the Akan assimilation of strangers; the Yoruba lack anything of the kind.

7 On the two conceptions of Asante, emphasizing matriliny and the local community on the one hand, and the political relationships of the Asante state on the other, see Klein (1981).

8 It might be truer to say that what emerged with the war conditions of the nineteenth century were less lineages (i.e. *descent* groups), but strongly corporate households, clientages formed round a big man which started slowly to evolve into lineages.

9 On these 'Salems' see Middleton's (1983) study of Akuropon.

10 On 'hot'/'cold' in cognitive change see Elster (1982: 126 ff.).

11 For a useful methodological review see Skocpol and Somers (1980).

12 I say this notwithstanding Moore's dislike of these Weber-derived explanations of economic development in terms of values, popular among modernization theorists. This dislike is justified; their source, *The Protestant Ethic and the Spirit of Capitalism*, may start off from a Mode V-type question — 'Why has only the West produced rational capitalism?' — but fails on a vital methodological requirement: it does not examine the operation of religious ideas in the social contexts where they were taken up. But Moore in fact combines his class analysis with much attention to national traditions, elite beliefs, ideologies, policies etc. (See Peel 1973: 288—90).

REFERENCES

Abimbola, W. 1976. *Ifa: an exposition of Ifa literary corpus*. Ibadan: Oxford University Press.

Anderson, P. 1974. *Passages from Antiquity to Feudalism*. London: New Left Books.

Bascom, W. R. 1969. *Ifa Divination: communication between gods and men in West Africa*. Bloomington: Indiana University Press.

Bendix, R. 1956. *Work and Authority in Industry*. New York: Wiley.

Binsbergen, W. van. 1981. *Religious Change in Zambia*. London: Kegan Paul International.

Bloch, M. 1967 [1928]. A contribution towards a comparative history of European societies. In *Land and Work in Mediaeval Europe*. London: Routledge and Kegan Paul.

Boas, F. 1896. The limitations of the comparative method of anthropology. *Science* 4: 901—8.

Bradbury, R. E. 1964. The historical uses of comparative ethnography, with special references to Benin and the Yoruba. Reprinted in R. E. Bradbury, *Benin Studies*. London: Oxford University Press.

___ 1973. *Benin Studies*. London: Oxford University Press.

Burton, R. F. 1966 [1864]. *A Mission to Gelele, King of Dahome* (ed.) C. W. Newbury. London: Routledge and Kegan Paul.

Busia, K. A. 1951. *The Position of the Chief in the Modern Political System of Ashanti*. London: Oxford University Press.

Cahiers d'études africaines 1982. Special issue 'Systèmes étatiques africains', Nos 87—8.

Cohn, B. S. 1980. History and anthropology: the state of play. *Comparative Studies in Society and History* 22: 198—221.

—— 1981. Anthropology and history in the 1980s. *Journal of Interdisciplinary History*. 12, 227—52.

Douglas, M. 1962. Lele economy compared with the Bushong. In *Markets in Africa* (eds) P. J. Bohannan and G. Dalton. Evanston, Illinois: Northwestern University Press.

—— 1967. Witch beliefs in Central Africa. *Africa* 37: 72—80.

Eades, J. S. 1980. *The Yoruba Today*. Cambridge: Cambridge University Press.

Edwards, A. C. 1984. On the non-existence of an ancestor cult among the Tiv. *Anthropos* 79: 77—112.

Eggan, F. 1954. Social anthropology and the method of controlled comparison. *American Anthropologist* 56: 743—63.

Elster, J. 1982. Belief, bias and ideology. In *Rationality and Relativism* (eds) M. Hollis and S. Lukes. Oxford: Blackwell.

Evans-Pritchard, E. E. 1949. *The Sanusi of Cyrenaica*. Oxford: Clarendon.

—— 1961. *Anthropology and History*. Manchester: Manchester University Press.

—— 1963. *The Comparative Method in Social Anthropology*. London: Athlone Press.

—— 1965. *Theories of Primitive Religion*. Oxford: Clarendon.

—— 1973. Fifty years of British anthropology. *Times Literary Supplement* 6 July: 764.

Fardon, R. 1984—5. Sisters, wards, wives and daughters: a transformational analysis of the political organization of the Tiv and their neighbours. *Africa* 54: 2—21; 55: 77—91.

Ferguson, A. 1966 [1767]. *An Essay on the History of Civil Society*. Edinburgh: Edinburgh University Press.

Field, M. J. 1960. *Search for Security: an ethnopsychiatric study of rural Ghana*. London: Faber.

Forde, C. D. and P. Kaberry (eds). 1967. *West African Kingdoms in the Nineteenth Century*. London: Oxford University Press.

Fortes, M. 1950. Kinship and marriage among the Ashanti. In *African Systems of Kinship and Marriage* (eds) A. R. Radcliffe-Brown and C. D. Forde. London: Oxford University Press.

—— 1959. *Oedipus and Job in West African Religion*. Cambridge: Cambridge University Press.

—— 1970. Pietas in ancestor worship. In *Time and Social Structure*. London: Athlone Press.

—— 1975. Strangers. In *Studies in Social Anthropology* (eds) M. Fortes and S. Patterson. London: Academic Press.

Fortes, M. and E. E. Evans-Pritchard (eds). 1940. *African Political Systems*. London: Oxford University Press.

Gbadamosi, T. G. O. 1977. Odu Imale: Islam in Ifa divination and the case of pre-destined Muslims. *Journal of the Historical Society of Nigeria* 8: 88—92.

Geertz, C. 1966. Religion as a cultural system. In *Anthropological Approaches to the Study of Religion* (ed.) M. Banton. London: Tavistock.

Ginsberg, M. 1961. The comparative method. In *Evolution and Progress*. London: Heinemann.

Gluckman, M. 1950. Kinship and marriage among the Lozi . . . and the Zulu. In *African Systems of Kinship and Marriage* (eds) A. R. Radcliffe-Brown and C. D. Forde. London: Oxford University Press.

Goody, J. 1971. *Technology, Tradition and the State in Africa.* London: Oxford University Press.

Hammel, E. A. 1980. The comparative method in anthropological perspective. *Comparative Studies in Society and History* 22: 145—55.

Herskovits, M. J. 1938. *Dahomey: an ancient West African kingdom.* 2 vols. New York: J. J. Augustin.

Heusch, L. de. 1982. *Rois nés d'un Coeur de Vache.* Paris: Gallimard.

Hobhouse, L. T., G. C. Wheeler and M. Ginsberg. 1965 [1915]. *The Material Culture and Social Institutions of the Simpler Peoples.* London: Routledge and Kegan Paul.

Hocart, A. M. 1970 [1936]. *Kings and Councillors.* Chicago: University of Chicago Press.

Horton, R. 1969. From fishing village to city state: a social history of New Calabar. In *Man in Africa* (eds) M. Douglas and P. Kaberry. London: Tavistock.

___ 1971. African conversion. *Africa* 41(2), 85—108.

___ 1975. On the rationality of conversion. *Africa* 45: 219—35, 373—99.

___ 1983. Social psychologies: African and Western. In M. Forkes, *Oedipus and Job in West African Religion* (re-issue of 1959 edn). Cambridge: Cambridge University Press.

Iliffe, J. 1984. Persecution and toleration in pre-colonial Africa: nineteenth century Yorubaland. *Studies in Church History* 21: 357—78.

Johnson, M. 1976. The economic basis of an Islamic theocracy: Masina. *Journal of African History* 17: 481—95.

Jones, G. I. 1963. *The Trading States of the Oil Rivers.* London: Oxford University Press.

Klein, A. M. 1981. The two Asantes: competing interpretations of slavery in Akan Asante society and culture. In *The Ideology of Slavery in Africa* (ed.) P. E. Lovejoy. Beverley Hills: Sage Publications.

Kopytoff, I. 1971. Ancestors as elders in Africa. *Africa* 41: 129—42.

Kuper, A. 1982a. *Wives for Cattle.* London: Routledge and Kegan Paul.

___ 1982b. Lineage theory: a critical retrospect. *Annual Review of Anthropology* 11: 71—95.

Law, R. C. C. 1976. Horses, firearms and political power in pre-colonial West Africa. *Past and Present* 72: 112—32.

___ 1977. *The Oyo Empire c. 1600 — c. 1836.* Oxford: Clarendon.

___ 1982. Making sense of a traditional narrative: political disintegration in the kingdom of Oyo. *Cahiers d'Etudes africaines* 87—8: 387—402.

Lewis, I. M. (ed.) 1968. *History and Social Anthropology*. London: Tavistock.

—— 1971. *Ecstatic Religion*. Harmondsworth: Penguin.

—— 1976. *Social Anthropology in Perspective*. Harmondsworth: Penguin.

Littleton, C. S. 1982. *The New Comparative Mythology*. 3rd edn. Berkeley: University of California Press.

Lloyd, P. C. 1960. Sacred kingship and government among the Yoruba. *Africa* 30: 221—38.

—— 1965. The political structure of African Kingdoms. In *Political Systems and the Distribution of Power* (ed.) M. Banton. London: Tavistock.

—— 1968. Conflict theory and Yoruba kingdoms. In *History and Social Anthropology* (ed.) I. M. Lewis. London: Tavistock.

—— 1971. *Political Development of Yoruba Kingdoms in the Eighteenth and Nineteenth Centuries*. London: Royal Anthropological Institute.

Maitland, F. W. 1936 [1899]. The body politic. In *Selected Essays*. Cambridge: Cambridge University Press.

Maupoil, B. 1943. *La Géomancie à l'Ancienne Côte des Esclaves*. Paris: Institut d'Ethnologie.

McCaskie, T. C. 1980. Time and calendar in c. 19 Asante: an exploratory essay. *History in Africa* 7: 179—200.

—— 1981. Anti-witchcraft cults in Asante. *History in Africa* 8: 125—54.

—— 1983. Accumulation, wealth and belief in Asante history. *Africa* 53: 23—4.

McKnight, J. D. 1967. Extra descent-group ancestor cults in African societies. *Africa* 37: 1—21.

Meek, R. L. 1976. *Social Science and the Ignoble Savage*. Cambridge: Cambridge University Press.

Mercier, P. 1954. The Fon of Dahomey. In *African Worlds* (ed.) D. Forde. London: Oxford University Press.

Middleton, J. 1983. One hundred and fifty years of Christianity in a Ghanaian town. *Africa* 53: 2—18.

Middleton, J. and E. H. Winter (eds) 1963. *Witchcraft and Sorcery in East Africa*. London: Routledge and Kegan Paul.

Mill, J. S. 1973 [1843]. *A System of Logic*. Toronto: University of Toronto Press.

Moore, B. 1966. *Social Origins of Dictatorship and Democracy*. London: Allen Lane.

Morton-Williams, P. 1968. The Fulani penetration into Nupe and Yoruba in the nineteenth century. In *History and Social Anthropology* (ed.) I. M. Lewis. London: Tavistock.

—— 1969. The influence of habitat and trade on the politics of Oyo and Ashanti. In *Man in Africa* (eds) M. Douglas and P. M. Kaberry. London: Tavistock.

Nadel, S. F. 1951. *The Foundations of Social Anthropology*. London: Cohen and West.

—— 1952. Witchcraft in four African societies: an essay in comparison. *American Anthropologist* 54: 18—29.

—— 1955. Two Nuba religions: an essay in comparison. *American Anthropologist* 57: 661—79.

Naroll, R. 1973. Galton's problem. In *A Handbook of Method in Cultural Anthropology* (eds) R. Naroll and R. Cohen. New York: Columbia University Press.

Needham, R. 1985. *Exemplars*. Berkeley: University of California Press.

Northrup, D. 1978. *Trade without Rulers: pre-colonial economic development in south-eastern Nigeria*. Oxford: Clarendon.

Otite, O. 1973. *Autonomy and Independence: the Urhobo kingdom of Okpe*. London: Hurst.

Peel, J. D. Y. 1967. Religious change in Yorubaland. *Africa* 37: 292−306.

―― 1971. *Herbert Spencer: the evolution of a sociologist*. London: Heinemann.

―― 1973. Cultural factors in the contemporary theory of development. *Archives Européennes de Sociologie* 14: 293−303.

―― 1980. Kings, titles and quarters: a conjectural history of Ilesha. Part II: institutional growth. *History in Africa* 7: 225−57.

―― 1983. *Ijeshas and Nigerians: the incorporation of a Yoruba kingdom 1890s− 1970s*. Cambridge: Cambridge University Press.

Radcliffe-Brown, A. R. 1951. The comparative method in social anthropology. *Journal of the Royal Anthropological Institute* 81: 15−22.

―― and C. D. Forde (eds) 1950. *African Systems of Kinship and Marriage*. London: Oxford University Press.

Rattray, R. S. 1923. *Ashanti*. Oxford: Clarendon.

―― 1927. *Religion and Art in Ashanti*. Oxford: Clarendon.

Runciman, W. G. 1983. *A Treatise on Social Theory*. Volume I. Cambridge: Cambridge University Press.

Sahlins, M. 1985. *Islands of History*. Chicago: University of Chicago Press.

Schapera, I. 1953. Some comments on comparative method in social anthropology. *American Anthropologist* 55: 353−62.

―― 1962. Should anthropologists be historians? *Journal of the Royal Anthropological Institute* 92: 143−56.

Shaw, T. 1978. *Nigeria: its archaeology and early history*. London: Thames and Hudson.

Skocpol, T. 1979. *States and Social Revolutions*. Cambridge: Cambridge University Press.

Skocpol, T., and M. Somers. 1980. The uses of comparative history in macrosocial enquiry. *Comparative Studies in Society and History* 22: 174−97.

Smith, A. 1964 [1776]. *The Wealth of Nations*. London: Dent.

Smith, M. G. 1960. *Government in Zazzau*. London: Oxford University Press.

―― 1962. History and social anthropology. *Journal of the Royal Anthropological Institute* 92: 73−85.

―― 1978. *The Affairs of Daura*. Berkeley: University of California Press.

Spencer, H. 1972. *Herbert Spencer on Social Evolution*. Selection edited by J. D. Y. Peel. Chicago: University of Chicago Press.

Stocking, G. 1968. *Race, Culture and Evolution*. Chicago: University of Chicago Press.

Touraine, A. 1977. *The Self-Production of Society* (trans.) D. Coltman. Chicago: University of Chicago Press.

Tylor, E. B. 1889. On a method of investigating the development of institutions; applied to laws of marriage and descent. *Journal of the Royal Anthropological Institute* 18: 245—56, 261—9.

Weber, M. 1968. *Economy and Society* (eds) G. Roth and C. Wittich, 2 vols. Berkeley: University of California Press.

Wilks, I. 1967. Ashanti government. In *West African Kingdoms in the Nineteenth Century* eds. D. Forde and P. Kaberry. London: Oxford University Press.

___ 1975. *Asante in the Nineteenth Century*. Cambridge: Cambridge University Press.

Wilson, M. 1951. Witch beliefs and social structure. *American Journal of Sociology* 56: 307—13.

Wyllie, R. W. 1980. *Spiritism in Ghana*. Missoula: Scholars Press.

Zwernemann, J. 1983. *Cultural History and African Anthropology*. Uppsala and Stockholm: Almqvist and Wiksell.

6

Anthropological Comparison

R. H. Barnes

Anthropology is permanently in crisis about the comparative method. Contemporary problems about comparison differ not at all from those which were discussed with a sense of urgency in a sequence of papers by European and American anthropologists in the 1950s and 1960s. Most of those authors were aware that there was little for them to say which had not already been said by *their* predecessors. This circumstance is to be expected, because the comparative method is the method of anthropology. As Evans-Pritchard remarked, 'there is no other method in social anthropology than observation, classification and comparison in one form or another' (1965: 31).

Disregarding shifts in fashion, anthropology is shaped and defined by a permanent set of questions at the centre of which is the relation between description and generalization. Writers sometimes seem to imply that the comparative method comes into play only in generalization. Yet most anthropologists would accept that there can be no description without comparison. Köbben, otherwise so percipient on the topic, therefore created a false opposition when he claimed that, 'in the anthropological fraternity there are two constantly warring factions which we may label the comparativists and the non-comparativists' (1970: 583). The method of participant observation is a particular, if crucial, instance of the comparative method (Evans-Pritchard 1951: 90). Anthropology is not just a part-time comparative discipline. It is intrinsically the comparative discipline among those which study human institutions. From this position it derives its own unity, as well as the unity of its method.

Traditional anthropological topics are not equally tractable or intractable to comparison. Different issues require different styles and techniques. Anthropologists have been tempted therefore to speak of as many comparative methods as there are thematic issues in anthropology (Eggan 1965: 359), as though anthropology could itself be fragmented into as many anthropologies as there are topics. To do so, however, is to lose sight of the extent to which general anthropological understanding derives from field observations as well as the fact that comparison really begins in the field.

Many, if not all, of the obstacles in the way of successful statistical comparison recently and meticulously examined by Köbben (1967), Naroll (1970) and Driver (1973) are basically problems in the technique and reliability of direct ethnographic research. The correct characterization and labelling of social features and countable ethnic units are problems which begin with the gathering of data. Even difficulties about multicausality and pluricausality would in principle be amenable to ethnographic determination, if information about the past were as readily accessible as it is about the present. More fundamental is the point, often made, that the technique of participant observation is the means by which the ethnographer places himself in an inextricably and, as it were, involuntarily comparative position. Incapable, at least at first, of responding except in terms of learned patterns of his own culture, unable to make these patterns fit the exigencies of the one he is attempting to study, the ethnographer finds that his paradoxical situation highlights unexpected predispositions of his own background by contrast with the new predispositions which he must make his own. No doubt the capacity to think and feel alternately as a local and as a foreigner is not easily acquired (Evans-Pritchard 1951: 82), if by that we mean with an easy control. However, those who have experienced fieldwork know the unpremeditated and painful lurch from one perspective to the other which often reveals more of value than carefully planned strategies of inquiry. What is to be gained, over and above factual knowledge, is that acquired ability to recognize the social in man which Dumont (1966: 20—1) calls the sociological apperception.

Köbben (1970: 585) misrepresents the position of field studies when he explains the holistic attitudes within anthropology as deriving from the trauma of fieldwork and the romantic personalities of the anthropologists. These features are real enough, but Köbben has left out the essential point, namely that the fieldworker is likely to be especially sensitive to differences, whereas many comparative studies place too much weight on similarities. 'Institutions have to be similar in some respects before they can be different in others,' (Evans-Pritchard 1965: 25) but, 'it is the differences which would seem to invite sociological explanation.' Anthropology is concerned with 'likenesses *and* differences' (Kroeber 1954: 285), not just with lists of likenesses and differences, but with particular configurations between them in a necessarily comparative perspective. Instead of losing the anthropologist in a flood of particular experiences, field research ought to and generally does expand his awareness of appropriate comparative themes.

The same spirit that animates, for example, the grand comparative enterprises of a Louis Dumont seems to reside in Kroeber's assertion that anthropological understanding is to be achieved only by 'meeting and mastering differences as well as likenesses' (1954: 286). For Dumont sociological understanding begins by setting instructively divergent civiliations in opposition. Dumont's comparative sociology exploits an unusual use of the notion of ideology (1966: 15), namely the system of ideas and values expressed through social action. Anthropology, he observes (1982: 237), is not committed to an absolute relativism. 'What happens in the anthropological view is that every ideology is relativized *in relation to others.*' A realization of the relativity of culture is an indispensable first step (Kroeber 1954: 286), 'because it means the break with dogmatism — with the attitude which refuses to see any problem because the answer is evident without investigation.' Relativism indeed leads to recognition of endless variety. Variety alone is uninteresting and uninformative. Kroeber however is right (1954: 286) to say that, 'variety must be overcome, not deplored, denied, or shrugged off.' Dumont encouragingly argues that limits are set to variation by the unity of mankind, not only postulated but slowly and painfully verified. The comparative method entails the complete and radical revision of comparative concepts, a job which cannot be done at once, causing some to doubt that it can be done at all. An all or none stance leads to the gloomy conclusion that a relativized anthropology could no longer communicate its results. The subject however has continually revised its perspectives and advanced. 'We have to work,' as Dumont says (1982: 229), 'piecemeal, and that is what anthropology had done, as history shows' (for further discussion of Dumont's comparativism see the essays in Barnes, de Coppet and Parkin 1985).

In his own essay on the comparative method, Evans-Pritchard (1965: 25) stated categorically that, 'any claim to universality demands in the nature of things a historical or psychological, rather than a sociological explanation.' We would do well not to confuse the universal with the general; for in that case Evans-Pritchard's position would indeed condemn us to producing merely local studies. The principle however is a valid one, of particular relevance when social anthropology turns from a Radcliffe-Brownian fixation with social structure to the especially difficult issues about metaphysical categories and the foundations of rational thought. Bloch (1977: 282) has recently noted the contrast between anthropological studies stressing the variation in systems of classification and the rather different productions of scholars such as Bulmer and Berlin and Kay which emphasize the universality of certain means of classifying the natural world. Indeed, since 1969 there has been a rush of development in the study of colour terms, appearing to overturn the previously prevailing relativism. Drawing a parallel between colour and time, Bloch asserts that if the relativity of concepts of time is upheld, then the conclusion is justified that *all* aspects of culture are relative. On the other hand Leech (1974) has drawn attention to a parallel between the notion of basic colour terms and the idea of 'universal kinship categories' as exemplified by the familiar extentionists' doctrine of primary referents for kinship terms. Although Leech (1974: 238) acknowledges that the situation of kinship terms is clearly different from colour terms, by placing both in the same chapter he implies that the similarities are of greater importance than the differences.

Time, colour and kinship are not however simply equivalent kinds of topics even though there are similarities. Conclusions about the universality or relativity of colour classification need have no implications for time or kinship. Indeed an objection which may be made to Leech's treatment of semantic universals is that it invites the inference that if Berlin and Kay are right about colour terms, then much the same may be true of kinship. Leech does not of course adopt this position, but neither does he successfully distance himself from it. Conklin (1973: 939) has also recently observed that colour categories are not organized in the same way as relationship terms. Though cautious about asserting that it is true, Leech outlines (1974: 247) a theory in which the nuclear family provides 'a universal or language-neutral conceptualization of basic kinship relations.' Componential analysis, in the fashion of Goodenough and Lounsbury mediates between a universal, but culturally neutral, level of kinship semantics and the relative level of cultural variation. In fact, nothing in Lounsbury's style of analysis (which is more traditional than it at first appears) depends upon his extensionist hypothesis. The latter is, strictly speaking, irrelevant to most anthropological work on kinship.

The same comment cannot be made about Berlin and Kay's doctrine of universal colour foci; for it serves as the basis of a comprehensive evolutionary hypothesis organizing all cultures on a sequential scale in respect of colour classification. No strictly comparable evolutionary scheme has currency in the area of kinship. Hickerson (1983: 27) summarizes the trend subsequent to the publication of *Basic Color Terms* as being toward the documentation of universal tendencies and underplaying specific historical and cultural developments. Recent work emphasizes biological determinants leading to the emergence of similar colour categories in separate languages, while attributing variations in category boundaries and numbers of categories to cultural factors. The place of culture has been understated therefore, not dismissed, and there is no reason to accept that the question of colour universals is any less complicated by cultural factors than kinship terminology (cf. Leech 1974: 262).

Sahlins (1976: 2) has generously conceded that Berlin and Kay's conclusions 'seem beyond the reach of the empiricists controversy they have occasioned.'

The study has been criticized for weaknesses in their method of gathering data and uncertainties in their definitions (Hays et al. 1972; Durbin 1972). The authors have themselves introduced major changes in their hypothesis in response to contrary ethnographic studies. They now emphasize not just foci, but the interaction of foci and boundaries, and they have conceded that there are alternative sequences of development possible through the range of yellow, green or blue (Kay 1975: 258; Berlin and Berlin 1975: 83). Witkowski and Brown (1977) have recently weakened their evolutionary sequence further by permitting green and blue to remain undifferentiated in languages containing words for brown, pink, purple or orange.

One such language is spoken by the Mursi of Ethiopia. Turton, who describes the Mursi, remarks (1980: 333) that as transformed by Witowski and Brown, the hypothesis has come to be hedged around with so many qualifications that it is unlikely to satisfy those who wish for an evolutionary or biological explanation of cultural differences in colour naming. Turton (1980: 332) also objects to the fact that Berlin and Kay's hypothesis equates general evolution with the historical development of particular languages. Ray's claim (1952: 259) that evolutionary schemes of colour vision are without foundation would seem more plausible now than it has in the last decade.

Naturally something remains of the sequential order of colour names. Three-term systems include dark, light and a hue focused in red; two-term systems distinguish dark and light rather than orange and pink. Anthropologists easily accept that physical and physiological factors of perception impose some regularity on the linguistic ordering of colour.

Anthropologists have also shown uneasiness about Berlin and Kay's distinction between basic and secondary colour terms (Panoff-Eliet 1971; Turton 1980: 332). Sahlins argues that colour terms take on the constraints imposed by nature and human physiology insofar as the terms are culturally meaningful, and that the units of differentiation are not just the terms so much as the relation between terms (1976: 3, 13). He exemplifies his position with reference to Turner's discussion (1965) of the Ndembu symbolic colour-triad of red-white-black (cf. Jacobson-Widding 1979). Another example is provided by Conklin who shows (1955: 343) that the Hanunóo colour system is reducible to four terms associated with lightness, darkness, wetness and dryness.

Anthropologists have more to learn by concentrating on colour as value, rather than as perception. Value, as Dumont (1982: 226) observes, is 'normally segmented in its application, except in specifically modern representations.' In non-modern regions, such as Hindu India, 'distinctions are numerous, fluid, flexible, running independently of each other, overlapping or intersecting; they are also variably stressed according to the situation at hand, now coming to the fore and now receding.'

Perhaps no better example of this pattern has been described than in Onvlee's article (1977) on eastern Sumba social organization and the ceremony of dam building, where groups and objects shiftingly represent male and female principles according to the level of generality upon which contrasts are drawn. There are two water courses, each associated with one of two groups in Mangili society, to whose fields it carries water. One water course is masculine in relation to the other, but both are masculine in relation to the wet rice fields, as is expressed by an explicit analogy between rice fields and symbolically female ear pendants on the one hand, and water channels and male woven wire chains on the other. Both groups are composed of men and women, and both work rice fields, but one is associated with the situationally male water channel and the other with the female course. The male channel lies higher than the other, but the female conduit is made to cross over the male course twice. A cosmological distinction between male and female principles organizes various levels of Mangili representations of society and the world.

An unexpected discovery concerning the two-term Dani pattern was that the basic terms were focused not in white and black, but in red or pink for the light term and in dark green and blue for the dark (Heider 1972: 451). Furthermore, half of the Dani informants had a more developed system including terms for red, yellow and blue. Sahlins (1976: 4) has suggested of course that the unusual Dani pattern is due to the properties of the Munsell colour chips in the experiment. The red chips reflect more brightly than blues and greens. Of the languages with only two terms listed by Heider (1972: 449), one is in Africa, another in India and the rest are in New Guinea, five of them belonging to the same language family as the Dani. It is probable therefore that some at least of these languages possess, like the Dani, greater colour resources than their situation as stage I languages in Berlin and Kay's evolutionary series would imply. The anthropological implications of the wider ability of the Dani to characterize colours remain at present unexplored. It is also possible that there are cultural reasons, going beyond matters of perception, why the Dani emphasize the opposition between light and dark, when they could if they wished identify hues.

There is a parallel of a kind between this optionally two-term colour system and binary number systems, which are found in New Guinea, Australia, Africa and South America. In Australia, such systems coexist with others capable of reaching higher numbers. Curr (1886: 1: 31—2) says of Australians who employ the binary system that they would hardly notice that two pins had been removed from a row of seven, but would immediately see that one is gone. It appears that binary systems reflect at least a preoccupation with pairing and are therefore connected with culturally determined evaluations. Evolutionary-minded commentators have also placed two-counting at the first stage of evolution. There are traces of dualism in Kédang, Indonesia, despite the fact that the Kédang employ an arithmetically and symbolically far more sophisticated decimal system (Barnes 1980a: 200—1; 1982a). Perhaps we could speak of binarism submerged by long processes of history. Austronesian languages distinguish odd and even number series as incomplete and complete, suggesting a connection, at least in logic, if not in origin, with two-counting.

Kédang colour words include green, blue, yellow, brown, as well as black, white and red (Barnes 1974: 167). The triad of black, white and red figures prominently in ceremonies, with red representing wickedness. Black and white when joined sometimes represent wholeness, as in the use of a black and white thread to represent a person's soul. Black can be opposed to red: cloth used in marriage gifts must in Kédang be black, not — as among the neighbouring Lamaholot — red. Sometimes black is opposed indifferently by red or white, as in a ceremony in which a black chicken replaced a goat (Barnes 1974: 137). Red and white strands together may represent the combination of male and female fertility (1974: 261). Blackness figures in various ways at birth and death. If a newborn infant has white fingernails, he is premature: his time in the womb was incomplete. Black (dirty) nails show that he was born at the right moment. At the funeral, black cloth represents agnatic ties. In daily usage, black and white often appear not to describe strictly colour properties. Colourless water for example is contrasted as black in opposition to the milky appearance of 'white' palm wine. On the other hand, freshly cut, green palm leaves are 'black' as opposed to the colourless or 'white' leaves that have dried in the sun.

These circumstances are not unlike Conklin's description (1955: 342) of Hanunóo usage where the distinction of light and dark is modulated by oppositions of desiccation and succulence as well as deep, indelible versus bleached or colourless. The Kédang use their opposition of black and white noticeably more broadly than we do in English, contrasting things without immediate regard to their specific hue. They do so, though, *not* because of any linguistic or perceptual inability to describe the true colours. These usages may well be said to be metaphorical. Even so, they represent characteristic predispositions to select for emphasis aspects of the colour world somewhat differently than speakers of English. There is no connection here, by the way, with the English cliché about moralizing all in black and white. The usages do express values, and they do so in a segmentary fashion which resembles Dumont's comment quoted above and is reminiscent of the Sumbanese references to male and female principles as described by Onvlee.

In an incautious moment, Warneck (1906) described the Toba Batak of Sumatra as having no colour sense and lacking most words for colour because Batak *birong* refers to black and all dark shades, including the blue of the sky and sea. In this respect the language is not different from Malay, where *hitam* is black or dark, or Kédang for that matter where even though they have a word for blue, *pahelong*, dark shades are commonly simply called *miteng*, even the dark blue of indigo dyed cloth. Brandstetter (1923: 8—9) refuted Warneck's assertion by citing an impressive list of colour words from Warneck's own dictionary and also from the language of the neighbouring Karo Batak. Bartlett (1929: 1) repeated the demonstration, but still accepted the possibility that, for example, the commonplace confusion of black and blue may have some basis in perceptual deficiencies. Van Wijk (1959: 131) presents tables in which languages emphasizing brightness, rather than colour terms, are located near the equator, though the impression he leaves that Toba Batak have only four brightness and no colour terms is in fact incorrect. Bornstein (1975: 789) has revived Rivers's theory (1901: 52) that languages which class together green or blue and black are associated with populations weak in blue perception because of pigmentation in the eye. In the recent reissue (1977) of Warneck's dictionary, the offending generalization has been removed, perhaps by Warneck himself.[1] It is individuals not populations who are colour-blind or weak. The wide use of brightness terms cannot be comprehensively accounted for by racial or perceptual factors. What remains are cultural predispositions. It would be most desirable to address Batak colour and brightness usage in the context of the values which they serve to express, and indeed the same is true for Indonesian languages generally.

Berlin and Kay's hypothesis has not withstood the challenge of scholarly criticism as well as writers sometimes suggest.[2] Such regularities as do exist can be related safely to physiological features in human perception. The proper field of anthropological concern with colour, namely the use of colour to express social value, remains untouched.

Colour does not provide a good parallel for anthropological treatment of metaphysical categories such as time or space (see Bloch 1977: 282; 1979: 166). Bloch (1977) has recently offered a strongly presented, and subsequently much discussed, attack on relativism in anthropological writing about time. It is easy to sympathize with aspects of his position. As with the other metaphysical categories, time presents issues which are more difficult than most anthropological problems. Anthropologists are generally well advised to leave them where possible to the experts, namely philosophers. But anthropological writing often reveals uncertainty about where the line is to be drawn between anthropological as opposed to philosophical concerns, and these doubts are typically exacerbated by critical ambiguities in choice of vocabulary. In principle these matters cannot be entirely left alone, because, as Durkheim so keenly sensed, they involve important questions concerning the definition of anthropology as a separate kind of scholarship.

On the whole Durkheim did not cope successfully with the origin of rational capacities, tending, especially in *The Elementary Forms of the Religious Life*, to have things both ways by claiming that in the first place they were of social origin, *but also* corresponded to reality. 'It is not necessary to conclude that they [time, space, class, number, cause, substance, personality] are devoid of all objective value. On the contrary, their social origin rather leads to the belief that they are not without foundation in the nature of things' (1915: 14, 19). Time is based on the rhythm of social life, which in turn is related to the rhythm of the universe.

Bloch (1977: 283) asserts that if anthropologists were right that other peoples had different concepts of time, we could not communicate with them. The quandary is broader even than that. By trying to attribute social origins to reason, Durkheim came close to undermining sociology as a form of rational scholarship. If categories and laws of reason derive from society, and potentially vary from society to society, then by what, or whose, standard do we decide that any statements we make about them are logical and correct? Durkheim's manner of preserving their 'speculative value' is just as *a priori* as the position of the rationalists he was attacking. Though a product of collective life, they imitate nature perfectly (Durkheim 1915: 19). Had Durkheim however *not* offered his social explanation, he would have run the risk of conceding that there was a large range of human concern (the metaphysical, including religion) which was not made up of social facts and therefore beyond the bounds of sociology.

Bloch's culprits are Durkheim, Boas, Lévi-Strauss and Evans-Pritchard. About Durkheim he appears to be wrong.[3] Durkheim's position seems to be that while rational categories may be perfected, they are essentially immutable, or at least that there is only one form to be achieved through evolutionary progress. As for logical thought, it has always existed (Durkheim 1915: 439). 'There is no point in history when men have lived in a chronic confusion and contradiction.' As for Lévi-Strauss, Bloch seems to be right. I have expressed my criticisms of Lévi-Strauss's discussion of time elsewhere (1976: 391—2; 1984: 222—3). Bloch's criticisms of Evans-Pritchard sent me back to the original, which exists in two forms: his article on Nuer time-reckoning (1939), which Bloch does not cite, and the chapter on time in *The Nuer* (1940). Many passages in the article which might appear to support Bloch's interpretation show up rewritten and less open to objection in the book. Even so, I think the reader is free to give a far less radically relativistic interpretation to Evans-Pritchard's remarks than Bloch has done.

The particular features of Evans-Pritchard's ethnographic description may in any case not be the object of dispute in Bloch's critique. Furthermore, many would surely agree with Evans-Pritchard's view (1939: 189) that the Nuer and Europeans have different interests and therefore different time-values or that Nuer time concepts are man-made, social notions referring to preponderant communal interests. It seems perfectly orthodox and good anthropology for Evans-Pritchard to say (1939: 190) that Nuer 'time-reckoning is a value, or norm, to which activities should roughly accord.' More open to controversy are his assertions that Nuer perceptions of time are culturally determined (1939: 209), that they have no concept of time (1939: 208), and that they have a different sense of time than our own (1939: 189). In Bloch's reading, Evans-Pritchard would seem to be writing at approximately the same level of abstract generality as Kant, and in radical contradiction to Kant, when Kant describes space and time as the pure *a priori* forms of sensuous intuitions (1781: 19—33). Perhaps Evans-Pritchard did have such issues in mind, but it seems very unlikely.

Whatever criticisms modern philosophers may make of Kant's philosophy, they seem to accept a single absolute system of space and time or of space-time more or less directly governing perception (Smart 1964: 4; Strawson 1966: 64). Anthropologists may tacitly agree, while still describing cultural (or historical) variations in time sense, such as those which E. P. Thompson (1967), in a Marxist study partially inspired by Evans-Pritchard, described as consciously instilled in the British workforce by directors of factories during the industrial revolution. The words 'sense' and 'concept' are no more precise than their partial synonyms 'thought', 'idea' and 'notion.' We regularly use all of these words at different levels of abstraction. Turton and Ruggles (1978: 585) for example say that most anthropologists, and Evans-Pritchard in particular, tend to assume that different ways of measuring time are proof of different perceptions of time. They later comment (1978: 591) that time is as a category of human understanding, like space and causality, a 'part of the mental equipment of all men' and therefore not subject to differing conceptualization. Plainly they too place Evans-Pritchard's observations about perception at the same extremely abstract level as does Bloch.

Even the most formally correct scientific or mathematical concepts come in different levels of abstraction. Since Kant's day (or, depending on interpretation, shortly thereafter), mathematicians have come to speak of different kinds of geometry without committing themselves to abandoning the idea of space. In so far as our experiences of space and time are verbalized and recorded in systems of time reckoning which reflect commonplace interests and values, then these more or less overt representations of them are very susceptible to historical change and cultural variation. A sympathetic reading of Evans-Pritchard in that vein turns his discussion of time from being an example of naive philosophical relativism into an instructive model of good anthropological description.

Anthropologists become side-tracked into metaphysical quandaries not simply through carelessness or because of the looseness of words. Simple empirical questions about time and space are systematically linked to the more difficult philosophical issues. Just where anthropological aspects of these problems leave off in principle, as opposed to healthy practice, may be a question without a final answer. Bloch (1977: 283) quotes Wittgenstein to the effect that if lions could talk, we would not understand them. Bloch then concludes that people with a different concept (N.B.: in Kant's sense) of time would be like Wittgenstein's lions. It seems more likely that if an anthropologist did run across a group with such a radically different metaphysical system, he would never know it or have any way of finding it out for sure.

More commonplace anthropological topics like politics, economics and kinship do not initially engage us in issues of the same degree of difficulty as do the metaphysical categories. Much of our working vocabulary in these areas is no more than ordinary expressions of daily language. I accept with Leach (1961) that a great deal of instructive comparative work can be done on marriage without any hope or need of a universally applicable definition, so long as each study makes clear what features direct the investigation at hand. Much the same is true of descent groupings. My own experience shows that the strictly sociological side of descent and marriage is concerned, as Evans-Pritchard claimed, with the recording and explanation of potentially unlimited variation in the application of common principles (see for example Barnes 1980b; 1980c). Real progress at a more general level has been made by considering the principles of descent and of marriage prescriptions or restrictions as logical sets. Many hands have been involved, and the more important contributions are so well known that they need not be cited here. The logical possibilities for positive marriage systems and for varieties of rules of descent may be unlimited. In any case they extend well beyond those actually found in empirical examples. As an empirically and sociologically minded anthropologist, I am most interested in the varieties which do find exemplification.

As an ethnographer, I am sensitive to differences, which I think should be given their due in generalized discussions. By no means do I think that a general view or comparison are thereby made impossible. In a recent book (Barnes 1984) on one of the central topics of anthropology, I have made the following points. Much which has recently been said about Omaha systems of descent and alliance is at complete variance with the facts of Omaha sociology.

A good deal more can be known about the Omaha from unpublished information that is available but so far has not been exploited. Although the Omaha are an interesting and important example of patrilineal descent, they should cease to be treated as the archetypal case of patrilineality and should no longer be regarded merely from the point of view of their unilineal institutions. What has been called 'Omaha alliance' by Lévi-Strauss and others has nothing to do with the Omaha. The analysis of Omaha society can be advanced by comparison with remotely situated societies which have elaborate marriage prohibitions, such as the Samo of the Upper Volta (Héritier 1981; Barnes 1982b), without needing to combine them in a common category. Comparison in any case would be more instructive if it were to focus on the systematic variations within different regions, rather than simply setting one tribe against another.

   An example of such regionally focused comparison guided by a set of shared features is what Dutch authors have called the *ethnologisch studieveld* or the 'Field of Anthropological Study' in the island world of Southeast Asia (J. P. B. de Josselin de Jong 1977; P. E. de Josselin de Jong 1984). There is no doubt that in the fifty years since its formulation it has led to considerable progress not only in local studies, but in general anthropological understanding of its themes, however much anthropologists may feel that it requires continual revision. (For a critique and rejoinder see Barnes 1985 and P. E. de Josselin de Jong 1985.) In a somewhat different vein, a series of articles in a recent book (Barnes, de Coppet and Parkin 1985) has carried through ramifying comparisons of widely separated societies in terms of a definition of hierarchy originally devised for the caste system of India. Progress in these areas, as well as that historically important set of questions about social classification and groups commonly called the Omaha problem, has been indeed, as Dumont says about anthropological progress generally, 'piecemeal,' but nevertheless sure. There is no more, nor less, occasion to worry about comparison in anthropology now than at any time in the past.

NOTES

1   The editor wrote to me (12 March 1979) that he does not know who removed the comment, but that Warneck, who was himself preparing the revised letter B before the Second World War, may have been responsible.
2   See for example Baines (1985: 289) who seems to take for granted the veracity of their evolutionary scale in order to use it as a standard by which to assess his own historical evidence for ancient Egyptian colour classification.
3   On Durkheim's rationalism, see Lukes (1973: 72—6, 486—7). Lukes writes (1973: 440), 'Durkheim saw clearly that there are criteria of truth and "objective"

explanation, as well as principles of logic, which are non-relative and non-context-dependent; and he further saw that these principles of logic are fundamental and universal to all cultures. As a firm rationalist, he did not succumb to the temptations of relativism.' In this phrasing Lukes displays his own tendency to treat empirical questions as matters of dogma (Durkheim could hardly empirically 'see' these principles as universal to all cultures) as well as his own quasi-religious commitment to rationalism, something outside empirical investigation. (His metaphorical reference to succumbing to temptations implies that relativism is the devil.) For more rhetoric of the same kind see Lukes (1982). For the counterblast see Geertz (1984) and the papers in Overing (1985).

REFERENCES

Baines, J. 1985. Color terminology and color classification: Ancient Egyptian color terminology and polychromy. *American Anthropologist* 87: 2: 282—97.

Barnes, R. H. 1974. *Kédang: a study of the collective thought of an eastern Indonesian people*. Oxford: Clarendon.

—— 1976. Dispersed alliance and the prohibition of marriage: reconsideration of McKinley's explanation of Crow-Omaha terminologies. *Man* (N.S.) 11: 384—99.

—— 1980a. Fingers and numbers. *Journal of the Anthropological Society of Oxford* 11: 197—206.

—— 1980b. Concordance, structure, and variation: considerations of alliance in Kédang. In *The Flow of Life* (ed.) James J. Fox. Cambridge Mass.: Harvard University Press.

—— 1980c. Marriage, exchange and the meaning of corporations in eastern Indonesia. In *The Meaning of Marriage Payments* (ed.) J. L. Comaroff. London: Academic Press.

—— 1982a. Number and number use in Kédang, Indonesia. *Man* (N.S.) 17: 1—22.

—— 1982b. Kinship exercises. Review of Françoise Héritier, *L'Exercise de la Parenté*. *Culture* 2: 113—18.

—— 1984. *Two Crows Denies It: a history of controversy in Omaha sociology*. Lincoln, Nebraska and London: University of Nebraska Press.

—— 1985. The Leiden version of the comparative method in Southeast Asia. *Journal of the Anthropological Society of Oxford* 16: 87—110.

Barnes, R. H., D. de Coppet, and R. J. Parkin (eds). 1985. *Contexts and Levels: anthropological essays on hierarchy*. (JASO Occasional Papers No. 4). Oxford: JASO.

Bartlett, H. H. 1929. Color nomenclature in Batak and Malay. *Papers, Michigan Academy of Sciences, Arts & Letters* 10: 1—52.

Berlin, B. and L. A. Berlin. 1975. Aquarana color categories. *American Ethnologist* 2: 61—87.

Berlin, B. and P. Kay. 1969. *Basic Color Terms: their universality and evolution*. Berkeley: University of California Press.

Bloch, M. 1977. The past and present in the present. *Man* (N.S.) 12: 278—92.

132   R. H. Barnes

___ 1979. Knowing the world and hiding it. Letter in *Man* (N.S.) 14: 165—7.
Bornstein, M. H. 1975. The influence of visual perception on culture. *American Anthropologist* 77: 774—98.
Brandstetter, R. 1923. *Wir Menschen der indonesischen Erde, III: der Intellekt der indonesischen Rasse.* Luzern: Haag.
Conklin, H. C. 1955. Hanunóo color categories. *Southwestern Journal of Anthropology* 11: 339—44.
___ 1973. Color categorization. *American Anthropologist* 75: 931—42.
Curr, E. M. 1886. *The Australian Race.* 4 vols. Melbourne: Ferres.
Driver, H. E. 1973. Cross-cultural studies. In *Handbook of Social and Cultural Anthropology* (ed.) J. J. Honigman. Chicago: Rand McNally.
Dumont, L. 1966. Introduction. *Homo Hierarchicus.* Paris: Gallimard.
___ 1982. On value (Radcliffe-Brown lecture 1980). *The Proceedings of the British Academy* (1980) 66: 207—41.
Durbin, M. 1972. Basic terms — off-color? *Semiotica* 6: 257—78.
Durkheim, E. 1915. *The Elementary Forms of the Religious Life* (trans.) J. W. Swain. London: Allen and Unwin.
Eggan, F. 1965. Some reflections on comparative method in anthropology. In *Context and Meaning in Cultural Anthropology* (ed.) Melford E. Spiro. New York: Free Press.
Evans-Pritchard, E. E. 1939. Nuer time-reckoning. *Africa* 12: 189—216.
___ 1940. *The Nuer.* Oxford: Clarendon.
___ 1951. *Social anthropology.* London: Cohen and West.
___ 1965. The comparative method in social anthropology. In *The Position of Women in Primitive Societies and other Essays in Social Anthropology.* London: Faber.
Geertz, C. 1984. Anti anti-relativism. *American Anthropologist* 86: 263—78.
Hays, D. G., E. Margolis, R. Naroll and D. R. Perkins. 1972. Color term salience. *American Anthropologist* 74: 1107—21.
Heider, E. R. 1972. Probabilities, sampling, and ethnographic method: the case of Dani colour names. *Man* (N.S.) 7: 448—66.
Héritier, F. 1981. *L'Exercice de la Parenté.* Paris: Gallimard.
Hickerson, N. P. 1983. Gladstone's ethnolinguistics: the language of experience in the nineteenth century. *Journal of Anthropological Research* 39: 26—41.
Jacobson-Widding, A. 1979. *Red-White-Black as a Mode of Thought: a study of triadic classification by colours in the ritual symbolism and cognitive thought of the peoples of the lower Congo.* (Upps. Stud. cult. Anthrop. 1) Stockholm: Almqvist and Wiksell.
Josselin de Jong, J. P. B. de. 1977. The Malay Archipelago as a field of ethnological study. In *Structural Anthropology in the Netherlands: a reader* (ed.) P. E. de Josselin de Jong. (KITLV Translations Series 17). The Hague: Nijhoff.
Josselin de Jong, P. E. de. (ed.) 1984. *Unity in Diversity: Indonesia as a field of anthropological study.* (KITLV Verhandelingen 103). Dordrecht and Cinnaminson, USA: Foris.

____ 1985. The comparative method in Southeast Asia: Ideal and practice. *Journal of the Anthropological Society of Oxford* 16: 197—208.

Kant, I. 1781. *Critik der reinen Vernunft*. Riga: Hartknoch.

Kay, P. 1975. Variability and change in basic color terms. *Language in Society* 4: 257—70.

Köbben, A. J. 1967. Why exceptions? The logic of cross-cultural analysis. *Current Anthropology* 8: 3—19.

____ 1970. Comparativists and non-comparativists in anthropology. In *A Handbook of Method in Cultural Anthropology* (eds) R. Naroll and R. Cohen. New York: Natural History Press.

Kroeber, A. L. 1954. Critical summary and commentary. In *Method and Perspective in Anthropology: papers in honor of Wilson D. Wallis* (ed.) R. R. Spencer. Minneapolis: University of Minnesota Press.

Leach, E. R. 1961. Polyandry, inheritance and the definition of marriage. In *Rethinking Anthropology*. London: Athlone.

Leech, G. 1974. *Semantics*. Harmondsworth: Penguin.

Lukes, S. 1973. *Emile Durkheim, His Life and Work: a historical and critical study*. London: Allen Lane.

____ 1982. Relativism in its place. In *Rationality and Relativism* (eds) M. Hollis and S. Lukes. Oxford: Blackwell.

Naroll, R. 1970. What have we learned from cross-cultural surveys. *American Anthropologist* 72: 1227—88.

Onvlee, L. 1977. The construction of the Mangili dam: notes on the social organization of eastern Sumba. In *Structural Anthropology in the Netherlands: a reader* (ed.) P. E. de Josselin de Jong. (KITLV Translation Series 17). The Hague: Nijhoff.

Overing, J. (ed.) 1985. *Reason and Morality*. ASA Monographs 24. London: Tavistock.

Panoff-Eliet, F. 1971. Review of Berlin and Kay, *Basic Color Terms*. *L'Homme* 11: 100—3.

Ray, V. F. 1952. Techniques and problems in the study of color perception. *Southwestern Journal of Anthropology* 8: 251—9.

Rivers, W. H. R. 1901. Primitive color vision. *Popular Science Monthly* 59: 44—58.

Sahlins, M. 1976. Colors and cultures. *Semiotica* 16: 1: 1—22.

Smart, J. J. C. (ed.) 1964. *Problems of Space and Time*. New York: Macmillan.

Strawson, P. R. 1966. *The Bounds of Sense: an essay on Kant's critique of pure reason*. London: Methuen.

Thompson, E. P. 1967. Time, work-discipline and industrial capitalism. *Past & Present* 38: 56—97.

Turner, V. 1965. Color classification in Ndembu ritual: a problem in primitive classification. In *Anthropological Approaches to the Study of Religion* (ed.) M. Banton. ASA Monographs 3. London: Tavistock.

Turton, D. 1980. There's no such beast: cattle and colour naming among the Mursi. *Man* (N.S.) 15: 320—38.

Turton, D. and C. Ruggles. 1978. Agreeing to disagree: the measurement of duration in a southwestern Ethiopian community. *Current Anthropology* 19: 585—600.

134   *R. H. Barnes*

Warneck, J. 1906. *Tobabataksch-Deutsches Wörterbuch*. Batavia: Landsdrukkerij.
—— 1977. *Toba-Batak-Deutsches Wörterbuch* (ed.) R. Roolvink. The Hague: Nijhoff.
Wijk, H. A. C. W. van. 1959. A cross-cultural theory of color and brightness nomenclature. *Bijdragen tot de Taal-, Land- en Volkenkunde* 115: 113—37.
Witkowski, S. R. and C. H. Brown. 1977. An explanation of color nomenclature universals. *American Anthropologist* 79: 50—7.

7

Caste in Bali and India:
Levels of Comparison

Leo Howe

Comparison is fundamental to both description and analysis since each depends on judgements concerning how events, processes and things are classified as either the 'same' or 'different'. Willy-nilly, then, we all compare. Generally the judgements made in any particular case rest on both implicit and partial criteria, but it must be noted that if our separate classifications disagree it is not our concepts of 'sameness' and 'difference' which are at stake but merely the criteria being used to apply them or, in Winch's terms, the rules being followed (Winch 1958: 24–33). More importantly, criteria are always partial since a comparison invariably involves selecting some criteria as salient whilst leaving aside others, for the time being anyway, as irrelevant. Equally we make comparisons from a particular point of view (Popper 1959: 420), because it is we who decide the criteria to be employed. This point was made by Nadel (1949: 224–5) and more recently by Barry Barnes who stresses that concept application, i.e. the decision to assign an item to this or that class, ultimately depends on one's goals and interests (1982: 101–14).

This perspective allows us to tackle a vexing problem, namely the sheer possibility of comparing at all. At least this was a paradox for Evans-Pritchard, if we are to believe Needham who quotes him as having said: 'There's only one method in social anthropology, the comparative method — and that's impossible' (Needham 1975: 365). Presumably when Evans-Pritchard commented thus he was more inclined to see the uniqueness of phenomena rather than the similarities between them, and to believe that if phenomena are unique they are also essentially incomparable. Evans-Pritchard's aphorism, however, is one-sided and we are better served by Kuhn, whom Barry Barnes quotes as having written somewhere: 'It is a truism that anything is similar to, and different from, anything else' (B. Barnes 1982: v). The import of this, as I see it, is that relations of similarity and difference are not given in the empirical phenomena themselves but are generated by those who act on them and decide, using criteria of their own choosing, to which class, category or concept they conform. In other words, uniqueness is not an inherent attribute of phenomena, whether these be natural or social. If something is unique it is so because we choose to classify it in terms of criteria which differentiate it from everything else; we could just as well select other criteria which would classify it as one of a kind. In short, the paradox which states that the comparison of similar phenomena leads to triviality while the comparison of different phenomena is impossible can be seen for the confusion it is. It is not a matter of looking for things which are similar or different and then comparing them; rather, the process of comparison, by virtue of the fact that certain criteria are chosen to the exclusion of others, creates or establishes relations of similarity and difference in the first place.

The function of comparison then is not so much to determine, from scratch as it were, the similarities and differences between phenomena (though this may be a stage in the process) but to illuminate one set of ill-understood phenomena by reference to another set more clearly comprehended. The choice of this latter set will be governed by several issues: the degree to which its institutions and social practices are understood; the researcher's theoretical purposes; historical precedent and the classification of traditionally influential concepts of anthropological analysis (which over time have already established relations of similarity between Hindu caste and Balinese hierarchy and thereby categorized India and Bali as essentially similar types of culture); and so on. Given this, any attempt to analyse Balinese hierarchy makes Hindu caste appear to be the natural point of comparative reference. But I hope to show that in many respects Balinese hierarchy can be conceived as a set of more or less incongruent rank orderings, and thereby to establish relations of considerable difference in regard to the Indian caste system.

THE COMPARISON

Although Bali is often designated a caste system and although its religion is regularly referred to as 'Hindu', there has been, with the partial exception of Lekkerkerker (1926), no systematic comparison of India with Bali in respect to these social and cultural domains. Most Dutch writers failed to address the question at all: the Geertzes devoted one paragraph of their 1975 monograph to it (1975: 21), whilst Boon discussed the problem in only two pages (1977: 147—9). Finally, while not treating comparison as an analytic question, Hobart (1979) drew explicitly on models constructed to deal with Indian data and thereby emphasized the connection between the two cultures.

Since the regions with which the comparison is to deal are many thousands of miles apart, are enormously different in size and, for the last 1500 years or so, have shared neither a historical, a political nor an economic background, the purpose of the present essay should not be seen as an attempt to provide definite answers to what are, obviously, very complex issues. Rather it should be viewed as an exploratory incursion designed to register some tentative remarks concerning caste in India and Bali, in the hope of stimulating further debate. A further aim is to demonstrate that simplistic assertions as to whether Bali is or is not a caste society are largely unhelpful, since different conclusions can be obtained by focusing on data drawn both from different aspects of the culture and from different levels of abstraction. Consequently the following analysis will concentrate, in turn, on conceptual, institutional and interactional data though, it hardly needs to be added, no hard and fast distinctions can be made between these different orders of abstraction as, in reality, they interpenetrate each other in complex ways.

The Conceptual Level

It is Dumont's opinion that the essential and defining feature of caste is the disjunction between status and power epitomized by the *brahman/kshatriya* relation (1972: 260). If this relation can be shown to exist in Bali, perhaps it can justifiably be argued that Bali possesses caste.

The presence of the status/power disjunction in Bali, however, is somewhat problematical because of the nature of kingship in that island. Certainly kings were all of the *satria warna* (these being the Balinese spellings) and did not themselves perform any religious ceremonies. These were conducted for them by *padanda* priests of the *brahman warna*. Moreover *padandas* have long been very active in the traditional Balinese law courts and been authorities on all religious matters (Korn 1960; Swellengrebel 1960). On the other hand the king was a divine king of the south-east Asian variety (Swellengrebel 1947); and according to Geertz (1980:126) priests are, or were, merely a part of the king's regalia. It remains then to ask whether Indian kings had magico-religious functions, even though they were representatives of temporal power. Dumont (1962: 61) contends that the developed relation between *brahman* and *kshatriya* was only attained when the magico-religious aspect was stripped from the notion of kingship, and Geertz (1980:126) asserts that this did not happen in Bali. Moreover Tambiah (1976: 83) argues that the brahmanical formula of *rajadharma* (in which the *brahman* sanctifies kingship) was transformed into the conception *dharmaraja* (in which *brahmans* serve as subordinate functionaries) in the states of Indic south-east Asia which, of course, includes Java and Bali.

The position seems to be that the *brahman/kshatriya* relation, fundamental

to Dumont's version of caste, is to some extent contaminated in Bali by the
Buddhist notion of divine kingship. Against this it can be said that in Bali
brahman priests were never, at the normative level at least, subordinate to
kings in religious and judicial matters. Furthermore, though Geertz denies
the existence of this relation in Bali, Boon (1977: 148—9) asserts that it is, in
fact, present. In short, at this level of analysis the data are at best equivocal and
at worst contradictory, and given the inadequacy of reliable and relevant
information it does not seem possible, for the time being anyway, to resolve
the conflict in the evidence. However, by focusing instead on village Bali a
rather different picture emerges for, it can be argued, the *brahman/kshatriya*
relation is only one manifestation of the status/power disjunction. In other
words, kings and priests are not the only locus of enquiry for determining
whether the relation is present; a case, no doubt disputable, can be made for
examining the structure of ideas in more localized spheres such as the village.

Inhabitants of lowland villages in south, west and east Bali possess titles
which, in specific but variable circumstances, can function as the basis for the
formation of caste-like social groups. Usually in such villages can be found
representatives of the *satria warna* with titles such as *cokorda, déwa agung,
anak agung, pradéwa*, etc. Such titles *(soroh)* are ranked hierarchically and in
the literature the highest ranking family is often glossed as the local princes or
the local lords. But I, at least, can find no information in the ethnographic
record which ascribes to these lords any sort of magico-religious nature or
function. Such villages often have no resident *padanda* priests, and in these
cases many family and villlage ceremonies must be conducted by *padandas*
brought in from other villages. Other ceremonies are performed by priests of
a different kind and standing, and I shall have something to say about these
later. Such an organization is in no sense conclusive evidence but, at the
village level, it is the kind of situation one might expect if the brahmanical, as
opposed to the Buddhist, definition of the *brahman/kshatriya* relation were
present. There is other evidence, though, which is perhaps more interesting
and more germane to the problem.

In Pujung, the village in which my own fieldwork was carried out, there is a
very significant and constant conceptual distinction between two very
important institutions, the *krama désa* and the *krama banjar*. Both are
organizations of people and they have an overlapping membership. The *désa*
is constituted by one man (and his wife or other close female kin) from each of
the compounds built on the consecrated village land *(karang désa)*. In some
sense these men have a religious authority over the ground on which their
house is built, and they also have total rights of usufruct on its products. They
do not 'own' this land (it cannot be sold privately or alienated in any other way)
and are only allowed to live and build on it by virtue of permission from the

village gods, though in practice compound land is inherited without any undue fuss. The point to remember is that membership of the *désa* is defined by a religious criterion, to wit the holding of authority, on behalf of the village gods, over a piece of sacred village land.

The *banjar*, on the other hand, is composed of all married men in the village together with their wives (or other close female relative). On marriage a couple is compelled to join the *banjar* though again, in practice, entrance is eagerly awaited and quite straightforward. Now, partly because of the acknowledged commencement of regular sexual relations, marriage is considered a stage in the life cycle at which people are at the nadir of their ritual purity (Howe 1980: chapter 6), and so it can be argued that marriage is a comparatively secular membership criterion.

These two organizations have very different statuses and perform very different functions, and the main contrast, in keeping with their respective membership criteria, is that the *désa* is concerned with religious affairs and the *banjar* takes responsibility for secular village affairs. For example, the monthly meetings of the *désa* are held within the precincts of a temple, and the main point of the meeting is to engage in a communal meal with the god or gods of that temple. It is said that the god consumes the invisible essence of the food whilst the members eat what is left over ('what is asked back' in the local idiom). Members often have informal discussions about various topics, but these are not part of the formal proceedings. *Désa* business is generally conducted at the end of work periods when the *désa* is engaged on temple repair work or on preparations for a temple festival. Finally, formal *désa* meetings are held every full moon.

In contrast the *banjar* meets every 35 days according to a very different calendar and it gathers in the *wantilan*, a non-religious building most regularly used for cock-fighting, rehearsals and drama performances. At these meetings all outstanding local village issues are debated, and government legislation is announced and explained. Whereas no overt politicking goes on at *désa* meetings, the *banjar* is the principal arena for such activity (Hobart 1975).

The distinction between the *désa* and the *banjar* is also strongly evident in the contrast between their respective officials and priests. *Désa* officials obtain office by virtue of holding certain hereditary titles; they are unpaid and serve for an indefinite period. *Banjar* officials are elected, paid by government, and serve for no more than five years in any one term, though they can be ousted before their appointment has terminated. The principal *désa* official must undertake a purificatory ceremony (*mawinten*) but this is optional for the *banjar* leader.

The *désa*, as already mentioned, is primarily concerned with temple affairs and each temple has a resident priest. The *banjar* also appoints priests, but their status and functions are, in many respects, quite different. Temple priests must wear white and/or yellow, though all those I knew wore white on the upper body. White is the pre-eminent symbol of purity and divinity and comes at the top, literally, of the colour hierarchy. *Banjar* priests may wear white but to wear all white is considered presumptuous, and it is thought far more appropriate to wear black on the upper body. Black is, in other contexts, associated with the night, with witches and with the genitalia.

Temple priests conduct services to the gods whilst *banjar* priests conduct life-crisis rites for the living and for the partly purified dead. It is, in fact, polluting for temple priests even to attend life-crisis ceremonies. Moreover, whereas both types of priest have to undergo the purificatory ceremony *mawinten,* the one for the temple priests is conducted at a higher level (i.e. with more offerings) than that for the *banjar* priests, and they are also held in different temples. As a consequence, temple priests are credited with a higher level of natural purity, and in funeral processions their remains take precedence over those of *banjar* priests. The superior status of temple priests is also indicated in language use. The Balinese language contains several lexical levels, hierarchically ranked, for about 1500 to 2000 key words. In general it is always more appropriate to speak to all priests in a more refined version of the language than is used among co-equals, but this injunction is expressed more emphatically for temple priests than it is for *banjar* priests. Indeed the latter should, and do, use higher levels of Balinese to address and refer to temple priests than they do for themselves. Such prescriptions apply more strongly in religious contexts than in secular ones. Finally temple priests are selected by some form of divine revelation and are therefore often young, whilst *banjar* priests are elected or appointed by the *banjar* after having shown themselves worthy, and they are thus almost always old.

That part of village law which has not so far been superseded by the national legal code is enshrined in books known as *awig-awig,* and in this particular village the *awig-awig* is kept in a temple shrine. The village legal code is based on religious values, and certain contraventions are considered an affront to the village gods, the place where the infringement took place becoming polluted. This legal code, enshrined in a *désa* temple, is also the legal code for *banjar* affairs.

Though far from complete, this evidence seems to point to the conclusion that there is an asymmetric conceptual contrast between spiritual authority and temporal power in the contexts described and such a contrast, if not identical to the *brahman/kshatriya* relation, nonetheless appears analogous to it or, perhaps better, structurally equivalent. To bolster the argument slightly, evidence from other parts of the archipelago, where such a contrast seems to exist, can be adduced: van Wouden for eastern Indonesia generally (1968:

29—30, 63—5, 133—4); Schulte-Nordholt for Timor (1971: 371—4); Fox for Roti (1971: 40—1, 48); and R. H. Barnes for Kédang (1974: 89, 92). Ironically the demonstration that such a distinction may have general relevance for eastern Indonesian societies, which no-one would dream of designating caste societies, would seem to indicate the possibility that the relation between this distinction and caste is contingent. Such a conclusion would be premature because it is not entirely clear that the *brahman/kshatriya* relation is a simple derivative of the distinction between spiritual authority and temporal power. If the former is not merely a more concrete expression of the latter but is essentially different, it is, nonetheless, difficult to see in what this difference consists.

In concluding this section it may be argued that there are grounds for classifying Bali as a caste society. Moreover the adoption of the standpoint used in this section enables us to see some of the significance of two very central Balinese institutions. Unfortunately the picture is more complicated than has so far been indicated, because Dumont's version of caste has been severely criticized in the past few years. I am aware, of course, that *Homo Hierarchicus* has been at the centre of debate ever since it was first published, but in recent years much material has appeared which brings into doubt various aspects of the theory. Thus Das (1977) bases Hinduism within a framework of relations (of equivalence, opposition and parellelism) between four major categories: *brahman,* king, *sanyasi* and a residual category of 'householders'. The relations between these categories are not determined solely by an opposition between the pure and the impure, which is what Dumont avers, but rather by this opposition in conjunction with the notions of rank and separation seen as being independent of one another. Burghart (1978), on the other hand, atomizes Hinduism into three incongruent systems personified by *brahman,* king and ascetic based on three independently and differentially coded hierarchies which in turn are embedded in three dissimilar domains of action. Both Fuller (1979) and Parry (1980) place doubt on the Dumontian version of caste by providing data on the relation of priests to god and priests to sin and pollution respectively, which tend to subvert the clearly bounded categories which Dumont perceives. Finally both Burghart (1978: 524) and Fuller (n.d.) contest Dumont's view that Indian kings had no magico-religious aspect.

The Institutional Level

A point has been reached where, depending on the level at which the analysis proceeds, it is difficult to decide unequivocally whether Balinese culture exhibits the relation between *brahman* and *kshatriya,* and even if a decision could be made there is the added complication that the so-called defining feature of caste is itself of doubtful use and validity. But the situation is perhaps worse still; for even should the complications be ignored (and there is no good reason to do so) and Bali described as a caste society in terms of Dumontian theory, there is still sense in the question: why then does it 'look' so different on the ground? Only a small number of relevant ethnographies need be consulted (on India, for example, Dumont 1957; Mayer 1960; and Parry 1979; on Bali, for example, Geertz and Geertz 1975; Boon 1977; and Hobart 1979) in order to reveal just how different the two areas are, and it is worth spending a moment on the examination of some of these differences.

According to Dumont (1972:81) Bouglé's (1927) three principles of caste structure can be reduced to a single 'true' principle, namely, the opposition between the pure and the impure. In Bali, though, the picture would appear to be somewhat different. Bouglé's first principle, the gradation of status or hierarchy, is obviously present in the Balinese *warna* scheme which, unlike that in India, does have a social, as opposed to a purely cultural, relevance. But the titles groups which compose each *warna* are not nearly as preoccupied with status ranking as are the Indian *jat*. The upper three *warna* in Bali, collectively known as the *triwangsa* and constituting less than ten per cent of the population, are much more concerned with ranking than those title groups which make up the *sudra warna*, for most of whom ranking is largely irrelevant in most contexts. Secondly, and in accordance with what has just been said, rules concerning the separation of title groups, (Bouglé's second principle), are few and lax for *sudras* but more restrictive for *triwangsa*. Next, the division of labour (Bouglé's third principle) is largely absent in Bali. Finally, even the opposition of the pure to the impure is not as dominant in Bali as it is in India, for the simple reason that other conceptual oppositions are relevant for the analysis of stratification. Perhaps the most widely used is that of *alus/kasar* (refined/coarse) which, though it can substitute for the pure/impure distinction in some contexts, is probably appropriate in a wider range of circumstances than is the latter (Howe 1984).

There are many other differences, some of the most important of which can be listed as follows:

1   In Bali there is no concept of untouchability and no notion concerning the accumulation of pollution for those at the bottom of the hierarchy who, in India, have to deal with grossly polluting substances.
2   Whereas in India brahman priests rank lower then non-priestly brahmans, in Bali the situation is the reverse.
3   Balinese religion is perhaps more aptly described as an ancestor cult than a peculiar version of Hinduism (Geertz and Geertz 1975; Boon 1977; Howe 1980).

4 While Balinese society does display patrilineal descent groups practising preferential endogamous marriage, by no means all Balinese are members of such groups. In general, kinship institutions and marriage practices in Bali are very different from those in India which, in any case, exhibit such tremendous variation that comparison at any level poses numerous problems.

5 Whereas in India sub-castes are generally corporate groups, in Bali people holding the same title form groups only under specifiable conditions (Geertz and Geertz 1975). As often as not, those with the same title, even though living in the one village, are no more than aggregates of 'similar' kinds of people. The Balinese word for title, *soroh,* has the same range of referents, 'kind', 'species', 'sort', as does the Hindi word *jat.*

6 The Balinese have a predilection for forming functionally specific voluntary social groups (which persist for varying lengths of time) which are open to all to join and which are, *de jure* at least, based on the democratic principle of one man, one vote. Organs of local government in village Bali are similar sorts of organization, though membership is often compulsory and much more permanent. India, it would seem, does not possess social formations of this character.

There are then numerous differences between the two societies, and it is the substantial nature of some of these which should caution against any dogmatic assertion that Bali constitutes a caste society. Just as there is a good deal of disparity between the conceptual and institutional forms of the two areas, so there are also many reasons which account, to one extent or another, for the dissimilarity. First, the available evidence points clearly to the fact that it was Sanskritic culture rather than Hindu social structure that was adopted by the Javanese and Balinese, and that it was brought to Java both by Hindu priests and by Indonesians who travelled to India (Bosch 1961; van Leur 1967). Second, such a culture eventually arrived in Bali via Javanese intermediaries. Third, it is probable that Bali already possessed a fairly well developed ancestor cult and ranked status titles on which this suitable culture could settle; and it is worth noting the complete absence in Java of any kind of caste-like groups now and in the past. Fourth, whatever was the nature of the culture adopted, there were in it significant strains of Buddhist influence. Fifth, there probably existed in Bali, prior to the advent of Hindu culture, a system of family, village and regional temples with its associated ritual and ceremony. Sixth, and very importantly, it is likely that there already existed the practice of wet rice agriculture and its associated irrigation organization (Swellengrebel 1960). All of these factors are, undoubtedly, crucial in providing Balinese hierarchy with its own particular characteristics and,

obviously, none of them can now be researched in any depth because of the
exiguous nature of the historical sources, be these documents or material
artefacts.

Summarizing it seems possible to conclude that (a) focusing on conceptual
criteria, for example the *brahman/kshatriya* relation, Bali could conceivably
be characterized as a caste society; (b) concentrating on the institutional
make-up of the island, at least one set of institutions, the *désa* and the *banjar,*
seems to embody this notion at a fairly concrete level, but (c) other institutions,
such as those concerning marriage, the nature of title groups, the extent of
ranking and the absence of the *jajmani* system, argue quite strongly against it,
and (d) the emergence of recent critical assessments of Dumont's theory of
the Indian caste system considerably complicates the picture.

The Interactional Level

So far the argument has centred on criteria of either a conceptual or an
institutional type, and I have, in essence, been comparing forms, ideas, and
cultural products. There is, of course, a third mode of tackling the problem,
and that is by focusing on social processes. Before proceeding, however, it is
necessary to supply some further data on titles and ranking.

As already mentioned, the Indian *varna* system is present in Bali although
there is no equivalent of the untouchable castes. All four *varnas* are represented,
but the major sociological divide is that between the *triwangsa* and the *sudra*
titles. *Brahman* and *wesia* titles are only found in some villages and the
further north one goes in south Bali the more the villages tend to be
composed entirely of *sudra* titles.

People who share a title only form corporate groups when they build
temples for the communal worship of their cremated and deified ancestors. In
such groups, known as *dadia* or *pamaksan,* endogamy is usually practised to a
greater extent than in the uncrystallized title aggregate, and the members
may often hold land in common (Geertz and Geertz 1975).

Ranking within the Balinese *warna* is really only important for *triwangsa*
and especially for those holding *satria* titles, amongst whom marriage contracts
can be fraught with relative status considerations. Preoccupation with ranking
is, moreover, relevant in a number of other contexts, for example, concerning
the amount, type and level of ritual paraphernalia, language use, physical
posture (in terms of relative head height), restrictions on commensality, and
so on.

As far as *sudra* titles are concerned, it is generally agreed that the *pandés*
(metal smiths) rank highest and that the various *pasek* titles follow. After
that, little attention is paid to ranking and, in contrast to what Geertz (1966)

has to say, I would argue that interaction between villagers in almost all contexts is quite relaxed. Thus, for instance, there is virtually no bar to marriage between holders of different *sudra* titles and very little trouble, if any, concerning the giving and acceptance of food. What problems exist concerning language are related, not so much to relative ritual rank, but to degree of acquaintanceship and to whether a person is a priest, other type of religious functionary or respected public official.

On the other hand, interaction between members of different *warna*, especially between *triwangsa* and *sudra*, is much more restricted by rules like those found in India, in form if not in content. Hypergamous marriages do take place, but have some significant social disadvantages, and hypogamous unions result in the decasting of the woman and, in previous times, even her death. Furthermore relative head height, language use and commensality are heavily standardized and therefore limit the freedom of interaction to levels more reminiscent of the Indian caste system. In short it can be argued, although it is something of a simplification to do so, that ranking is a preoccupation only when *triwangsa* are involved, and it is this circumstance which lends Bali the appearance of an attenuated caste society.

The last remark is a simplification not merely because the rules relating to ranking may be manipulated for political and economic ends (Hobart 1979), but also because, even in villages composed entirely of *sudras,* ranking may still be a significant aspect of social relations in certain contexts. In Pujung there are only three titles (all *sudra*) represented, *pandé, pasek gélgél* and *pasek batuan,* but these account for only 24 of the 93 village compounds. Those who have no title, to whom I shall return in a moment, are designated as *jaba* ('outsiders'). The status ranking of these aggregates is rarely a topic of conversation, but when questioned villagers almost unanimously placed *pandé* at the top, *gélgél* and *batuan* equally just below and *jaba* at the bottom, and this ordering was constant irrespective of the title of the person providing the information. The only contexts in which status is a significant issue are a very small number of inter-title marriages (disapproved of by the family of higher rank), the type of ritual accessories at major life-crisis rites (tooth filing, marriage, cremation) and the type of terms used to address and refer to other people, those of higher status being accorded respect by the use of terms from more refined *(alus)* levels of the language. What this seems to indicate is that this village, at least, displays a rank system rather than a caste system. According to Barth (1960: 113) 'caste is characterised by the simplicity of its basic schema, and its comprehensiveness' while 'systems of rank, though single in the scale which each defines, are generally restricted in their fields of relevance'. In short, if status considerations are confined to a rather narrow range of contexts, as they seem to be in this village, then there is no need for elaborate rules to govern social interaction in other contexts and, to that extent, it may be doubted that Bali has a caste system.

This argument is by no means conclusive because, as already mentioned, only a minority of the village's population acknowledge that they possess a title at all. The rest of the population either confess to possessing no title or, though having one prefer not to divulge it because, they attest, titles are unimportant and the less said about them the better. Indeed there is a significant body of opinion, from both title-holders and those without titles, which maintains that an excessive interest in titles, and in the consequent inevitable disputes over ranking, will have a deleterious effect on the apparent egalitarian ideology of the village. This ideology is well established in village origin myths, in rituals enacted during annual temple ceremonies and in certain other contexts, all of which are avidly and proudly pointed out by villagers owing allegiance to different title groupings (Howe 1980: chapters 1,15). That being the case, it could be argued that the seeming suppression of titles and title ranking is something of a deliberate strategy, and that therefore this village is an inappropriate example on which to base the kinds of arguments here being advanced. In fact there is some evidence that the situation in this village may be changing to one in which titles are likely to take on an increased significance (Howe 1984). However, two points need to be added. First, the evidence for such a change is scanty and equivocal and second, even in villages further south, where status ranking appears to be more important, it is nevertheless confined to the same kinds of contexts as it is in this village. In other words, granted that a change is taking place in the direction of a greater emphasis on status considerations, this does not necessarily imply that it will find application in a broader range of contexts than is presently the case; an intensification of the interest in ritual status will not inevitably signify a qualitative change in the character of hierarchy. If these arguments are valid then there is no reason to characterize this particular village as exceptional. Indeed many of the surrounding villages to the west, north and east appear to be even less interested in status and ritual ranking than is Pujung. In villages such as these, while notions of rank order govern relations between holders of different titles in only a weak way, ranking nevertheless is important in other contexts, such as in the asymmetrical oppositions between right and left, between *désa* and *banjar*, between god and demon, between above and below, etc (Howe 1980; 1981; 1983). In short, for parts of Bali (villages nearer the mountains) analysis in terms of rank seems most appropriate. In other areas (the lowland, more prosperous villages in many of which holders of *triwangsa* titles reside) analysis in terms of caste might prove more profitable because the presence of *triwangsa* considerably increases the pressures towards more standardized forms of social interaction.

It is possible to take the analysis a little further, at least as far as Pujung is concerned, by focusing on an institution which is not present in Bali, namely the *jajmani* system. Most writers who have had anything to say about caste in Bali and its relation to caste in India have made only passing reference to the absence of such a division of labour. Usually it is merely enumerated as one of several differences and, because it is not present, there is thought to be little of interest to say about it. However, there are grounds for arguing that it is the absence of a *jajmani* system which has resulted, to some degree, in the lack of the kind of status differentiation which is to be found in India. Of course the explanation of the absence of one phenomenon which is based on the absence of another is not the usual way in which anthropologists proceed, but in this particular case there are good reasons for following such a course. Bali does seem to differ from India, as far as caste is concerned anyway, in terms of institutions and social practices which are curtailed or absent in the former but present or emphasized in the latter, and indeed this is why I have already referred to Bali as an attenuated caste society.

In regard to the *jajmani* system, part of the difference between India and Bali is that villages in India are often characterized by the presence of a dominant caste of land owners. Some of these work their own land, others hire wage labour and still others tenant it out. Land owners receive services from various other castes, some of whose members pursue traditional occupations. In return for their services they are paid partly in kind on an annual basis and partly in cash. Ranking of castes is, to some extent, determined by such traditional occupations since these are themselves ranked in terms of both purity and prestige (Mayer 1960). It should be added that in many cases members of service castes own land in their own right and that therefore the degree of concentration of land ownership by the dominant caste varies widely over India (Mayer 1960; Parry 1979: 57).

The distribution and cultivation of agricultural land (mostly wet rice land) in Pujung provides quite a contrast. Only six per cent of families own no land at all, but a majority of these are nevertheless well off; four per cent own a good deal (I do not have accurate data on the holdings of these families as much of their land is scattered about in different villages); and fully 90 per cent own between one-half and two-and-one-half acres. Hence in Pujung, and probably in Bali as a whole, land is distributed far more evenly across the whole population than is the case in India.

In regard to the occupations which people follow, while in India there is a strong ideological and practical link between traditional occupations and both *varna* and caste, in Bali the link is evident only at the *warna* level. It is true that smiths generally pursue that particular trade, but many of them are also farmers. As far as can be ascertained, no other title group has a linked traditional occupation, although certain religious and public offices, such as *bendésa* for example, do tend to be restricted to one or two title groups. Overwhelmingly the vast majority of Balinese are farmers. However because of the relatively small amounts of land owned, farming does not consume much time (except at certain stages of the rice cycle), and it is therefore in their interests for the Balinese to engage in other, money-making, activities. Indeed most villagers are constantly on the look-out for such oportunities. It should also be emphasised that these undertakings are embedded in a cash/market nexus, and consequently individuals do not have a stable, traditional clientele. Services such as hair-cutting, basket-making, rope-making, production and distribution of palm and rice wine, carpentry, musicianship, tailoring, shop-keeping, bus and taxi driving, carving, building, etc. are therefore open to members of any and all titles. So far then it is possible to conclude that neither the ownership and distribution of land nor the distribution of occupations, except in one or two isolated and untypical cases, are linked to ritual status as indicated by title.

Systems of rank may also be based on wealth and power, so it is worth spending a moment in documenting some facts concerning how these are correlated with ritual rank. First, it would seem that in Pujung land ownership is correlated to wealth and power only at the extremes of the distribution and sometimes not even then. Thus there are a number of landless families which are also poor and politically impotent. However, there are also a number of landless families that are quite prosperous, their wealth being based on business activities, especially statue carving, transport services and retailing. Second, of those with large holdings of land some are politically powerful in the sense that they have an organized faction which is active in village politics. Other families with equally large holdings, while powerful in terms of their ability to provide employment, tend to have little influence in village affairs. Moreover certain individuals with small holdings have, for one reason or another (intelligence, integrity, accredited supernatural power, etc.) become prominent in these local arenas, Third, the *pandés,* who are undisputedly at the summit of Punjung's ritual hierarchy, are nevertheless some of the poorest in the village and, as a group, are politically insignificant. Finally, for only two families can it be said that large land holdings, wealth and political patronage are united. These two families are, respectively, the heads of the *pasek gélgél* and *pasek batuan* title groups. By comparison with the rest of the village they enjoy enormous wealth and a dominant role in village, and in the former case, supra-village affairs. Notwithstanding these two cases, however, the general trend is that ritual rank, wealth and political power are only contingently related at best.

The point of this descriptive exercise is to show that whereas in India certain statuses and practices are combined and ordered in a particular way within a single institution, the *jajmani* system, in Bali they are, to a very significant extent, independent of each other. The evidence seems to indicate that, for the Balinese, statuses associated with title group membership, occupation, land ownership, wealth and political power are not closely correlated, nor do they cluster together in a manner reminiscent of Indian castes. In Barth's terms (1960: 145) these statuses are freely combined, and according to him this combination results in what he calls a complex system quite different from a caste system in which 'caste position is characterized by a cluster of statuses relevant in different sectors of life and frameworks of organization' and in which 'incumbency of one status also necessarily implies incumbency of a series of other statuses forming the cluster'. In other words, in a caste system high caste rank, wealth, land ownership, political patronage and prestigious occupation all tend to cluster together, as do low caste rank, poverty, little land, political clientship and despised occupation. In India then, caste status is all-embracing and manifests itself in a wide variety of contexts whilst in Bali, taking Pujung as an example, the influence of ritual rank is, generally speaking, confined to a relatively small number of contexts and, in particular, does not appear to affect statuses determined by land ownership, wealth, occupation or political influence. However it must be pointed out that whilst the ethnographic record on Bali is now very extensive, a great deal of it is not entirely relevant to the present discussion, and there is thus a pressing need for modern studies of village social organization. In the absence of comparative material it would be unwise to proffer any definitive conclusions concerning the relationships between the rank orderings based on the various statuses discussed above. The issue here does not so much concern the range of application or significance of ritual rank, which would appear from available evidence to be much the same all over south Bali, but the extent to which these orderings are or are not correlated into clusters reminiscent of the Indian caste system. It could well be, for example, that in villages containing large concentrations of *triwangsa* title holders there might be found strong positive correlations between the different rank orderings, but even then it would still have to be determined whether such correlations are based on contingent and situational factors or on ideological ones.

CONCLUSION

If anything has been achieved by these meanderings through various aspects of Balinese ethnography it is, I hope, something of a concrete demonstration of Parkin's notion of comparison as 'endless perspectives'. The issue has not been to decide whether Bali is or is not to be characterized as a caste society, but in relation to any perspective adopted, to argue the merits of the case for saying so (one way or the other). Or, in other words, by shifting the perspective from one level of abstraction to another and from one set of data to another, relations of similarity and difference with Indian caste have been created. It could be argued that the word 'created' is inappropriate, and that something like 'revealed', 'exposed' or 'discovered' should have been used, since some may think these similarities and differences between the two societies really do exist. But this formulation disregards the fact that the comparison is not between these two societies or even between sets of 'raw', 'objective' data, but rather between various representations of these societies, or between interpretations of data (mine, Dumont's, Geertz's, Mayer's, etc.) already selected and interpreted in the very processes of being recorded, analysed and reported. If we take seriously the view that facts are 'joint constructions of the anthropologist and the people studied' (see Holy, this volume), then the relations between our data must also be joint constructions.

In the terms of Barry Barnes's (1982) immensely satisfying account of 'concept application' I am arguing that a combination of past usage, routine, and the authority of anthropological tradition points in the direction of applying the concept of caste to the Balinese instance. However, present interests and the burgeoning reaction to positivism inhibit this sort of simplistic classification. In response to this the data have been used in such a way as to produce a more or less interpretive account, and one which gives due recognition to cultural diversity and specificity. The data at my disposal clearly indicate that there is an intractable complexity involved in the analysis of Balinese hierarchy; it simply will not stand still, it seems to change in form and content depending on the direction from which it is approached: is it caste? is it a set of asymmetrical oppositions? is it a series of (more or less) incongruent rank orders? The available literature allows for all of these interpretations (in part), not because Balinese society is what it is (whatever that means) but because the data are as they are.

There is a kind of vertiginous feeling generated by arguments of this sort, for they seem to imply that one can say anything about everything and it is all equally good or bad, and indeed there is a certain scholastic validity in this logic. Fortunately in and of itself logic has no compelling force. What counts as good or bad anthropology depends on a range of different and constantly changing criteria, but few of these have anything to do with logic. Anthropology, like the worlds it attempts to comprehend, is a socially constructed enterprise, and as such it is founded on various conventions. But these conventions are not arbitrary and they are not easily changed, nor can anything be made into a convention; social credibility and practical utility are severe constraints (Bloor 1976: 37—9). Moreover the demands which anthropology makes of its practitioners are not generated solely from within the discipline, but to one extent or another permeate all the social and natural sciences. To grasp this is to understand that we are not trying to describe the world once and for all. Instead, within the frameworks and resources we have at our disposal, we are attempting not only to construct interpretations of our world and those of other peoples, but also to gain insight into how these worlds, including the world of anthropological practice, are themselves socially constructed.

REFERENCES

Barnes, B. 1982. *T. S. Kuhn and Social Science*. London: Macmillan.
Barnes, R. H. 1974. *Kédang, a study of the collective thought of an eastern Indonesian people*. Oxford: Clarendon.
Barth, F. 1960. The system of social stratification in Swat, north Pakistan. In *Aspects of Caste in South India, Ceylon and north-west Pakistan* (ed.) E. Leach. Cambridge: Cambridge University Press.
Bloor, D. 1976. *Knowledge and Social Imagery*. London: Routledge and Kegan Paul.
Boon, J. 1977. *The Anthropological Romance of Bali 1597—1972*. Cambridge: Cambridge University Press.
Bosch, F. D. K. 1961. *Selected Studies in Indonesian Archaeology*. The Hague: Nijhoff.
Bouglé, C. 1927. *Essai sur le régime des castes*, 2nd edn. Paris: Alcan.
Burghart, R. 1978. Hierarchical models of the Hindu social system. *Man* (N.S.) 13: 519—36.
Das, V. 1977. *Structure and Cognition: aspects of Hindu caste and ritual*. Delhi: Oxford University Press.
Dumont, L. 1957. *Une Sous-Caste de l'Inde du Sud: organisation sociale et religion des Pramalai Kallar*. Paris: Mouton & Co.
—— 1962. The conception of kingship in ancient India. *Contributions to Indian Sociology*, No 4.
—— 1972. *Homo Hierarchicus*. London: Paladin.
Fox, J. J. 1971. A Rotinese dynastic genealogy. In *The Translation of Culture* (ed.) T. O. Beidelman. London: Tavistock.
Fuller, C. 1979. Gods, priests and purity: on the relation between Hinduism and the caste system. *Man* (N.S.) 14: 459—76.
—— (n.d.) The King, the law and the priest. Seminar paper delivered at the Department of Social Anthropology, Queen's University, Belfast, 1983.
Geertz, C. 1966. *Person, Time and Conduct in Bali*. New Haven: Yale Southeast Asia Studies.
—— 1980. *Negara: the theatre state in nineteenth-century Bali*. Princeton: Princeton University Press.

Geertz, C. amd H. Geertz. 1975. *Kinship in Bali.* Chicago: Chicago University Press.

Hobart, M. 1975. Orators and patrons: two types of political leader in Balinese village society. In *Political Language and Oratory in Traditional Society* (ed.) M. Bloch. London: Academic Press.

—— 1979. A Balinese village and its field of social relations. Unpublished PhD thesis, University of London, School of Oriental and African Studies.

Howe, L. E. A. 1980. Pujung, an investigation into the foundations of Balinese culture. Unpublished PhD thesis, Edinburgh University.

—— 1981. The social determination of knowledge: Maurice Bloch and Balinese time. *Man* (N.S.) 16: 220−34.

—— 1983. An introduction to the study of traditional Balinese architecture. *Archipel* 25, 137−58.

—— 1984. Gods, people, spirits and witches: the Balinese system of person definition. *Bijdragen tot de Taal-, Land- en Volkenkunde* 140: 193−222.

Korn, V. E. 1960. The consecration of a priest. In *Bali, studies in life, thought and ritual.* The Hague: W. van Hoeve.

Lekkerkerker, C. 1926. De kastenmaatschappij in Britisch-Indie en op Bali. *Mensch en Maatschappij* 2: 175−213, 300−34.

Leur, J. C. van. 1967. *Indonesian Trade and Society.* The Hague: W. van Hoeve.

Mayer, A. 1960. *Caste and Kinship in Central India.* Berkeley: University of California Press.

Nadel, S. F. 1949. *The Foundations of Social Anthropology.* London: Cohen and West.

Needham, R. 1975. Polythetic classification: convergence and consequences. *Man* (N.S.) 10: 349−69.

Parry, J. 1979. *Caste and Kinship in Kangra.* London: Routledge and Kegan Paul.

—— 1980. Ghosts, greed and sin: the occupational identity of the Benares funeral priests. *Man* (N.S.) 15: 88−111.

Popper, K. 1959. *The logic of Scientific Discovery.* London: Hutchinson.

Schulte-Nordholt, H. G. 1971. *The Political System of the Atoni of Timor.* The Hague: Nijhoff.

Swellengrebel, J. L. 1947. *Een Vorstenwijding op Bali.* Leiden: Brill.

—— 1960. Introduction. In *Bali, studies in life, thought and ritual.* The Hague: W. van Hoeve.

Tambiah, S. J. 1976. *World Conqueror and World Renouncer.* Cambridge: Cambridge University Press.

Winch, P. 1958. *The Idea of a Social Science and its Relation to Philosophy.* London: Routledge and Kegan Paul.

Wouden, F. A. E. van. 1968. *Types of Social Structure in Eastern Indonesia.* The Hague: Nijhoff.

8

Pastoralism and the Comparative Method

Philip Burnham

When first asked to contribute to this volume, I must confess to having had ambivalent feelings about the topic. As Barnes points out in his paper, it is easy to take the view that everything of interest about the comparative method has already been said several times over. On the other hand, in British social anthropology since the pronouncements of Evans-Pritchard in his Marett (1950) and Simon (1961) lectures (see Evans-Pritchard 1962), it is clear that there has been something of an avoidance taboo applied to discussion of the comparative method, despite the many manifest uses to which it continues to be put in 'everyday' anthropology. And so, operating on the Malinowskian principle that the anthropologist should pay special attention to situations in which informants say one thing while doing another, I came around to the view that it would be interesting to do some stocktaking (if you will forgive the pun) with regard to the uses of the comparative method in an area of anthropology that is of interest to me — pastoralism.

Before moving to the more substantive section of this paper, however, I feel that it is necessary for me rapidly to sketch out my position on a number of issues to which, although they are of considerable relevance to the theme in question, I do not wish to devote much space in the present paper. First of all, I believe that there has been a tendency in certain anthropological circles to overinterpret, or misinterpret, Evans-Pritchard's remarks on the comparative method, which I take to have been directed principally at the inappropriateness of the natural science model of anthropological theory building advanced by Radcliffe-Brown (and based on a particular reading of Durkheim). Although Evans-Pritchard felt that anthropology should give up the quest for laws of social behaviour in Radcliffe-Brown's purportedly inductive and very positivistic sense, social anthropology was still to be concerned with generalization, understood in a more interpretive manner, and the comparative method, once it had been shorn of its role as the anthropological equivalent of the laboratory experiment, would inevitably still play a central part in anthropological approaches to knowledge construction. Evans-Pritchard's position here is one with which I have little trouble in agreeing, and his further comments on the combination of generalizing versus particularizing dimensions of social anthropological study also need to be kept in mind:

> Indeed I do not see how there can be an abstraction which is not a generalization as well. No events are unique. The battle of Hastings was fought only once, but it belongs to the class "battle", and it is only when it is so considered that it is intelligible, and hence explicable, for, for the historian, intelligibility is explanation; and this, I suppose, is why Cassirer calls historical knowledge a branch of semantics or hermeneutics. Another version of the generalizing versus particularizing sciences theme is the statement sometimes made that social anthropology is much more comparative than history and that this is as it should be, since it is the object of a natural science to pick out similarities and of history to pick out differences. The truth of the matter is this: both sociological historians and social anthropologists are fully aware that any event has the characters of uniqueness and of generality, and that in an interpretation of it both have to be given consideration.
>
> (Evans-Pritchard 1962: 48—9)

But this implicit comparison argument does not give one licence simply to treat social facts as things nor to engage in the 'butterfly collecting' and 'reificatory typologies' derided by Leach (1961: 2) and Needham (1974: 70). The longstanding strength of a participant-observation-based anthropology has been its repeated demonstration of the situationally malleable quality of actors' cultural vocabularies (even if much of 'mainstream' social anthropology has not sufficiently incorporated this perspective into its theorizing.) This prime feature of practical anthropological understanding has been further strengthened by insights derived from several recent theoretical perspectives, including phenomenological sociology and ethnomethodology (Schutz 1970; Garfinkel 1967), Geertzian interpretive anthropology, and writings on ideology by certain Marxist and Weberian writers (e.g. Bourdieu 1977; Habermas 1976). On the other hand, we should also remember in passing that Evans-Pritchard's remarks on generalization and categorical thinking were hardly novel even at the time they were written and are reminiscent of, for example, those of Max Weber concerning problems of historical and sociological interpretation published almost a half century earlier (Weber 1949: 113—88, English translation).

PASTORALISM AS A COMPARATIVE CATEGORY

Having touched briefly on some of the general issues related to the use of comparison in present-day anthropology, it is time now to move to a more specific level of discussion. I have decided to focus my paper on the problem of 'pastoralism' as a social and analytic category since it is an area of study in which I have some firsthand experience and also one that has been plagued by more than its fair share of problems relating to the use of the comparative method.

As categories bequeathed to modern anthropology by the nineteenth-century evolutionists (not to mention earlier social theorists as diverse as Montesquieu (1959) and Ibn Khaldun (1958)), pastoralism and its close relative, pastoral nomadism, are charged with a heavy load of preconceptions. It would be fair to say, I think, that much of the literature on this theme, both past and present, operates on the implicit premise that pastoralism is a 'natural' category of society, clearly distinguishable from other social forms. This impression of the 'purity' and distinctiveness of pastoralism as a way of life is, indeed, often reinforced by the ideologies of pastoralists themselves. Thus, for example, both Stenning (1959: 56—7) and I (Burnham 1972) have documented the Fulani self-image, which goes as far as to connect the ideal pastoral Fulani lifestyle with idealized Fulani physical traits to produce a thoroughgoing racist theory of society, albeit an indigenous one. In my opinion, many ethnographers who incline to the 'natural category' view of pastoralism have tended to focus to an unwarranted extent on such ideologically motivated statements of their informants (see R. Dyson-Hudson 1972 who argues a similar point.)

Fundamental to many anthropologists' views of pastoralism in this highly typological sense (dare I say, 'naturally enough'!) is the notion that there is something very special about a pastoral economy — the idea being essentially that such a mode of livelihood is hedged about with ecological constraints particular to itself. As a consequence, the literature on pastoralism continues to display numerous examples of strongly typological thinking. Correlatively, much time is still expended at conferences in discussing questions of such excessive generality as whether pastoralism is associated with predatory behaviour, individualistic temperament or other features of 'modal personality'. I say 'excessive generality' because it is clear that when 'explanations' or 'hypotheses' are formulated in this way, they fall prey to the trap of comparativism to which I have already alluded. (See Asad 1979: 419 for a rejection of such typological approaches.) When one attempts to employ such broadly phrased category words to illuminate a particular ethnographic case, an anthropologist whó is alive to the cultural complexities and nuances of the society in question will almost certainly come to the conclusion that such labels obscure more than they clarify. Or, to phrase the problem in Evans-Pritchard's terms, the explanatory advantages gained through such generalizations do not outweigh the disadvantage of the loss of particularized understanding.

One way of attempting to deal with this problem of excessive generalization is to try to be more specific about the particular attributes singled out in discussions of pastoralism as a taxon. Such efforts can assume a rather essentialist character, being based on the reasoning that if one could only isolate those attributes that are both necessary and sufficient to define a society as pastoral, one might be able to arrive at fruitful comparative generalizations. Thus, for example, a common approach is to attempt to isolate a category of 'pure' pastoralism — which is taken to refer to those societies or communities (or social units however defined) that live entirely from the products, direct or indirect, of the herd (see N. Dyson-Hudson 1972: 8, 23 for a critique of such an approach in relation to the category 'nomadism'). The reasoning behind such an analytical step is clearly expressed by Irons:

Given the fact that pastoral nomads exhibit such a variety of ecology, economy, social organization, and political organization, one might raise the question of whether it is worthwhile at all to try to generalize about pastoral nomadic societies. The answer is that one can hope to generalize only about certain features of such societies. Specifically one can only generalize about characteristics which are closely interconnected with a pastoral economy or a nomadic residence pattern.

(1979: 362)

Ultimately, the attempt here is to build the foundations of the comparative category of 'pastoralism' on the apparently solid rock of biology, for as Monod states:

The constraints of the environment, acting first on the animal and through the animal on the herdsman, provide the conditions for the well being of the herd, conditions that will guide all nomadic activity. No attempt at explanation, or merely at description, of the working of different types of pastoralism can therefore afford to ignore this necessary basis for the system, the ecology of the herbivore.

(1975: 105)

Leaving aside the pitfall of essentialism which surely is to be avoided, I must say that I (in company with other writers such as Dahl and Hjort or

Ingold) am broadly in sympathy with Monod's emphasis on the importance of an understanding of ecology in the analysis of pastoral societies, and I would not agree with Asad's (1979: 419) contrary view that the dependence of pastoral nomads on animals for their livelihood is simply a 'rather banal common-sense fact' which the anthropologist can rapidly pass over. However, Monod surely goes too far in arguing that environmental constraints 'guide all nomadic activity' — a position which clearly underestimates the social component in such systems. A major difficulty, therefore, which plagues the comparative analysis of pastoral systems is that of achieving an adequate analytical integration of environmental and social factors — a problem which we will now consider further in relation to the concept of minimum herd size.

MINIMUM HERD SIZE

Following logically from the concept of a purely pastoral economy, the literature offers many examples of attempts to define the minimum or basic herd size per capita that would be necessary to sustain a group practising this form of livelihood (e.g. Stenning 1958: 100; Barth 1961: 16—17; Allan 1965: 307—9; Monod 1975: 113—15, 120—1). By reference to data on rates of livestock reproduction, milk production, human nutritional needs, etc., such minimum herd size estimates have been produced for different forms of pastoralism, although even the more ardent supporters of this approach freely admit that, at best, such estimates indicate only rough orders of magnitude. As N. Dyson-Hudson notes (1972: 11, 12), the available data for such quantitative estimates are generally weak. Moreover, as Dahl and Hjort's (1976) simulations of herd production and reproduction rates suggest, even if minimum levels of required herd could be estimated more exactly in practice, they would be subject to very major fluctuations over time, given unpredictable climatic and/or demographic shifts.

One is therefore entitled to ask whether such a biologically derived concept as minimum herd size can have any utility as a basis for anthropological comparisons. This question is clearly of wider significance in that it applies to the use of a broad range of ecological concepts, including carrying capacity and energetic measures, as comparative anthropological tools (see, for example, Brush 1975). Answers to this question can be framed at several different levels, which I would like to explore briefly in turn.

It may be interesting at the outset to consider whether pastoralists themselves make any consistent reference to the minimum herd size concept in organizing their lives. The answer to this question is rather equivocal. Monod (1975: 120—1), citing various contributors to the *Pastoralism in Tropical*

Africa volume, emphasises that such actors' judgements are often not very explicit (although some are, like those of the Maasai) or may vary situationally. It seems also to be the case that in situations of relative plenty, pastoralists tend to be more interested in maximizing herd sizes, rather than in minimal limits, although in the opposite case, that of the Sahel drought of 1973, I found that destitute Fulani herders had very clear views on the minimum herd size and types of stock they would require before attempting to readopt a pastoral life style. As this range of pastoral opinion clearly illustrates, use of the minimum herd size approach in broad-ranging comparisons within the pastoral category would run into substantial difficulties if it depended on comparison of actors' formulations on this theme, and many pastoral ethnographers who use this approach have paid scant attention to collecting such opinions from their informants. On the other hand, as we shall see in a moment, the thinking of certain anthropologists in this connection (e.g. that of Fredrik Barth) has clearly been developed as a fieldwork dialogue between their informants' folk models and their own 'scientific' views — a fact which illustrates the complex nature of the process of concept formation and typification in a participant-observation-based anthropology.

In contrast to an emphasis on actors' models of their own systems, a strongly functionalist usage of the minimum herd size concept or of other purported pastoral 'requisites' is frequently employed, effectively to argue that the institutions of a pastoral society are functionally structured as adaptations to the requisites of a pastoral economy. A good example of such an approach is that adopted by Goldschmidt and his co-workers as the theoretical basis for their massively funded 'Culture and Ecology in East Africa Project'. As Goldschmidt explains:

... functional theory assumes that the institutions of a society are integrated wholes, that changes in one sector require adjustments in other sectors of the social system. This was the set of ideas which we are endeavouring to test. Let us put it this way: we treat environment as the independent variable; then, assuming a repertoire of techniques available, the pattern of economic exploitation becomes the intermediate variable, while the institutions of society, cultural attitudes and behaviour patterns, become the dependent variables.

(1965: 403)

Goldschmidt goes on to state:

Let me set forth some of the major elements in our model for pastoral life. This must be a logical model, a construct of institutional and behavioral relationships in terms of the requisites of the system.

(1965: 403)

Given such a functional requisite approach to comparison, Goldschmidt argues:

Pastoralism is a very good subject for our investigation; being relatively confined into a narrowly defined environment and ecology, it has a more specific set of sociological requirements and a closer unity of institutional forms than most economic life-modes.

(1965: 403)

Aside from their explicit functionalism, such arguments are frequently associated with the strongly typological position which I have already mentioned, since such a functionalist position provides a convenient rationale for the distinctive qualities that are considered to be associated with the pastoral category. Thus, in a later article, Goldschmidt (1979: 18) espouses precisely this viewpoint in the course of developing a 'pastoral model' that functionally interlinks the social and economic attributes that he considers to be distinctive of pastoral societies world-wide.

GENERATIVE MODELS AND OTHERS

Moving beyond such strongly functionalist approaches, probably the most influential use of the minimum herd size concept has been that of Barth (1961) in his work on the Basseri sheepherders. Using rough estimates of household budgets and rates of herd replacement supplied by the Basseri, Barth (1961: 16—17) presents a relatively simple economic rationale for the Basseri view that an average-sized household requires about 100 sheep and goats to maintain a satisfactory style of life. Basseri 'informants agreed that it was impossible to subsist on less than 60 (sheep)' (Barth 1961: 16) although no detailed nutritional or budgetary data were offered to defend this estimate. On the other hand, maximum herd sizes are said to be determined essentially by the behavioural characteristics of sheep and the availability of herdsmen's labour — since it is difficult for a single herdsman to control a flock of more than 400 head (Barth 1961: 22). Rich men therefore resort to the hiring of paid herdsmen and split their flocks (see Ingold 1980: 179, 180 and Swidler 1972: 74 for similar discussions of these issues).

   Although Barth was to present his concept of the generative model more formally in 1966, this work on herd sizes among the Basseri would certainly qualify as an example of such a model. In the 1961 monograph, he presents quite a comprehensive model of pastoral social structure among the Basseri and their neighbours which is ultimately derived in large measure from his analysis of the social entailments of herd size variations, used in conjunction with Stenning's (1958) concept of household viability among the pastoral Fulani. In particular, Barth (1961: 124—7) argues that form of property holding, inheritance, tendencies toward sedentarization of certain Basseri tribesmen, as well as particular features of tribal political organization, can be seen as social forms generated by the character of Basseri pastoralism. Barth also clearly considers this social ecological model to have utility as a form of comparative method, applicable to other Iranian sheepherding societies (cf. Swidler 1972: 72—4). And moving to the broadest possible canvas, Spooner (1973), following Barth, has attempted to produce a generative model of nomadic pastoralism that is applicable on a world-wide scale — an exercise that is not unrelated to Goldschmidt's pastoral model mentioned above.

If we now attempt to reduce to their essentials the strongly functionalist and the Barthian generative model approaches, it is possible to see, I think, that they rest on two contrasting, but somewhat linked, rationales:

Either (a) The minimum herd can be seen as a universally valid minimal limiting condition affecting pastoral societies, despite the fact that the details of each particular society's limit will vary, given variation in local environments and types of stock held. This interpretation rests directly on a set of biological circumstances, which can be seen as independent of a given cultural context.

Or (b) While starting from the same set of biological circumstances as outlined in (a), the minimum herd size approach can be interpreted in a more socially contextualized and culturally relative manner. In this approach, a clearer recognition is given to the fact that the 'minimum' is only a minimum relative to culturally defined needs and that pastoralists' failure to achieve the prescribed minimum herd size normally results only in a change in social state (e.g., change from a pastoral economy to some other economy, change from a nomadic lifestyle to a sedentary one, etc.) rather than death. Indeed, one could go further and show that transgression of the 'minimum' herd size figure will necessarily take place from time to time in all pastoral communities, given a set of reasonable assumptions concerning herd and human demographic rates. Despite the apparently more culturally relative character of the (b) position, many authors espousing it would still argue for the universal value of the minimal herd size notion as a comparative analytical technique for pastoral societies on the grounds that, however culturally interpreted, the biological limit must still operate to the extent that the society remains pastoral. To some authors (presumably Asad (1979) would count himself among this group), such an 'insight' would border on the banal or tautological, but I believe it cannot be disregarded.

In the case of the strong functionalist rationale for minimum herd size analyses and related functional requisites, we are dealing with a logic phrased in terms of the word 'must'. In its most pure form, this reasoning is becoming relatively rare in the modern anthropological literature since it represents an extreme functionalism whose drawbacks are now well known. On the other hand, reasoning of this nature can still creep in in certain statements within larger anthropological works and is common in non-anthropological writing of a technicist, development-oriented kind. It is the second approach which is by far the more common and, looking beyond pastoralist ethnography, can be seen to have close parallels with many other well-known analytical approaches in social anthropology — including the developmental cycle of domestic groups and analyses of carrying capacity and energy flow.

In the generative model and related approaches, although traces of functionalism may often creep in, we are principally dealing with a more contingent 'if — then' logic. In this latter form, the reasoning runs that *if* a system consists of a set of prescribed attributes (although there is no necessity for or analyst's commitment to its being so constituted) *then* certain other features, minimal conditions, etc. can be seen to be entailments of this defined state. Such 'if — then' reasoning can be seen to be common to a wide variety of post-war anthropological structuralisms including those of Lévi-Straussian studies of kinship, mythology and symbolism, the structural approach to politics and history of M. G. Smith (1978), the Althusserian Marxist analyses of social reproduction (see Friedman's 1976 discussion of this point), as well as the generative model approach developed by Barth. On the other hand, although these approaches all share an interest in analysing the logical entailments of sets of social attributes, be they termed models, structures, modes of production or whatever, they clearly differ concerning the forms and sources of the logics they employ to derive these entailments. While most would not hesitate to use formal logical concepts such as implication, contradiction, etc. as bases for their reasonings, they would disagree over their uses of logics derived from presumed human psychic properties, biological principles, or economic laws. Indeed, to give only one illustration of particular relevance to this paper, Ingold (1980: 211—17) has argued that, although Barth's comparative ecological analysis of Iranian pastoral systems pinpoints many of the relevant factors, it is invalidated by Barth's inadequate understanding of the ecological logic underlying man-herd relations. Clearly, in the context of the problems of the comparative method, there is scope for fruitful discussion of these themes, since it may be at the level of such logical properties that useful theoretical comparisons can be pursued.

Supporters of Barth's transactional approach might object to my bracketing of his generative model with other structuralisms — particularly in view of the fact that Barth (1981: 4) explicitly states that he developed his purportedly more actor-focused approach as a way of overcoming what he viewed as the shortcomings of structuralism. However, as Barth (1981: 84) has also pointed out, his approach consists of 'alternating between (but not confusing) logical operations on models, and empirical observation of processes and patterns.' In fact, I would suggest that due to Barth's tendency to skate rapidly over the problems of implicit comparison and typification in transactional analysis, as well as a decidedly cavalier attitude to the problem of aggregation of behaviour (Barth 1981: 23, 25), Barth himself would be hard pressed not to confuse these two levels. In this regard, I have long felt that he would be better advised to give explicit attention to the very close similarity between his concept of generative model and Weber's (1949: 90-2) concept of the ideal type. (Indeed, most of Barth's theoretical writing can be viewed as a direct elaboration of Weber's own theoretical position, although Weber is rarely cited explicitly.) Admittedly, the Weberian *verstehen* position sits uncomfortably with Barth's positivistic language, as in the following passage (1981: 119), 'Such comparisons are fruitful because they lead to empirical generalizations, they expose analytical problems, and they allow for the *falsification of hypotheses* (my emphasis).' However, if closer attention to Weber could convince Barth to modify this aspect of his own thinking, this would, in itself, be helpful.

Returning, then, to the minimum herd size notion, my own feeling is that, treated in an ideal-typical, 'if — then' way, such concepts can be of substantial value for understanding the social and ecological dynamics of pastoral systems. But I must sound a warning note here, since there is an unfortunate tendency among some writers on pastoralist themes (see N. Dyson-Hudson 1972 and R. Dyson-Hudson 1972, for example) to use the concept of the ideal type in a caricatured manner — one which has nothing in common with Weber's original meaning and which is more related to Durkheimian approaches of social typology. Weber's concept of the ideal type was developed explicitly to escape from the 'monism' (Weber 1949: 86) of the notion in the natural sciences of a causality operating outside of history and of actors' subjective consciousnesses. Through the use as an ideal type of the minimum herd size model, which contains both social and ecological elements, the analyst's attention is directed to many of the logical and functional entailments of a herding economy. At the same time, explicit recognition is given to the heuristic and socially contingent character of the model, in which the many factors operating within pastoral systems are mediated by the actors' subjective understandings of their situations.

A FULANI EXAMPLE

As an illustration of this ideal type approach to social comparisons, we can refer to the ethnographic data collected by Dupire, Stenning and myself on patterns of intergenerational transfer of livestock among the Fulani of West Africa and consider, albeit very briefly, the extent to which the minimum herd size logic provides a useful way of understanding these phenomena. Here, one is engaged in an exercise in regional comparison touching a large ethnic group (upwards of six million people) which includes communities subsisting both entirely from pastoralism and entirely from agriculture, as well as many combinations in between. If we begin by looking at Fulani communities that are relatively wealthy in cattle, e.g. the Wodaabe communities of Niger, Nigeria and Cameroon, we can see that intergenerational stock transfers tend toward a pattern of 'anticipatory inheritance' (Barth 1961: 19), in which most herd resources are transferred from the senior generation to the junior generation during the lifetime of the seniors. Thus, an infant boy receives his first gifts of cattle from his father at his naming ceremony shortly after birth, and these gifts are followed by further bestowals of cattle at circumcision and at the 'graduation' ceremony from Koranic school during boyhood. As Dupire (1970: 26) notes, marriage among these groups involves further important prestations, which can be described succinctly under the following four headings: (1) cattle given by the husband's group and killed for marriage feasting; (2) cattle and other gifts given by the husband's group to the new wife to provide for the domestic economy of the new household; (3) gifts of money and kind (not cattle) from the husband's group to the wife's group (brideprice proper); and (4) gifts of money and kind (not cattle) from the wife's group to the new couple as a form of dowry. The wife will also bring with her in marriage the cattle which she had been given as a child by her own parents at points of transition in her life.

As Stenning (1958) clearly noted, this pattern of intergenerational transfer of livestock among pastoral Fulani is manifestly oriented toward the creation of an independent domestic unit, replete with sufficient stock to ensure its livelihood (i.e. household viability). However, when we broaden our comparative considerations and look at other eastern Fulani groups with mixed farming and pastoral economies, it becomes apparent that there is a tendency for the bridewealth aspects of wealth transfer at marriage to be accentuated as the pastoral component of the economy declines and, correlatively, the anticipatory inheritance of stock is reduced or eliminated (Dupire 1970: 26). Similar correlations may be noted in the data on more westerly Fulani groups in Guinea, Upper Volta, Senegal, and Mali, although the relatively well developed stratification of many of these Fulani groups also clearly plays a role in determining patterns of stock transfer and marriage payment (Dupire 1970: 44). Indeed, in formulating an ideal type analysis of Fulani stock holdings and transfers, it is important systematically to consider, for both eastern and western groups, both the large-scale patterns of social stratification that obtain and the effects of individual variations in stock holdings within groups. Looking briefly at the individual level of variation in stock holding, it rapidly becomes apparent that actors in different economic positions tend to place different subjectively defined meanings on the concept of minimum herd size, and this will have direct implications for patterns of stock transfer and accumulation in these different cases. Moreover, on a closely related theme, the attitudes toward cattle stocking, minimum herd sizes, wealth transfers, and choice of stock varieties can be shown to be different among Fulani groups that manage their herds principally with a view toward milk production as opposed to beef production for the market (Burnham 1980: 166).

CONCLUSION

Rather than delve further into the detail of Fulani stock transfers, which is a very large topic in itself, I shall rapidly sum up several of the points which this brief ethnographic comparison illustrates. To begin with, an ideal-type approach has value as a means of considering the possible mutual effects of different aspects of an ethnographic situation, seen as an ecological system. In this way, biological constraints, actors' motivations, and social structural features may be interrelated with less risk of falling prey to unacceptable functionalist thinking. Already at this stage, one is involved with implicit comparisons but, in my opinion, a Weberian ideal-type approach is most helpful in reminding the analyst of the problems of subjectivity and typification that must be kept in view. Also of central importance here are intensive and repeated experiences of fieldwork by participant observation, combined with as explicit an awareness as possible of the socially constructed nature of ethnographic data.

At a second level of abstraction, such a model can also provide a method for more explicit comparisons, although one must be aware that in so doing, one is inevitably further sacrificing depth of understanding of particulars for perceived gains at the level of generalization. In view of this unavoidable problem, regional or other forms of controlled comparisons are likely to be the more fruitful.

The Fulani example also illustrates, I believe, that cross-category comparisons are often as useful as those which remain rigidly circumscribed by the definitional boundaries of a taxon like 'pastoralism'. One could as easily have made this point with regard to the related category of 'nomadism', a fact which I have discussed in previous papers (Burnham 1975; 1979), although discussion of pastoralism is especially cogent in view of the determinedly typological thinking displayed in much of that literature.

In conclusion, I think it is important to at least raise the issue of the relevance of our discussions of the comparative method for work in the applied anthropology field. My own experience in this regard is limited to Third World development and, viewed from this perspective, it appears that the 'natural science/comparative method as an experimental method' position is still predominant. This is not unconnected, of course, with the desire of certain applied anthropologists to portray their expertise as 'scientific' in a 'hard' science sense. In contrast, the position I have espoused in this paper is a decidedly weaker one, so far as providing quick and easy answers is concerned, although I would argue that it is likely to produce better insights into the development process in the long run since it gives explicit attention to the perceptions and values of those toward whom this process is (at least supposedly) directed. Finally, if we take seriously the dimensions of subjectivity and typification implied in the ideal-typical approach suggested above, we will also realize the value of frequent periods of fieldwork and especially, to quote Barth (1981: 10), the importance of the opportunity to 'expose our scholarship to the demands of practical action'.

REFERENCES

Allan, W. 1965. *The African Husbandman*. London: Oliver and Boyd.
Asad, T. 1979. Equality in nomadic social systems. In *Pastoral Production and Society* (eds) Equipe ecologie et anthropologie des sociétés pastorales. Cambridge: Cambridge University Press.
Barth, F. 1961. *Nomads of South Persia*. Boston: Little, Brown & Co.
___ 1966. *Models of Social Organization* (Occasional Papers of the Royal Anthropological Institute No. 23). London: R.A.I.
___ 1981. *Process and Form in Social Life: selected essays of Fredrik Barth*. Vol. I. London: Routledge and Kegan Paul.
Bourdieu, P. 1977. *Outline of a Theory of Practice*. Cambridge: Cambridge University Press.
Brush, S. 1975. The concept of carrying capacity for systems of shifting cultivation. *American Anthropologist* 75: 799—811.

Burnham, P. 1972. Racial classification and ideology in the Meiganga region: North Cameroon. In *Race and Social Difference* (eds) P. Baxter and B. Sansom. Harmondsworth: Penguin.

—— 1975. *Regroupement* and mobile societies: two Cameroon cases. *Journal of African History* 16: 577—94.

—— 1979. Spatial mobility and political centralization in pastoral societies. In *Pastoral Production and Society* (eds) Equipe ecologie et anthropologie des sociétés pastorales. Cambridge: Cambridge University Press.

—— 1980. Changing agricultural and pastoral ecologies in the West African savanna. In *Human Ecology in Savanna Environments* (ed.) D. Harris. London: Academic Press.

Dahl, G. and A. Hjort. 1976. *Having Herds*. Stockholm: Department of Social Anthropology, University of Stockholm.

Dupire, M. 1970. *Organisation Sociale des Peul*. Paris: Plon.

Dyson-Hudson, N. 1972. The study of nomads. *Journal of Asian and African Studies* 7: 2—29.

Dyson-Hudson, R. 1972. Pastoralism: self image and behavioral reality. *Journal of Asian and African Studies* 7: 30—47.

Evans-Pritchard, E. E. 1962. *Essays in Social Anthropology*. London: Faber.

Friedman, J. 1976. Marxist theory and systems of total reproduction. *Critique of Anthropology* 2: 3—42.

Garfinkel, H. 1967. *Studies in Ethnomethodology*. Englewood Cliffs, New Jersey: Prentice-Hall.

Goldschmidt, W. 1965. Theory and strategy in the study of cultural adaptability. *American Anthropologist* 67: 402—8.

—— 1979. A general model for pastoral social systems. In *Pastoral Production and Society* (eds) Equipe ecologie et anthropologie des sociétés pastorales. Cambridge: Cambridge University Press.

Habermas, J. 1976. *Legitimation Crisis*. London: Heinemann.

Ibn Khaldun. 1958. *The Muqaddimah: an introduction to history*. New York: Pantheon.

Ingold, T. 1980. *Hunters, Pastoralists and Ranchers*. Cambridge: Cambridge University Press.

Irons, W. 1979. Political stratification among pastoral nomads. In *Pastoral Production and Society* (eds) Equipe ecologie et anthropologie des sociétés pastorales. Cambridge: Cambridge University Press.

Leach, E. 1961. *Rethinking Anthropology*. London: Athlone Press.

Monod, T. 1975. Introduction to *Pastoralism in Tropical Africa*. London: Oxford University Press for the International African Institute.

Montesquieu, C. Baron de. 1959. *The Spirit of the Laws*. New York: Hafner.

Needham, R. 1974. *Remarks and Inventions*. London: Tavistock.

Schutz, A. 1970. *Reflections on the Problem of Relevance*. New Haven: Yale University Press.

Smith, M. G. 1978. *The Affairs of Daura*. Berkeley: University of California Press.

Spooner, B. 1973. The cultural ecology of pastoral nomads. *Current Topics in Anthropology* (Module No. 45). Reading, Mass.: Addison-Wesley.

Stenning, D. 1958. Household viability among the pastoral Fulani. In *The Developmental Cycle in Domestic Groups* (ed.) J. Goody. Cambridge: Cambridge University Press.

___ 1959. *Savannah Nomads*. London: Oxford University Press for the International African Institute.

Swidler, W. 1972. Some demographic factors regulating the formation of flocks and camps among the Brahui of Baluchistan. *Journal of Asian and African Studies* 7: 69–75.

Weber, M. 1949. *The Methodology of the Social Sciences*. New York: Free Press.

9

'African Ethnogenesis': Limits to the Comparability of Ethnic Phenomena

Richard Fardon

ETHNICITY AND COMPARATIVE ANTHROPOLOGY

Recently there has been a profusion of books and articles concerned with ethnicity; exercises in global comparative anthropology also continue to make their appearance, although these seem less numerous than once they did. But the twain meet rarely: few anthropologists have explicitly addressed the relationship which should obtain between ethnicity and comparison.[1] At first sight the omission appears puzzling. Ethnic terms furnish the benchmarks for comparative anthropology — the appendices to any book in the *Human Relations Area Files* tradition of comparison contain long lists of ethnic labels which refer the presence or absence of particular cultural traits to human societies as they presently exist or once existed. The ethnic labels stand as guarantors of the relation between the characteristics isolated and people to whom the characteristics can be attributed. These names are tokens of reality which we assume can be redeemed. Take away the ethnic labels, and you also remove the link between the culture and its carriers. The rhetorical role of naming seems obvious in the case of the American exemplars of comparative method, but it must be true of all comparisons which employ ethnic tags. Comparison depends upon ethnic tags having a constant 'reality value'.

Recent approaches to ethnicity, on the other hand, tell us that ethnic labelling is a complex process. Questions about the status and fixity of ethnic boundaries and the internal homogeneity of ethnic cultures cannot be answered *a priori*. In this light, the anthropologists' practical approach to comparing institutions (kinship systems, marriage rules, productive units or whatever) seems to rely upon a startling, even wilful, naïvety about the ethnic units compared. Explicit approaches to ethnicity and implicit uses of ethnicity as a benchmark for comparison hardly seem to belong to the same 'episteme'. Troubling questions arise: 'Does the viability of comparative anthropology rest upon the comparability of ethnic identities?'. Or, to put it differently: 'If there is not a unitary ethnic phenomenon, how are units for comparison to be isolated?' To respond to these questions it is necessary to recall some elements of the career which ethnicity has enjoyed in anthropology and to draw attention to three related assumptions which inform much contemporary anthropology. I regard all three with deep suspicion.

1 The 'ethnic phenomenon' describes a relatively distinct and universal circumstance which can be abstracted from the welter of appearances for comparative purposes.
2 Ethnicity also furnishes the basis for isolating units to be compared in other terms.
3 Ethnicity has subsumed a collection of earlier distinctions which had different labels (race, tribe, culture, nation etc.). For a variety of reasons this is a good thing.

I shall discuss these assumptions in the abstract, then in relation to a specific (ethnically defined) ethnographic context and, finally, with respect to African ethnicities in general. I begin with the existence of an 'ethnic phenomenon' (van den Berghe 1981).

WHY ETHNICITY IS DIFFICULT TO DEFINE

To start with the obvious — ethnic terms are elements in the practical philosophy and sociology of the peoples studied by anthropologists. Anthropologists press such distinctions into comparative service at second hand; like Lévi-Strauss's mythical *bricoleur*, they find themselves doomed to construct from the debris of other people's previous creations. Thus, a practical difference may be invoked in a context which calls for objective collation and comparison — a task for which it was never designed. Long before current preoccupations with *la différence*, Georg Simmel had neatly summed up the issue:

It is above all the practical significance of men for one another that is determined by both the similarities and differences among them. Similarity, as fact or tendency, is no less important than difference. In the most varied forms, both are the great principles of all external and internal development. In fact, the cultural history of mankind can be conceived as the history of the struggles and conciliatory attempts between the two.
(Simmel 1950: 30)

When anthropologists appropriate indigenous terms for the business of comparison, they implicitly alter the practical significance of those terms. This is to ignore what I shall call Nietzsche's pocket problem: 'As if every word were not a pocket into which now this, now that, now several things at once have been put!' (Nietzsche 1977: 153)

Precisely because ethnic terms serve and inform practical significances, which are liable to change, they share with Nietzsche's pocket the characteristic of sometimes containing this, sometimes that, and sometimes several things at once. Contents tend to reflect the habits of the user, subject only to the broad constraint of the design of the pocket. Like pockets, ethnic terms have complex histories of use.

Such complex use histories mean that ethnicity shares with a kindred concept, nationalism, the property of being virtually impossible to define in a way that is not either ambiguous or tautologous (Seton-Watson 1977: 5; Anderson 1983: 9). Nonetheless, anthropologists appear to experience little difficulty in deciding that certain types of distinction constitute ethnic discriminations. Perhaps here, as elsewhere, we may suppose that anthropologists implicitly draw on a polythetically constructed category. The clustering of a goodly number of the characteristics we hold typical of the set labelled ethnicity suffices for us to recognize another member of the set (Needham 1975; Southwold 1978). Most of the generalizations we are able to make about ethnicity might be properties of a polythetic definition we implicitly use. The polythetic definition would be something like this,

Ethnic categories are broad classifications of people; they are frequently mapped according to a series of binary discriminations which oppose an 'us' to a 'them'. (R. Cohen 1978)

Although ethnic discriminations appeal to shared characteristics of the inclusive category, we have no way in advance of the facts, to specify what these characteristics will be in particular cases. (Experience of comparative cases leads us to anticipate that language, common history, descent, race, or some aspects of culture or religion will be used to 'naturalize' the commonality of the inclusive category. (Isajiw 1974))

The characteristics of the exclusive categories are also stereotyped, frequently in a pejorative manner. In extreme cases, we find the demonization or animalization of out-categories (Kuper 1977). In less extreme cases, we may find that the social and cultural habits, sexual morals and so forth of exclusive categories have been found wanting under the lens of the inclusive category's perception of its own life habits. Ethnic stereotypes are usually based in the self-regard of the classifiers.

However, the sum of these characteristics is not sufficient to account for our ability to discriminate a class of ethnic distinctions; most of the criteria could apply equally to race, class, or gender classifications. Implicitly, our definition must contain a clause which removes from the ethnic set any types of distinction which can be attributed to other sets. Ethnicity may be a residual polythetic category. But even if this is dismissed as fanciful, ethnicity is clearly not amenable to essential definition. We could also look at the arbitrariness of ethnicity from the perspective of the broader contexts in which terms of distinction are employed. Ethnic discriminations are elements of more general classifications which identify relations of similarity and difference within social universes. As such they are always 'adjacent' to other elements of these classifications which we choose to treat as non-ethnic. Ethnic idioms draw sustenance from and plagiarize these other idioms (all our neighbours are witches; our neighbours are effeminate . . .), while themselves serving as metaphors for internal classification (witches are like our neighbours rather than ourselves; women are strangers amongst us . . .). Both in practice and in principle, the cut-off point for the application of the term ethnic to bodies of social classification can be decided only on the merits of individual cases and in the light of the proclivities of particular analyses. Somehow, the ethnic has to be wrenched from its adjacent idioms if it is to label a people and a potential comparative instance.

Despite, or perhaps because of, its inchoate senses, ethnicity has become a vogue term.

HOW ETHNICITY JUST GREW AND GREW

Once there was a large vocabulary to describe types of differences (of race, of language, of nation (in its old sense)[2] and so on). These categories were often ill-defined and sometimes pejorative, but they did preserve the important, and I think justifiable, sense that not all of these differences were of the same type. Since ethnicity gobbled up these distinctions and regurgitated them as variants of a single type of 'ethnic' difference, it seems that many notes on the scale of difference have become muted if not lost. The contemporary coherence of the ethnic phenomenon in anthropology stems from the rejection of earlier distinctions and, in particular, the term 'tribe'. 'Tribe' used to connote a particular type of ethnicity characteristic of the people whom anthropologists traditionally studied and of a dim and distant period in their own national histories. It has virtually disappeared from professional usage under a barrage of criticisms, at the same time as 'tribalism' has become a politically loaded term purporting to describe and explain the chronic dissensus supposed to exist in many new states. The developments are not independent, and anthropologists have been justified in distancing themselves from appearing to endorse a popular prejudice. Nonetheless, I shall argue that acceptance of some of the reasons anthropologists have given for abandoning the term 'tribe' does not necessarily imply endorsement of a universal ethnic phenomenon. I shall review anthropological discontent with 'tribe' under four headings.

The Nominal Objection

One of the arguments of a series of important papers which Aidan Southall wrote on African ethnicity during the 1970s was that many of the terms which found their way into the literature as tribal epithets were not genuine ethnic terms (Southall 1970; 1976; for reception of the point see for example Young 1976). Some of these terms were bestowed by neighbours or by colonial authorities; others designated language groups without ethnic salience; others simply meant something like 'the people'. In the broadest sense, this objection is empirical. Ethnographic techniques have failed to represent indigenous societies by their own ethnic terms; although it could also be argued that the abusive usages of neighbours, or the misunderstandings of colonial authorities, become instrumental terms in their own right and equally subject to analysis. Southall, but not all those who repeated his criticism, recognized this.

The Reificatory Objection

A second charge against 'tribe' was part of the more general attempt anthropologists made to recognize and expunge the unacceptable elements of their structural-functional heritage. Earlier anthropologists, so the argument goes, had naïvely supposed a concordance of boundary phenomena, and so implicitly introduced the coincidence of tribal identity, culture, social and political organization. The reified tribal units could be directly compared with other units isolated in the same way. Charitable observers noted that influences ran the other way also, and the current understanding of comparison had probably led to the reification of tribes (Cohen and Middleton 1971: 4—5). Writers like Fortes (1945) and Nadel (1935) had paid explicit attention to the non-coincidence of boundary phenomena in classic structural-functional works, and Leach's influential critique of tribal reifications was published by 1954. However, in 1978 Ronald Cohen was able to see the replacement of tribe by ethnicity as indicative of a paradigm shift. If the reification of tribes had resulted from the older understandings of comparison it remained unclear how comparison was to take place under the new ethnic paradigm. As well as to the comparative method, the blind spot in structural-functional analyses could also be attributed to the neglect of history, which would have revealed changing tribal terms and referents, to the tendency of colonial administrative methods to create tribes in the process of administering them and, perhaps, also to an implicit export of some of the tacit assumptions underlying European notions of nationality. Like the nominal objection, the reificatory objection supposes a failure of ethnographic technique. Once identified, such a failure is remediable. It has no bearing on the existence of a universal ethnic phenomenon.

The Derogatory Objection

A further set of objections is directly critical of 'tribe' as a term which is held to be imbued with derogatory and evolutionary implications. Glazer and Moynihan, in the preface to a collection of essays that was itself a symbolic landmark in the legitimation of ethnic rights, attribute the first use of the term to David Riesman in 1953 (Glazer and Moynihan 1975: 1). The 'ethnic revival' describes a process by which more and more categories of people have been persuaded to see ethnic identity as an argument about which to mobilize claims to specific types of entitlement (A. Smith 1981; 1983). Anthropologists found themselves compromised as the proponents of a distinction within what was generally supposed, especially in the nationalists' and ethnic revivalists' own rhetoric of 'primordial sentiment', to be a universal phenomenon. Ethnicity could be construed as an element of 'personhood', and ethnic groups could appear as the natural carriers of rights (see, for instance, '*les droits des ethnies*' in Breton 1981: 122—4). It seemed as if everyone had ethnic groups unless they were studied by anthropologists, in which case they had tribes. Since no-one was willing to say what distinguished an ethnic group, or strictly ethnic category, from a tribe (other than the dubious privilege of attracting the attention of an anthropologist rather than a political scientist or sociologist) it seemed right that the distinction be dropped and everyone admitted to a world order of ethnic categories. 'Tribe' appeared as another of the devices which, Fabian has more recently claimed, tend to deny coevalness in time between societies (Fabian 1983). In a surprisingly short time, ethnicity cornered the market in forms of social distinction that were argued from a backward glance.

Apart from a populist use associated with anthropology via the exotic, 'tribe' also suffered from implication in more academic theories of evolution. In terms of a broad theory of evolution, tribes were supposed to intervene between bands and states. Conceived residually in this fashion (more than a band, less than a state), the category of tribe necessarily lacked coherence

(Godelier 1977). The tribal stage may have encompassed more organizational forms than the rest put together, and it became difficult to understand how such an assortment could constitute a step on the way anywhere.

'Tribe' may be irrevocably compromised as a term both inside and outside anthropology, but this is not tantamount to an argument that there are no distinctions to be drawn between modern and pre-modern ethnicity, only that 'tribe' cannot draw these distinctions with appropriate connotations.

The Situational Objection

A fourth set of objections relates closely to the charge of reification levelled against writers in the structural-functional tradition described above. Analyses by members of what we now recognize as the Manchester School, to a large extent in the Copper-belt and southern Africa, stressed the situational character of ethnicity.[3] According to this view, ethnic identity is a claim negotiated in the course of events which occur in determinate settings. The settings, the types of identity to which a claim is made, the referents of the ethnic terms, the symbols representative of ethnic identity and the contribution which these make to the construction of personal identities, are all subject to variation. The thrust of the Manchester critique is against the essentialist reading of tribal entities and towards the circumstances in which claims to a category membership can be envisaged as a useful, pointed, persuasive and coherent argument about something. This train of thought can be pursued more or less far. It would be possible to argue that ethnicity has no existence other than in the rhetorical claims made upon it during events; Manchester writers, on my reading of them, stop short of this conclusion and prefer to look upon ethnicity as situational to a degree rather than absolutely. Most typically, the situations have been defined by polarities of rural and urban location, often in a context of labour migration.

The realization that ethnicity is 'situational' cogently supplements the reification objection described above, but it is mute about the possibility of difference between types of ethnicity.

SUBJECTIVE AND OBJECTIVE ETHNICITY

Anthropologists drew two main conclusions from objections made to the use of the term 'tribe'. Firstly, that the term 'tribe' and category of societies it was supposed to designate were both indefensible, and that tribal discriminations should be shifted into an undifferentiated class of ethnicity. Secondly, they decided that the debate had been dealing with two senses of ethnicity which needed to be distinguished: these came to be labelled subjective and objective ethnicity. Subjective ethnicity was 'subjective' because it was defined in terms of meanings and intentions attributed to social actors by anthropologists. Objective definitions of ethnicity, on the other hand, were solely to be defined in terms of the agency of analysts, consisting of sober judgements about the distribution of features of culture, language and dialect, historical processes, institutionalized forms of organization and so forth. Objective analyses might accord with subjective judgements, which would thereby be validated, or they might alternatively denounce subjective judgements, or propose ethnic distinctions which were subjectively unrecognized.[4] Since ethnic discriminations were held to constitute a universal phenomenon, it followed that the subjective/objective distinction could be used globally and that comparisons could be joined on the basis of the distinction. It was then open to different commentators to declare themselves either as purists or as being in favour of varied mixes of the subjective and objective approaches.[5] I shall argue that this whole train of reasoning is flawed; and worse, that its conclusions are ideological.

The objections made to earlier uses of the term 'tribe' certainly told against a western tradition of representation of other peoples crucially predicated upon key associations of tribalism, in particular atemporality, atavism and isolation. This tradition was, and continues to be, a legitimate target. But, and this also is typical of criticisms of representative styles, the critique was hijacked by interests which found any representation of difference suspect.[6] Earlier anthropologists may often have reified tribes, ignored the situational nature of ethnic loyalties, used names other than those used self-referentially by the people about whom they wrote, and some of them may have subscribed to evolutionary presuppositions, explicitly or implicitly, but the acceptance of these points singly or together does not logically imply the existence of a universal ethnic phenomenon. Without such a phenomenon, it is not possible to argue that the subjective/objective distinction can be applied in all cases. To this extent the propositions are interrelated. But I shall argue that, anyway, the propositions are flawed both individually and collectively:

1   The subjective/objective distinction cannot be maintained on the grounds proposed.
2   Not all distinctions with 'ethnic intention' have the same significance and, therefore, there is no universal ethnic phenomenon.
3   The application of a concept of universal ethnicity is ahistorical and so obfuscates the course of historical change.

I call the sum of these errors ideological, rather than simply wrong, because it has the effect of distorting our perceptions by including the pernicious and non-pernicious in a single category. Even if the logic were unassailable (which it is not), the result would not assist us to act in terms consistent with common humanity. By creating a universal ethnic phenomenon we falsely naturalize ethnicity and may even put ourselves in the absurd position of seeking a literally natural solution to this falsely naturalized entity (van den Berghe 1981). Here, I would want to make a distinction between objectifying the common position of a group of people and reifying or naturalizing that common position. However, I think my argument about the error of some implications of the conventional anthropological approach to ethnicity might find support even where my opinion about the ideological nature of this error would not.

To start with the subjectivist position: this position seems to have much in its favour. Since ethnic boundaries do not necessarily coincide with cultural distributions, and since these boundaries are situational, when looked at in contemporary terms, and unstable, if looked at historically, then it follows that it is counterproductive for anthropologists to try to legislate regarding their locations. Ethnic boundaries are between whoever people think they are between. I have no quibble with this, but to call the phenomenon subjective is suspect. Ethnic ideas are, presumably, no easier to attribute than any other kinds of ideas, and conventional anthropological caution warns that it is not possible to move from what people may 'do' or 'say' to what they 'think' without an interpretative leap. Quite how this is to be made continues to be contested. Because 'subjective' ethnicity is attributed to social actors on the basis of our theories about their speech and activity, I would prefer to relabel it 'performative ethnicity', recognizing that it is deduced from a performative basis. But 'objective' ethnicity is also deduced from performative evidence. The difference between the two concepts lies not in the type of evidence upon which they draw, but in the assumption that the status of an actor's conceptual category can be attributed to 'subjective' ethnicity. However, such a reattribution of concepts would have to be justified and faces a significant hurdle.

People whom anthropologists study do not necessarily distinguish a category of differences akin to our ethnic differences. When we attribute 'ethnic ideas' to subjects we do more than simply translate, we also attribute a technique of social distinction, and one that we have only managed to define in our own culture as a polythetically constructed residual class (and then by dint of charitable interpretation). To argue that subjective ethnicity is universal is covertly to globalize the category of ethnicity, and I am not aware of the research base which permits us to do this. Our own societies did not discover the general form of a universal difference, rather they invented this form of difference. Once ethnicity was objectified and given autonomy as a form, to borrow terms from Simmel in translation (Simmel 1980), actors were able to pursue ethnic goals or adopt ethnic stratagems. Such goals and stratagems are a part of what ethnicity now means as a practical relationship of similarity and difference. But the presupposition of a universal class of ethnic difference attributes the same potential for action to those who do not read their differences in terms of ethnicity. This error is only compounded by calling the upshot 'subjective ethnicity'.

NATIONALISM AND THE AUTONOMIZATION OF ETHNICITY

> The great, but valid, paradox is this: nations can be defined only in terms of the age of nationalism, rather than, as you might expect, the other way around.
>
> (Gellner 1983: 55)

It is always possible to argue developmental (archaeological) views of history against disjunctive (epistemological) views. After all, the identification of change takes place from an interested point of view. My interest here is to extend Gellner's view of nationalism to ethnicity in general and to argue that the growth of nationalism, the 'ethnic revival' and the acceptance of the national state as an international norm, have created forms of national and sub-national ethnicity differing significantly from the styles of distinction current in earlier periods.

Contemporary nationalism is generally held to be the legacy of the Enlightenment and the European 'Age of Revolution' abetted by the development of industrial society (Hobsbawm 1962: chapter 7). The diffusion of nationalist sentiments in European societies has been related to the development of literacy and the circulation of ideas through print in several ways: through the creation of a common literate culture, the wider dissemination of ideas and the development of the capacity to imagine identity in terms of a community larger than that of the immediate circle of fellows (Gellner 1983; Anderson 1983). Imperialism and colonialism were responsible for delineating Third World states and encouraged nationalist sentiment within them, both by intention and despite it. Decolonization, often attended by struggles for a 'national' liberation, tended to encourage the growth of these sentiments, and state systems of education, national armies and bureaucracies have continued this process as much through their manifest purposes as by offering advancement to new elites through state sponsored channels. Internal mechanisms have been consistently reinforced by the exigencies of international and regional realpolitik, as well as by the presupposition of the national state as an international norm (polycentric nationalism in A. Smith's

1971 terms). It is from this political, economic and cultural background that the 'ethnic revival' derives its sense of unity. The failure of nationhood to be realized and the rhetoric of more successful nationalists equally draw upon and endorse the idea that ethnic identity furnishes an argument for rights which the ideal of nationhood guarantees: of which equal rights, cultural autonomy, personal dignity and political self-determination are felt to be amongst the more important (Kedourie 1960).

I have emphasized the political conditions under which ethnicity crystallized as an autonomous form, and most especially the role of the State in this; some other writers have given prominence to the economic conditions associated with the spread of capitalist organization of production and marketing (van Binsbergen 1985; Ranger 1982). The difference may result from regional focus, since my immediate problems have come from an economically underdeveloped area of west Africa, whereas emphasis upon economic factors occurs in analyses of southern Africa. (However, others have seen limitations in Marxist approaches to nationalism in Europe: Nairn 1977: chapter 9; Anderson 1983). In either case, the emergence of modern ethnicity seems to occur with other changes of perspective; the past has to be read as history, and to it must be attributed the force of an argument with respect to the evaluation of present conditions and the possibility and desirability of changing them. Nationalisms may be construed as 'old' by association with idealized notions of tradition and the collective destinies of 'peoples' and their culture presented as actors on a historical stage. Alternatively, 'newer' nationalisms may be construed as projects the inception of which is to be invoked in events more immediate than 'primordial' (a common heritage of oppression or struggle for liberation). The rhetoric of contemporary nationalism and ethnicity is inherently limited in its dependence upon a stream of exclusive first person plural possessives. It has to precipitate a new high age of the 'invention of tradition' (Ranger 1983). As the statuses of nations are defined in relation to a world order of United Nations, so are the saliences of ethnic groups homologized with reference to the State. National states exhaustively and exclusively partition the world, and there is an expectation that ethnic groups should be capable of doing the same in a national territory.[7]

Pre-colonial notions of distinction were rarely party to the same kinds of argument. Their practical significances and adjacencies were defined differently. We read ethnic intention into them with the benefit of hindsight, but in themselves these distinctions were not part of a unitary ethnic phenomenon. By ignoring the essentially local conditions of emergence and persistence of pre-colonial idioms of difference, we manage to fit them into a crudely tailored Nietzschean ethnic pocket. But with the help of an example, I want to show that the pocket in which they properly belong is part of a garment of an altogether different cut.

CHAMBA ETHNOGENESIS

Today the name Chamba is used in self-identification by perhaps a quarter of a million people living in Nigeria and Cameroon. The term presupposes for its users and listeners an entity on a logical, if not numerical, par with Yoruba, Ibo, Bamileke or Fulani: a recognized identity within one of two West African republics. Used of relations outside the Chamba people, but inside Nigeria or Cameroon, it is scarcely subject to situational variation. Individuals belong to a people, to a state or region very weakly, and then to a nation. Matters were not always so clearcut, and Chamba was not traditionallly a term of practical salience. Several writers have demonstrated how, in different parts of Africa, new ethnic terms and identities emerged during the colonial period and have persisted into the present (for example, Lancaster 1974). Like most such terms, Chamba has a historical genealogy but, in the senses in which it is currently employed, it also is a recent invention. Presently, it refers to people whose cultures, traditional political institutions, dialects and even languages varied widely. It is worth reiterating that current ethnic identities often emerged from the colonial process, but I pursue the argument further. I think that the ethnic modern term Chamba refers to an isolable type of difference which was not distinguished in a pre-colonial context.

Limitation of space forces me to supply background in very broad strokes (for detail see Fardon 1983; forthcoming). Most Chamba live in an area of almost exclusive Chamba settlement which straddles the Nigeria/Cameroon border. By far the larger part of this area is in Nigeria. In the west, these Chamba speak a language which has come to be known as Chamba Daka, in the east Chamba speak Chamba Leko (Meek 1931). Recent linguistic research suggests that the two languages may not belong to the same class (Bennett 1983). The, apparently correct, implication to be drawn is that the central Chamba were formed by the fusion of speakers of the two languages. Other Chamba live to the south and southwest of the main area of settlement, below the River Benue in Nigeria and in the Bamenda Grassfields of north-west Cameroon. Chamba presence was introduced to these areas by mounted raiders during the nineteenth century. Where a Chamba language has been preserved amongst these people this has been the easterly, Chamba Leko speech. On the face of it, we have evidence for a pre-nineteenth-century convergence, followed by nineteenth-century migrations, which together account for the present distribution of a recognized Chamba ethnic identity. Chamba oral traditions tend to support such a view. The intermingling of Leko and Daka speakers is accounted for by the migration of a Daka-speaking chiefly family into a Leko area, where they founded a chiefdom (Yeli) and adopted Leko speech before becoming the source of other western chiefdoms. The impact of Leko upon Daka was reinforced during the early part of the nineteenth century when the Fulani *jihad* waged in Adamawa forced the easterly Leko speakers to abandon their homelands: taking refuge in the hills, joining the Daka speakers to the west, or else taking part in one of the migrations which led to the implantation of a Chamba presence outside the older homelands. The upshot of these movements was the socially and culturally varied patchwork of peoples who now call themselves Chamba.

Chamba possess an extensive set of terms with which to discuss differences amongst themselves. Two of them have furnished the terms by which the languages are conventionally distinguished in published works:

1 Following Meek, I use Daka to refer to the language of the western central Chamba; this usage reflects that of the Leko speakers towards their western neighbours, speakers of the other Chamba language, whom they call Daka (or some variant or synonym of this term). However, this term is not accepted by members of the Daka-speaking chiefdoms which trace an origin from Yeli or some other Leko source. These groups call themselves Ñnakenyaré or, more simply, Sama (Chamba); they would claim the Daka to be the people living to their west. Daka, which is without etymology, connotes for them hill-dwelling backwardness, and they find the term insulting when applied to themselves. Only amongst the most westerly of the Chamba does Daka appear to be accepted as a term of self-identification.

2 The popular etymology of the term Leko derives it from a way of introducing a statement in that language: *mə baa lé ko*, 'I say that'. If there are no indications to the contrary (home of) Daka and Leko can mean west and east. Like Daka, Leko can refer to speech, culture, or people; unlike Daka, Leko does not have pejorative implications, but synonyms, like *Jûngbu* used of Leko by the Ñnakenyaré (and also by southerly Leko of northerly Leko) has similar connotations to the pejorative sense of Daka. Like the Ñnakenyaré, the Leko preferentially call themselves Chamba (Samba in Leko).

3 Ñnakenyaré is simply the normal greeting in Chamba Daka; its sense is close to the English 'How are you doing?'. The term is also used to refer to the dominant dialect of Chamba Daka in the central Chamba homelands, to the culture of the people speaking this dialect, or to the people themselves. As a term of self-identification, Ñnakenyaré tends to be assimilated to Leko when contrasted to Daka. Leko and Ñnakenyaré may, in some contexts, consider themselves collectively Chamba in distinction to Daka.

4   Sama (in Chamba Daka) or Samba (in Chamba Leko) is the term from which Chamba appears to have derived, initially through corruption by Hausa sources, and then by adoption in different spellings into German, French and English. With the possible exception of the westernmost Daka and very minor groupings, all speakers of a Chamba language preferentially lay claim to a Sama or Samba identity. Only this identity is prestigious regardless of context, and a sense of 'More Chamba than thou' pervades the Chamba area. Each Chamba group interprets its own culture, language and history as uniquely and estimably Sama or Samba and classifies other communities according to their divergence from this self-centred ideal.

The four terms can be accounted for historically according to the series of migrations I mentioned above: a convergence, followed by the foundation of chiefdoms from Yeli and the establishment of the Ñnakenyaré identity mediating the Leko/Daka distinction, in turn followed by a second set of migrations. These historical circumstances furnished the broad parameters of present relativistic usages. Some early writers attempted to withhold the status of Chamba from one of the language groupings (usually the Daka, for example Frobenius 1913), but in order to reflect Chamba's own usage we have to recognize explicitly that Sama and Samba were members of a relativistic set which became more absolute only after the establishment of the colonial and then national state. But I want to say more than this, and pursuing the example a little further is a way of illustrating the point.

The four relativistic terms are also found in contexts from which we might choose to withhold the term ethnic. In accordance with standard Africanist practice, it is not difficult to distinguish levels of differentiation amongst Chamba which we can call patriclans and patriclan clusters. Chamba also recognized levels of distinction, but they assessed them in terms of the relativistic ethnic terms analysed above. Some of the patriclans had no names other than Leko (Jûngbu), Daka (Daka-bu, Doobu) or Chamba (Samabu). In terms of anthropological categories, the ethnic terms were sometimes also patriclan names and often ways of grouping or evaluating patriclans. If we look at the usages amongst the nineteenth-century migrants now settled outside Chambaland, the variety is yet wider. Amongst the Bali Chamba, Sama and Ndagana have become terms in a dualistic organization which essentially contrasts chiefly and priestly sections of the community (Chilver and Kaberry 1968; Fardon forthcoming). Terms like Kaga and Pere (which operate as 'ethnic' terms for Bata and Koutine in Chambaland) have become terms for patriclans of people considering themselves Chamba. In the Donga chiefdom of the Benue Chamba, Sama occurs as the name of the royal patriclan, and, in reports of a reconvergence between the Benue and Bali streams of migration in the 1830s around a place called Takum, we find the Benue Chamba referring to the Bali Chamba as Daka, although the groups spoke the same Chamba language (Garbosa n.d.: 16−17; Fremantle 1922: 29−40). These usages, like the emergence of Chamba as a modern ethnic term, can be elucidated historically, although it would not be to the point to do so here. In terms of my present argument, the variations illustrate the extreme heterogeneity of purposes for which a few terms can be worked. The Chamba uses share little more than the assertion of a kind of difference which, in a given context, is irreducible. Had I space to expand the argument, I could show that other Chamba idioms of difference, especially those traced through women or more broadly through matriclanship, are interpreted to be far more biddable, and that within Chambaland the Chamba work with a notion of matriclanship which encompasses not only the maximal identity of Chamba but several of the Chamba's neighbours in a single grid of differences. This would be to labour the point that Chamba speech and practice suggest that they had no informing presupposition equivalent to our notion of ethnic difference. Rather, they recognized more and less irreducible forms of difference which were qualities of all types of relationship. Translating only one part of this complex usage as ethnic simply rends the fabric of Chamba notions of distinction in the interests of finding a chunk which fits the Nietzschean pocket of ethnicity. The plausibility of this translation effort is enhanced because the circumstances of incorporation into nation states, partly through the use of European languages, have caused the Chamba to do something similar themselves.

AFRICAN ETHNOGENESIS

My argument has been that the Chamba did not exist in the nineteenth century, not just because Chamba describes people whose origins, languages and cultures are diverse (the Chamba are an extreme rather than abnormal or atypical case in this sense), but because ethnic entities which have the form of the modern Chamba ethnicity are modern inventions. This invention did not take place in a vacuum − invention never does, and the term Chamba has historical precedents − but it resulted in a form different from those before it, one which was predicated upon the existence of unitary, essentially ethnic, boundaries. The effect of this invention was to curtail, perhaps even end, the processes of 'African Ethnogenesis' which had been a pervasive feature of political change prior to the imposition of the nation state.

I am not alone in arguing along these lines; a number of writers on Africa have recently stressed similar points, although not all have been concerned with the dynamic implications of idioms of difference.[8] They agree that traditional terms of distinction seem to have applied pervasively to the differences between individuals, groups of people and localities; they were relatively reactive to events, where modern ethnicity is relatively unreactive to events which it tends to inform. In all probability, the way in which anthropologists define units of study for research, pursue their investigations in practice and write about their results tends to conspire in the reification of ethnic entities (van Binsbergen 1985). The exigencies of comparison work towards the same outcome: if the 'so and so' exist they must have a kinship system, political system and other institutions which can be compared with those of another 'so and so'. But how would the logic of this position stand up to a recognition that identities crystallize transiently and in terms of different registers of difference? That only our reading in of ethnic intention to elements of these classifications taken out of context reinforces the starting assumption of a unitary ethnic phenomenon? Surely, comparative method on the grand scale draws implicitly upon the most naïve version of the invention and reification of ethnic units? Is the comparative method so vital to anthropology that gross reification can be accepted as a necessary cost? This would appear to be a dangerous argument. Should we limit comparisons to regions to draw upon a network of interrelated emergences of difference? This would seem to be a more controllable and nuanced procedure. Perhaps globalist aspirations to comparison can be preserved only by recognizing that comparison intrinsically defines units. Kinship systems, for instance, are contrasted analytically, and comparison between them implicates people to whose practices the analytic categories can be attributed. There is no necessity for the group of people implied to be an ethnic group, or for people to fall into the same groups for the purposes of different comparisons. On this argument it could be claimed that our comparisons only ever seemed to be based upon the contrasts between tribes, when they truly emerged in terms of analytic contrasts which were attributed to named units of people.[9]

The rejection of 'tribe' in 'favour' ethnicity seemed to be a liberal step which emphasized a subjective viewpoint and a situational grasp of context. But the gain was achieved at a cost. Reading ethnicity in textual terms diverted attention from its practical informing of activity, while the liberal generalizing of ethnicity was achieved on the fragile basis of assuming that differences can only be of a single type. Although many factors played their part, the major reason for these shortcomings may have been the failure sufficiently to take to heart the probability that, 'Europe's most enduring legacy to Africa is the nation state' (Mazrui and Tidy 1984: 373).

ACKNOWLEDGEMENTS

An early version of this paper was read at the University of Kent in autumn 1980 when I benefited from the comments of a seminar group led by Roy Ellen. Final revision of the version given to the St Andrews conference in December 1983 is indebted to participants' comments, notably Bob Barnes for a reference and Mark Hobart and David Parkin for points in the argument. I especially recall conversations with Barrie Sharpe when we were both writing up middle-belt materials a few years ago; his recent article is an important contribution to understanding the colonial manufacture of ethnicity. Marilyn Strathern kindly read and commented on the paper.

Research amongst different Chamba and neighbouring people was carried out in 1976—8, 1984, 1985 with financial assistance at various times from the Social Science Research Council, Economic and Social Research Council, Central Research Fund of the University of London, Hayter Fund of the University of St Andrews, and Carnegie Trust for the Universities of Scotland. I am also grateful for official affiliations and support in Cameroon and Nigeria.

NOTES

1 Galton's problem presupposes the identification of units in a region and so begs the question with which I am concerned.
2 The history of the term is reviewed by Kedourie who writes that, '*Natio* in ordinary speech originally meant a group of men belonging together by similarity of birth, larger than a family, but smaller than a clan or people. Thus, one spoke of the *Populus Romanus* and not of the *natio romanorum*' (1960: 13).
    The term has a further complex history of use before its emergence in modern guise around the beginning of the nineteenth century. The sense of race also appears to crystallize at this period, so we might be able to argue that a set of discriminations in terms of birth concurrently assumed something like their contemporary pattern.
3 I have in mind the early classics on situational analysis by Gluckman (1940) and Mitchell (1956). The Manchester tradition is maintained in later works such as Abner Cohen (1969; 1981) and Epstein (1978). For a review of the work of the school in Africa, see Werbner (1984).
4 See, for instance, van den Berghe's attempt to adjudicate genuine ethnicity in the case of American Blacks, and genuine nationhood in the case of new nations (1981). I prefer to align with Gellner, who sees the attempt to withhold national status from new states as a naturalization of the nationhood of old states (1983).
5 Ardener (1974) and Ronald Cohen (1978), who form the distinction with particular clarity, are basically subjectivists; proponents of the *Human Relations Area Files*

style of comparison are necessarily objectivists (e.g. Naroll 1964; 1970). Barth, as Okamura (1981: 459) has observed, is inconsistent. In theory, Barth is a subjectivist; his practice is objectivist (Barth 1969a and b). Van den Berghe holds ethnicity to be subjective and objective (1981). The aims of theories of pluralism, which lie outside the scope of this paper, mean they tend to objectivism (e.g. M. G. Smith 1971).

6 M. G. Smith has voiced objections to the assimilation of racial difference to a form of ethnic difference (1982). In a related vein, Clifford, in a largely sympathetic review of E. Said's *Orientalism*, points to the difficulties which the representation of difference poses to analyses sensitive to the political implications of admitting difference at all (1980).

7 For an instructive attempt to establish precise mapped boundaries for Nigerian ethnic groups (a national version of the international division of territories), see Gandonu (1978).

8 In a West African context, Brain and Kopytoff have emphasized the mutability of ethnic boundaries (both in Tardits 1981: Vol. II); the summaries of discussion amongst participants in that conference, as well as a recent review (Pontié 1984), point out the degree of ethnic diversity amongst the constituent clans of local Cameroonian communities. R. Cohen has related the emergent Pabir and Bura identities to growing political differentiation (1980); Tonkin has discussed the creation of Kroomen within a network of changing economic relations (1985). For East Africa, Southall has called attention to the shifting boundary between peoples we know as Nuer and Dinka (1976), and Ranger has drawn from many sources to document the manufacture of 'tribal' groups by colonial administration (1983: especially 247—52). Coquery-Vidrovitch has argued forcefully for a political contextualization of ethnicity and the recognition of a disjunction in the practical significances of ethnic difference, but at the cost of invoking a rather idealized notion of pre-colonial ethnic sentiment (1983: 57—8).

9 Naroll's development of his notion of culture-bearing unit appears to sever the ethnic knot by recognizing various criteria for the definition of units. But the results of the exercise tend to read as a justification for going on as before (Naroll 1970). Köbben's notion of a unit appropriate to the level of comparison may correspond to my contention that the definition of units is intrinsic to the analytic content of the comparison, but I am unclear how he would put the idea of appropriateness into practice (Köbben 1967, and especially 1970).

REFERENCES

Anderson, B. 1983. *Imagined Communities. Reflections on the origin and spread of nationalism*. London: Verso.

Ardener, E. 1974. Social anthropology and population. In *Population and its Problems* (ed.) H. P. Parry. Oxford: Clarendon.

Barth, F. 1969a. Introduction to *Ethnic Groups and Boundaries: the social organisation of culture difference*. London: Allen and Unwin.

—— 1969b. Pathan identity and its maintenance. In Barth 1969a.

Bennett, P. 1983. Adamawa-Eastern: problems and prospects. In *Current Approaches to African Linguistics* (ed.) I. R. Dihoff. Dordrecht: Foris.

van den Berghe, P. 1981. *The Ethnic Phenomenon.* Amsterdam: Elsevier/North Holland.

Binsbergen, W. van. 1985. From tribe to ethnicity in Western Zambia: the unit of study as an ideological problem. In *Old Modes of Production and Capitalist Encroachment* (eds) W. van Binsbergen and P. Geschiere. London: Routledge and Kegan Paul.

Brain, R. 1981. The Fontem-Bangwa: a Western Bamileke group. In *Contribution de la Recherche Ethnologique à l'Histoire des Civilisations du Cameroun* (ed.) C. Tardits. Paris: Editions du CNRS.

Breton, R. 1981. *Les Ethnies. Que sais-je?* Paris: Presses Universitaires de France.

Chilver, E. M. and P. K. Kaberry. 1968. *Traditional Bamenda.* Ministry of Primary Education and Social Welfare and West Cameroon Antiquities Commission, Cameroon.

Clifford, J. 1980. Review of *Orientalism* by E. W. Said. *History and Theory* 2: 204—23.

Cohen, A. 1969. *Custom and Politics in Urban Africa. A study of Hausa migrants in Yoruba towns.* Berkeley and Los Angeles: University of California Press.

—— 1981. *The Politics of Elite Culture. Explorations in the dramaturgy of power in a modern African society.* Berkeley: University of California Press.

Cohen, R. 1978. Ethnicity: problem and focus in anthropology. *Annual Review of Anthropology* 7: 379—403.

—— 1980. The natural history of hierarchy: a case study. In *Hierarchy and Society* (eds) G. M. Brittan and R. Cohen. Philadelphia: Institute for the Study of Human Issues.

Cohen, R. and J. Middleton. 1971. Introduction to *From Tribe to Nation in Africa.* Scranton, New Jersey: Chandler.

Coquery-Vidrovitch, C. 1983. A propos des racines historiques du pouvoir: 'Chefferie' et 'Tribalisme'. In *Les Pouvoirs Africains. Pouvoirs* 25: 51—62.

Epstein, A. L. 1978. *Ethos and Identity: three studies in ethnicity.* London: Tavistock.

Fabian, J. 1983. *Time and the Other. How anthropology makes its object.* New York: Columbia University Press.

Fardon, R. O. 1983. A chronology of pre-colonial Chamba history. *Paideuma* 29: 67—92.

—— (forthcoming). *Raiders and Refugees.* Washington: Smithsonian Institution Press.

Fortes, M. 1945. *The Dynamics of Clanship among the Tallensi.* London: Oxford University Press.

Fremantle, J. M. 1922. *Gazetteer of Muri Province.* London: Waterlow and Sons.

Frobenius, L. 1913. *Und Afrika Sprach.* Vol. 3, revised edition. Berlin: Vita Deutsches Verlagshaus.

Gandonu, A. 1978. Nigeria's 250 ethnic groups: realities and assumptions. In *Perspectives on Ethnicity* (eds) R. E. Holloman and S. A. Arutinov. The Hague: Mouton.

Garbosa, B. S. (n.d.). *Labarun Chambawa da Al'Amurransa.* Privately published.

Gellner, E. 1983. *Nations and Nationalism.* Oxford: Blackwell.

Glazer, N. and D. Moynihan. 1975. Introduction to *Ethnicity: theory and experience.* Cambridge, Mass. and London: Harvard University Press.

Gluckman, M. 1940. The analysis of a social situation in modern Zululand. *African Studies* 14: 1—30; 147—74.

Godelier, M. 1977. The concept of 'tribe': a crisis involving merely a concept or the empirical foundations of anthropology itself? In *Perspectives in Marxist Anthropology.* Cambridge: Cambridge University Press.

Hobsbawm, E. 1962. *The Age of Revolution.* London: Abacus.

Hobsbawm, E. and T. Ranger (eds). 1983. *The Invention of Tradition.* Cambridge: Cambridge University Press.

Isajiw, W. W. 1974. Definitions of ethnicity. *Ethnicity* 1: 111—24.

Kedourie, E. 1960. *Nationalism.* London: Hutchinson.

Köbben, A. 1967. Why exceptions? The logic of cross-cultural analysis. *Current Anthropology* 8: 3—19.

___ 1970. Comparativists and non-comparativists in anthropology. In Naroll, R. and R. Cohen 1970.

Kopytoff, I. 1981. Aghem ethnogenesis and the Grassfields ecumene. In *Contribution de la Recherche Ethnologique à l'Histoire des Civilisations du Cameroun* (ed.) C. Tardits. Paris: Editions du CNRS.

Kuper, L. 1977. *The Pity of it all: polarisation of racial and ethnic relations.* London: Duckworth.

Lancaster, C. S. 1974. Ethnic identity, history and 'tribe' in the Middle Zambezi Valley. *American Ethnologist* 1: 707—30. (Special number on *Uses of Ethnohistory in Ethnographic Analysis*).

Leach, E. R. 1954. *Political Systems of Highland Burma.* London: Athlone.

Mazrui, A. and M. Tidy. 1984. *Nationalism and New States in Africa.* Nairobi, Ibadan, London: Heinemann.

Meek, C. K. 1931. *Tribal Studies in Northern Nigeria.* Vol. 1. London: Kegan Paul, Trench and Trubner.

Mitchell, J. C. 1956. *The Kalela Dance: aspects of social relationships among urban Africans.* Rhodes Livingstone Papers No. 27. Manchester: Manchester University Press.

Nadel, S. F. 1935. Nupe state and community. *Africa* 8: 257—303. Reprinted in *Comparative Political Systems* (eds) R. Cohen and J. Middleton. 1967. New York: The Natural History Press.

Nairn, Tom. 1977. *The Break-up of Britain.* London: Verso.

Naroll, R. 1964. Ethnic unit classification. *Current Anthropology* 5: 283—91.

___ 1970. The culture bearing unit in cross-cultural studies. In Naroll, R. and R. Cohen 1970.

Naroll, R. and R. Cohen (eds). 1970. *A Handbook of Method in Cultural Anthropology.* New York: Columbia University Press.

Needham, R. 1975. Polythetic classification: convergence and consequences. *Man* (N.S.) 10: 347—69.

Nietzsche, F. 1977. *A Nietzsche Reader* (ed.) R. J. Hollingsworth. Harmondsworth: Penguin.

Okamura, J. 1981. Situational ethnicity. *Ethnic and Racial Studies* 4: 452—65.

Pontié, G. 1984. Les sociétés païennes. In *Le Nord du Cameroun. Des hommes, une région* (eds) J. Boutrais et al. Paris: ORSTOM.

Ranger, T. 1982. Race and tribe in Southern Africa: European ideas and African acceptance. In *Racism and Colonialism* (ed.) R. Ross. Leiden: Nijhoff.

—— 1983. The invention of tradition in colonial Africa. In Hobsbawm, E. and T. Ranger 1983.

Seton-Watson, H. 1977. *Nations and States. An enquiry into the origins of nations and the politics of nationalism.* London: Methuen.

Simmel, G. 1950. *The Sociology of Georg Simmel* (trans.) K. H. Wolf. New York: Free Press.

—— 1980. *Essays on Interpretation in Social Science* (trans.) G. Oakes. Manchester: Manchester University Press.

Sharpe, B. 1986. Ethnography and a regional system: mental maps and the myth of states and tribes in North-Central Nigeria. *Critique of Anthropology* VI (3): 33—65.

Smith, A. 1971. *Theories of Nationalism.* London: Duckworth.

—— 1981. *The Ethnic Revival.* Cambridge: Cambridge University Press.

—— 1983. *State and Nation in the Third World.* Brighton: Wheatsheaf Books.

Smith, M. G. 1971. The institutional and political conditions of pluralism, and, Some developments in the analytic framework of pluralism. In *Pluralism in Africa* (eds) L. Kuper and M. G. Smith. Berkeley: University of California Press.

—— 1982. Ethnicity and ethnic groups in America: the view from Harvard. *Ethnic and Racial Studies* 5: 1—22.

Southall, A. 1970. The illusion of tribe. *Journal of African and Asian Studies* 5: 28—50.

—— 1976. Nuer and Dinka are people: ecology, ethnicity and logical possibility. *Man* (N.S.) 11: 463—91.

Southwold, M. 1978. Buddhism and the definition of religion. *Man* (N.S.) 13: 362—79.

Tonkin, E. 1985. Creating Kroomen: ethnic diversity, economic specialism and changing demand. In *Africa and the Sea* (ed.) J. Stone. Aberdeen: Aberdeen University African Studies Group.

Werbner, R. 1984. The Manchester School in Central Africa. *Annual Reviews in Anthropology* 13: 157—85.

Young, C. 1976. *The Politics of Cultural Pluralism.* Madison: University of Wisconsin Press.

10

Khoisan Kinship: Regional Comparison and Underlying Structures

Alan Barnard

In this paper I shall try to demonstrate the utility of regional comparison as an aid to the understanding of kinship systems. My special concern is with the kinship systems of the Khoisan peoples of southern Africa. The problem is particularly complicated, due to the diversity of Khoisan kinship systems: according to conventional wisdom, they exhibit no uniform rule of descent, rule of marriage, or structure of kin classification. Yet this in fact is what makes the problem so interesting. I shall argue, against conventional wisdom, that specific Khoisan kinship systems are best seen as products of a regionally specific underlying kinship structure.

The Khoisan peoples are a large cluster of southern African nations. Some of them are pastoralists, others are hunter-gatherers or hunter-gatherer-fishermen, and virtually all today include individuals who work as herdsmen or labourers. But in spite of differences associated with their economic pursuits, as well as differences in language and other aspects of culture, many otherwise diverse Khoisan peoples share a great number of common features with respect to kinship. These represent elements of kinship structures held in common across economic, cultural, linguistic and 'racial' boundaries.

The term 'Khoisan', popularized by Schapera (1930), reflects the traditional ethnological division of the groups. *Khoi* (old orthography) or *khoe* (modern orthography) is the Nama word for 'person'. In the English compound 'Khoisan' it refers to the Nama themselves and other cattle-herding Khoekhoe or 'Hottentots'. *Sa-n* is the Nama word for 'Bushmen' or 'foragers' (though not always with the best connotations).

The distinction between Khoe and San is not as clear as it might seem. For example, the 'typical Bushman' is said to be characterized by:

diminutive proportions, slight habit, light yellowish skin, steatopygia, and hair in sparse peppercorn tufts; . . . and by speaking languages of an isolating, non-inflectional type, phonetically remarkable for the great prevalence of 'click' consonants; and . . . by living in small nomadic bands which lead a purely hunting and collecting existence, practising neither agriculture nor pastoralism.

(Schapera 1939: 69)

But as Schapera points out (1939: 69−72), there is really no such person as a 'typical Bushman'. The usual descriptions of physical characteristics seem to apply mainly to the extinct Bushmen of the Cape Province. Such well-known groups as the !Kung, who live 1500 kilometres north of Cape Town, have a very different appearance. A number of Bushman groups do speak isolating languages, but those of the central Kalahari, the Okavango delta, eastern Botswana and other areas speak inflecting languages, related not to those of 'typical Bushmen', but to those of the Khoekhoe.

Only Schapera's last characterization, that of Bushmen as hunter-gatherers who live in small nomadic bands, is useful for comparative purposes; yet even if we accept this as a basic definition, there are problems. Many Bushmen who have lived at one time by hunting and gathering have now settled permanently at waterholes, where they cultivate gardens or raise livestock. I retain the word 'Bushman' for members of such groups, although in the strictest sense the word applies to their traditional and not their present lifestyle. 'Bushman' is much more of an odd-job word than 'Khoekhoe'. The Khoekhoe all speak closely related languages, and their culture and social organization are relatively uniform; they are comparable in diversity to the Southern Bantu-speakers. The Bushmen, however, speak a variety of perhaps unrelated (or at least very distantly related) languages. Furthermore, 'Khoekhoe' is a word which the designants apply to themselves, whereas 'Bushman' has always been a collective term for peoples who generally have no equivalent in their own languages.

One final point is worth mentioning here: the problem of the Damara. Schapera (1930: 3) notes that the inhabitants of southern Africa before 1652 'are customarily classified into four separate groups, known respectively as the Bushmen, the Hottentots, the Bergdama [Damara], and the Bantu'. Again, classification is 'on the basis of racial, linguistic and cultural distinctions' (1930: 3), and apparently because of the 'racial' differences, the Damara are excluded from the category Khoisan. Yet I think this is a mistake.

Culturally, the Damara are a Khoisan people. They have long lived in close association with the Nama; they speak the Nama language; and their rituals, their mythology, their social organization, and indeed their kinship system, are easily identified as Khoisan.

KHOISAN KINSHIP

There are two ways in which the kinship systems of the Khoisan peoples could be classified. The more obvious is in terms of social organization, including economics, group structure and rules of descent. For reasons which I hope will become clear, this method can only illustrate the relatively superficial similarities and differences between the systems. A more useful and interesting way is in terms of underlying structures of kin categorization and rules of marriage. These structures closely parallel the linguistic classification. Consequently, the *major* division to be made is between Khoe-speakers and non-Khoe-speakers, rather than between herders and foragers, or between patrilineal clan-based societies and cognatic band-based societies. The Khoe-speaking peoples, who are by far the largest linguistic grouping, are more uniform than the non-Khoe-speaking Bushmen in relationship terminology structure and rules of marriage, but less uniform in group structure.

The Khoe-speaking peoples include the Khoekhoe, the Damara, the Bushmen of the central Kalahari and Okavango, the Hai-//om Bushmen of Etosha pan, and other groups. Similar relationship terminology structures are found among all these peoples, and in each case the marriage rule is either to matrilateral or to bilateral cross-cousins. The Khoekhoe nations, who include the Nama and the Korana (!Ora), traditionally hunted, gathered, and herded cattle and sheep. They lived in circular encampments which were made up of patrilineally related kin, in-married wives, and in-married husbands (often performing bride-service). Their tribes, clans and lineages were hierarchically ranked and each tribe had its own independent, and often powerful, chief. The Damara, who had been servants and blacksmiths for the Nama, also herded livestock, although many Damara groups in the late nineteenth century lived entirely by hunting and gathering and by stock-theft. Their encampments were like those of the Khoekhoe, but without patrilineal organization. The Khoe-speaking Bushmen, or Khoe Bushmen, inhabit the vast central region of the Kalahari desert, areas east of the Kalahari, and the Okavango swamps to the north. The desert-dwellers live by hunting and gathering, and the swamp-dwellers by hunting, gathering and fishing. Although the social organization of the Khoe Bushman is to some extent reminiscent of that of other, non-Khoe-speaking Bushman groups, in many respects the affinities of Khoe Bushman kinship systems are with those of the Khoekhoe. Little is known of the Hai-//om, but they seem to be a hybrid group. They were probably !Kung who for some reason forsook their language and some aspects of their kinship system for those of the Nama. Such Khoekhoe characteristics as patrilineal local organization and exogamous cross-descent name lines have been reported among them.

The non-Khoe-speaking Bushmen include the !Kung, the !xõ, the Eastern ≠Hoã, the /Xam, and remnants of the Bushman groups of the Cape. All were traditionally hunter-gatherers. The !Kung are well known for their leisurely, loosely structured camp life and band organization, their so-called 'Eskimo-type' relationship terminology, and their alternate-generation naming system by which kin categorization is extended throughout society. The !xõ are less well known. They live in the harsh south-central Kalahari, and have a system of kinship classification which places great emphasis on the rule that a joking partner's avoidance partner must be an avoidance partner. The 'Eastern ≠Hoã' received their name in order to distinguish them from the !xõ, who are also sometimes called '≠Hoã'; the fact that they speak a different language from the !xõ was discovered little more than a decade ago. Very little is known about the Eastern ≠Hoã kinship system as a whole, though their relationship terms for consanguines have been recorded and analysed by Gruber (1973). The /Xam are now culturally and linguistically extinct, and the other Cape Bushman groups are either culturally extinct or acculturated to Bantu and Cape Coloured ways.

Our knowledge of Khoisan groups is not at all uniform. We know a great deal about some systems and virtually nothing about others. While it is worthwhile to try to redress this balance, for reasons of practicality I have chosen to examine only a small number of Khoisan kinship systems in this paper. In particular, I shall concentrate on the kinship systems of some of the Khoe-speaking peoples, but with a view towards uncovering the regional underlying structures common to the Khoisan peoples generally (see also Barnard 1980). Before illustrating the method of analysis, a brief look at the theoretical problems of regional kinship comparison is in order.

THE INTERPRETATION AND COMPARISON OF KINSHIP SYSTEMS

Only a small percentage of theoretical writings on kinship have dealt with Khoisan data. Models derived from the study of Australian Aborigines, South American and North American Indians, Micronesians, etc., are far more common. In studying Khoisan kinship systems, I have often found that the rigid application of such traditional models obscures interesting features. Traditional methods of analysis, e.g., of relationship terminologies or of alliance structures, can explain only some of the features of particular kinship systems. An approach which takes into account similar features across societal boundaries may reveal underlying structures which add just as much to our understanding of kinship as the surface structures which are the subject of conventional methods of analysis. Common features of kinship behaviour, for example, may be expressed terminologically in one language, but not in the language of a closely related, neighbouring group. One group may distinguish relationships by a large number of relationship terms; another may employ one term for a large number of relationships, while distinguishing jurally between different genealogical positions within the same relationship category.

There have, of course, been many earlier comparative studies of kinship systems which at least imply some notion of underlying structure. Radcliffe-Brown's (1913; 1930—1) comparative and theoretical studies of Australian Aboriginal social organization, Josselin de Jong's (1977 [1935]) argument for the study of the East Indies as an 'ethnographic field of study', Eggan's (1950) *Social Organization of the Western Pueblos*, Goody's (1959) essay on the mother's brother in West Africa, and Kuper's (1982) *Wives for Cattle* are cases in point. Yet few such studies have made explicit either the generative principles or the constraining rules which such underlying structures entail. A few remarks on my usage of the notion of underlying structures may therefore be useful.

First, the concept, as I employ it, is a heuristic one; its precise formulation will depend on its context. Secondly, the concept may be used to characterize kinship systems which are similar in structure, in various ways, and it tends to be most useful when looking at those systems whose populations are linguistically related. In other words, an underlying structure is not generally unique to a particular kinship system, but may be found in common among several linguistically related peoples. In this sense my notion of underlying structure is not to be taken as analogous either to that of 'deep structure' (of a particular language) or to that of 'universal grammar' in linguistics; an underlying kinship structure is neither specific to one kinship system nor universal. Thirdly, the concept of underlying structure presupposes a contrasting concept of surface structure. The latter is especially useful as a characterization of aspects of kinship which are implied directly by relationship terminologies. As such, each speech community has its own surface kinship structures. Conventional kinship analyses, and especially traditional 'componential' analyses of terminologies, deal only with these. I shall argue for the interpretation of Khoisan systems in terms of underlying categorical components which are often submerged, generating the expected surface relationship terminology structures only when *not* superseded by culture-specific rules which override those of the underlying structures.

Kinship studies should be comparative, not just in the sense of elucidating superficial similarities and differences between systems, but, more importantly, in defining these features as manifestations of underlying structures. Underlying kinship structures may be held in common between otherwise diverse, linguistically unrelated and geographically separated peoples, but very often these structures seem to be formed on the basis of a regional or linguistically bounded system. Such a system may not be readily apparent to those ethnographers who tend to make their comparisons on a surface level, particularly when such comparisons are made on a global scale. For example, typologies of descent systems or terminology structures entail a notion of comparability only at a surface level and frequently fail to reveal either underlying differences within 'types' or underlying similarities across typological boundaries (see Barnard and Good 1984: 59–66).

KHOE KIN CATEGORIES AND RELATIONSHIP TERMS

The structure of Khoe kinship is remarkably uniform. Khoe relationship terms identify only a small number of kinship categories which, with certain accountable differences, are defined similarly in terms of both genealogical position and socially approved behaviour for all Khoe-speaking groups. Another common feature is the practice of designating category membership by reciprocal in addition to egocentric relationship terms. For example, there will be a term meaning 'brothers to each other', as well as one for 'my older brother' and one for 'my younger brother'. Most Khoe systems also allow for the extension of kin category membership beyond known consanguineous or affinal links (e.g., through namesake equivalence), and most Khoe-speaking peoples recognize a jural rule of marriage to members of one specific relationship category. This will be either that of bilateral or that of matrilateral cross-cousins. However, since affines and consanguines are distinguished from each other, Khoe kinship systems are not 'prescriptive' in the sense in which Needham uses the term; they do not possess an 'absolute constituent relation which orders their social categories' (Needham 1973: 179).

There are two levels of categorization. I term these the 'higher level' and the 'lower level'. The higher level consists of two mutually exclusive categories, JOKING and AVOIDANCE, whose respective designations in many Khoe languages might be more literally translated 'non-avoidance' and 'avoidance'. The intensity of joking and avoidance behaviour within the categories depends on precise genealogical relationship and on which particular kinship system is being considered. Several, if not all Khoe-speaking peoples, classify every member of society by relationship terms, on both higher and lower levels. Among these peoples, each person stands in either a JOKING or an AVOIDANCE relation to any other given individual.

Each of the two higher-level categories may be divided into up to four lower-level categories. Not every Khoe system will possess all eight possible lower-level categories. JOKING includes the reciprocal categories which I shall call GRANDRELATIVE, JOKING SIBLING, SPOUSE and JOKING IN-LAW. AVOIDANCE includes those I shall call PARENT/CHILD, AVOIDANCE SIBLING, RESPECT RELATIVE and AVOIDANCE IN-LAW (see table 10.1).

Among the Khoe-speaking peoples, category GRANDRELATIVE always includes grandparents, grandchildren, MBs and MBWs, a man's ZC and a woman's HBC, and same-sex namesakes. FZs, FZHs, and a man's ZC and a woman's HZC are RESPECT RELATIVES in those systems with patrilineal clan organization, and GRANDRELATIVES in the others. Except possibly for a man's FZDs or a woman's MBSs among the Korana (who forbid patrilateral cross-cousin marriage), cross-cousins on both sides are GRANDRELATIVES. Where category JOKING IN-LAW does not occur, spouse's JOKING relatives and JOKING relatives' spouses are also GRANDRELATIVES. Only GRAND-RELATIVES are marriageable.

JOKING SIBLING includes same-sex siblings and same-sex parallel cousins, as well as some more distant relatives. Similarly, category SPOUSE includes ego's own husband or wife, ego's spouse's same-sex siblings, and ego's same-sex siblings' spouses.

Spouse's JOKING relatives and JOKING relatives' spouses are in most systems classified as GRANDRELATIVES. However, the Central Khoe Bushmen and possibly some other groups have a separate category JOKING IN-LAW. This category includes spouse's same-sex siblings and same-sex siblings' spouses, who are also, and more specifically, categorized as (classificatory) SPOUSES. For the Khoekhoe, it is not entirely clear whether these relatives were in the past called by the GRANDRELATIVE terms //*nao* or //*nuri* or by the term otherwise used for AVOIDANCE IN-LAWS, /*ui*. Nama-speakers today tend to use /*ui*. /'*Ui*, /*ui* or /*wi* is a distinctly affinal term in all Khoe languages. In some, for example, Nharo, it is used exclusively or especially for AVOIDANCE relatives, and in others it has the more general sense of 'relatives by marriage', whether AVOIDANCE or JOKING.

Category PARENT/CHILD includes parents and children, parents' same-sex siblings and parents' same-sex siblings' spouses, and same-sex siblings' children. For the Khoekhoe and Hai-//om, among whom 'great names' pass from father to daughter and mother to son (by alternating or cross-descent), the category also includes all opposite-sex namesakes. In these systems, as in

TABLE 10.1 Genealogical referents of Khoe kin categories

Joking

GRANDRELATIVE: grandparent, MB and MBW, FZ and FZH (Khoe Bushman), cross-cousin (except Korana FZD [ms] and MBS [ws], who are regarded as RESPECT RELATIVES), spouse's JOKING relative (Western Khoe Bushman and Khoekhoe), same-sex namesake; and the reciprocals of all of these

JOKING SIBLING: same-sex sibling, same-sex parallel cousin

SPOUSE: spouse, spouse's same-sex sibling, same-sex sibling's spouse

JOKING IN-LAW: spouse's JOKING relative and JOKING relative's spouse (Central Khoe Bushman)

Avoidance

PARENT/CHILD: parent, parent's same-sex sibling, child, same-sex sibling's child, opposite sex namesake (Khoekhoe)

AVOIDANCE SIBLING: opposite-sex sibling, opposite-sex parallel cousin

RESPECT RELATIVE: FZ and FZH and their reciprocals, close AVOIDANCE relatives (Khoekhoe)

AVOIDANCE IN-LAW: spouse's AVOIDANCE relative and AVOIDANCE relative's spouse.

---

those Khoe Bushman systems in which names are inherited exclusively within the GRANDRELATIVE category (for example, Nharo), same-sex name-sakes are always GRANDRELATIVES.

Category AVOIDANCE SIBLING includes opposite-sex siblings and opposite-sex parallel cousins, among other relatives. Often the same lower-level relationship terms are used for both AVOIDANCE SIBLINGS and JOKING SIBLINGS, although the higher-level terms will, of course, be different. This is strong evidence for the validity of the notion of an underlying relationship terminology structure among the Khoe-speaking peoples.

The RESPECT RELATIVE category occurs only among those groups who trace descent patrilineally, i.e. among the Khoekhoe and possibly the Hai-//om. The primary genealogical referent is FZ, who as senior female agnate had in the past a particularly important role in keeping discipline over her brothers, and ultimately, over her brothers' children. FZs, FZHs, and reciprocally, a man's WBC and a woman's BC, were all placed in this category. In a more general sense, the category does include other close AVOIDANCE relatives, such as unmarriageable cousins, who are also (especially in the case of parallel cousins) classified as AVOIDANCE SIBLINGS. The choice of category or relationship term seems to depend on which potential relationship ego wishes to emphasize. *Tàra*, the defining morpheme of the RESPECT RELATIVE category, can in fact be employed in its widest sense for the higher-level category AVOIDANCE as a whole. Interestingly, although the Nama still use the term in its general sense, they nowadays classify FZ, FZH, BC(ws) and WBC(ms) as GRANDRELATIVES, rather than as RESPECT RELATIVES. Since the disintegration of the patrilineal clan organization after the 1904 War, the peculiar relationship of the FZ has disappeared among the Nama and this genealogical position has reverted to the category determined by the underlying structure of all Khoe relationship terminologies, that of GRANDRELATIVE.

Finally, the AVOIDANCE IN-LAW category comprises spouse's AVOIDANCE relatives and AVOIDANCE relatives' spouses. In particular, this category includes parents-in-law, children-in-law and same-sex siblings-in-law. Opposite-sex siblings-in-law are (classificatory) SPOUSES or JOKING IN-LAWS.

RECIPROCAL RELATIONSHIP TERMS

In Khoe languages it is possible to express relationship in either egocentric or reciprocal form. Reciprocal relationship terms may in fact be unique to the Khoe language family. Although a category will include several egocentric relationship terms, there is always just a single morpheme which designates it in reciprocal usage. The brother/brother relationship was mentioned earlier in this context, and all other reciprocal relationships follow the same pattern. Thus, for instance, the father/son relationship may be expressed egocentrically as 'He is my father' or 'I am his son', or reciprocally as 'He and I are in a PARENT/CHILD relationship to each other'. In the latter case, a single morpheme (*g//u* in most Khoe languages) will represent the concept PARENT/ CHILD. A reciprocal relationship term will contain a stem such as this one, followed by the suffix *ku* or *gu*, meaning 'to each other'.

The same construction is frequently used outside the kinship domain in phrases like 'to see each other' (Nharo: *mo-ku*) or 'to give to each other' (Nharo: *//aī-ku*). A phrase like the latter one, *//aī-ku*, may be used either with a verbal particle, giving a translation like 'We give to each other', or with a copula, 'We are gift-giving [partners] to each other'. In both senses, *//aī-ku* expresses a quasi-kin relationship in Nharo society (see Barnard 1978:

TABLE 10.2 Khoe reciprocal relationship terms

Khoekhoe (Nama)	Central Khoe Bushman (G/wi)	Western Khoe Bushman (Naro)
Joking: (no general term)	*Joking:* !oa-ku-kjima	*Joking:* g//ai-ku !au-ku-tama
(1) //nuri-gu [n//uri-ku] /ai-gu [/'ai-ku] (marriageable; archaic or taboo)	(1) n//odi-ku	(1) tsxõ-ku (or) mama-ku
(2) !gã-gu [!ã-ku]	(2) gijaxu-ku (?)	(2) !kwĩ-ku
(3) xae-gu [xae-ku] (archaic or taboo)	(3) se-ku	(3) se-ku
(4) – (or) /ui-gu [/'ui-ku]	(4) /wi-ku	(4) –
Avoidance: tàra-gu [tàra-ku] (or) !oa-gu [!'oa-ku]	*Avoidance:* !ao-ku	*Avoidance:* !au-ku (or) papa-ku
(1) //gu-gu [//u-ku]	(1) g//o-ku	(1) g//o-ku (or) papa-ku
(2) !gã-gu [!ã-ku]	(2) gijaxu-ku (?)	(2) !kwĩ-ku
(3) tàra-gu [tàra-ku]	(3) –	(3) –
(4) /ui-gu [/'ui-ku] !na-gu [n!a-ku]	(4) /wi-ku	(4) /wi-ku
Source: my fieldnotes, standard orthography with phonetic transcription in square brackets; cf. Schultze 1907: 299–303; cf. Hoernlé 1925: 18–23	*Source:* my fieldnotes	*Source:* my fieldnotes

625—6). However, as far as I am aware, reciprocal relationship terms in all Khoe languages are normally used with a copula and not with a verbal particle. Unlike gift-giving, kinship is not a deliberate *act* which can be expressed by a verb; thus it can only be expressed copulatively. Although the verbal (as opposed to nominal) constructions employing -*ku* or -*gu* are well documented in the grammars of Khoe languages, the reciprocal relationship terms have not been widely recorded.

For the purposes of illustration, three Khoe terminologies — Nama, G/wi and Nharo — are given here as examples. The Nama are a *Khoekhoe* people; the G/wi exemplify a *Central Khoe Bushman* structure; and the Nharo, a *Western Khoe Bushman* one. Their reciprocal terms are shown in table 10.2. Lower-level JOKING categories are numbered: (1) GRANDRELATIVE, (2) JOKING SIBLING, (3) SPOUSE, (4) JOKING IN-LAW. Lower-level AVOIDANCE categories are numbered: (1) PARENT/CHILD, (2) AVOIDANCE SIBLING, (3) RESPECT RELATIVE, (4) AVOIDANCE IN-LAW. A dash indicates that no such category exists in the system being described. Where category JOKING IN-LAW does not exist, its genealogical referents are absorbed into GRANDRELATIVE. Where category RESPECT RELATIVE does not exist, its primary genealogical referents (FZ and reciprocals) are, for reasons to be discussed later, transformed from AVOIDANCE to JOKING and placed in category GRANDRELATIVE. This transformation is permitted by a rule of the underlying structure of all Khoe systems, namely that an AVOIDANCE partner's AVOIDANCE partner is classified as JOKING.

EGOCENTRIC RELATIONSHIP TERMS

The egocentric relationship terms are employed according to the same rules of categorization as the reciprocal relationship terms. There are, of course, many more of them, since in egocentric usage both points of a reciprocal relationship can be distinguished and since the egocentric terms may also take into account degree of familiarity or other elements of social context. Egocentric usages in Nama, G/wi and Nharo are illustrated in table 10.3. In the G/wi and Nharo terminologies I have indicated the grammatical necessity of person-number-gender possessive prefixes by placing hyphens before the appropriate terms. In all Khoe languages number-gender suffixes are normally used with egocentric relationship terms. For simplicity, however, these have been omitted from table 10.3.

As both table 10.2 and table 10.3 show, there is a remarkable similarity among the systems. Cognate relationship terms abound and, with few exceptions, always occur in exactly the same categories. The exceptions are *ao* or *au* (primary meanings: 'man', 'husband' in Nama; 'my father' in Nharo);

TABLE 10.3 Khoe egocentric relationship terms

Khoekhoe (Nama)	Central Khoe Bushman (G/wi)	Western Khoe Bushman (Nharo)
Joking: (no general term)	Joking: -!ai-kjima	Joking: -g//ai
		-!au-tama

(1) //nao [n//ao] (senior, and sometimes MBC)
 //nuri [n//uri] (equal or junior)
 //nuri-!gã [n//uri-!ã] (cross-cousin)
 /ai [/'ai] (marriageable; archaic or taboo)
	(1) -baba (m., senior)
	 -mama (f., senior)
	 -n//odi (generally, equal or junior)
		(1) -tsxõ (or) mama
		 -ki (elder)
		 -!kwĩ (younger)

(2) !gã kai [!ã kai] (senior) !gã ≠kami [!ã ≠khami] (or) !gã-sa [!ã-sa] (junior)	(2) -gjibaxu (elder) -gijaxu (younger)	(2) -khwe (or) -g//ai -k'au (m.)
(3) xae [xae] (archaic or taboo) ao [ao] (m.) tará [tará] (f.)	(3) -k'ao (m.) -g//eis (f.)	(3) -g//ais (f.)
(4) — (or) /ui [/'ui]	(4) -/wi	(4) —

Avoidance: tara [tara] (or) !oa ['!oa]

(1) //gu [//u] (elder, someone else's; very formal)
sao [sao] (elder, someone else's)
ai [ai] (or) ī [ī] (elder, respect)
abo [apo] (m., elder, one's own; archaic)
dada [tata] (m., elder; often with relative age suffix)
mama [mama] (f., elder, familiar; often with relative age suffix)

(2) /gõa [/õa] (or) õa [õa] (younger)
!gã kai [!ã kai] (senior)
!gã ≠kami [!ã ≠khami] (or) !gã-sa [!ã-sa] (junior)

(3) tàra [tàra] (f., especially senior)
dada [tata] (m., senior or elder)
ai kai [ai kai] (f., senior; archaic)
tàra õa [tàra õa] (junior or younger)

(4) /ui [/'ui]
!na [n!a] (formal)

Avoidance: -!ao (or) ≠ao (cf. Silberbauer 1972: 310; 1981: 143)

(1) -ba (m., senior)
-gje (f., senior)
-/kwa (junior)
(2) -gjibaxu (elder)
-gijaxu (younger)
(3) —
(4) -/wi

Avoidance: -!au (or) papa

(1) -g//o (or) papa
au (m., elder, one's own)
ai (f., elder, one's own)
sau (elder, someone else's)
-/kwa (younger)
(2) -ki (elder)
-!kwī (younger)
(3) —
(4) -/wi

Sources: Hoernlé 1925: 18–23; Schultze 1907: 299–303; my fieldnotes; standard Nama orthography with phonetic transcription in square brackets

Sources: Silberbauer 1972: 309–13; 1981: 142–9; my fieldnotes

Source: my fieldnotes

ba, baba or *papa* (variously either a senior male GRANDRELATIVE term or a PARENT/CHILD term); and *ma* or *mama* (either a GRANDRELATIVE term or a senior female PARENT/CHILD term). Within the categories, terms almost invariably have the same meaning with reference to generation, relative age, and sex. The Nama stem *!na* and some of the sibling terms may be loan or substratum words, but of the others only the Nharo terms *tsxõ* and *mama* are probably not of Khoe origin. These latter terms were most likely borrowed, together with the system of personal naming, from the !Kung.

There is a general rule, applicable to all the Khoe kinship systems, that same-sex sibling, spouse and same-sex namesake links retain higher-level category, and that parent/child, opposite-sex sibling and opposite-sex namesake links change higher-level category. For example, in the Nharo system if alter is *!au* (AVOIDANCE), then this *!au*'s spouse is also *!au* in relation to any given ego, but his or her parent is *g//ai* (JOKING). By extension of this principle, ego's JOKING partners' JOKING partners and ego's AVOIDANCE partners' AVOIDANCE partners are ego's JOKING partners, and ego's JOKING partners' AVOIDANCE partners and ego's AVOIDANCE partners' JOKING partners are ego's AVOIDANCE partners. In all Khoe societies these rules hold true for most relationships, the most notable exceptions being in the classification of cross-cousins. In fact such rules are consciously employed by Western and Central Khoe Bushmen (for example, Nharo and G/wi respectively) when tracing relationship to distant kin.

SOME DIFFERENCES AMONG THE SYSTEMS

Three main differences between the egocentric terminologies are apparent. Two of these distinguish Central from Western Khoe Bushman systems: (a) the categorical distinction in the Central Khoe Bushman systems between JOKING consanguines and JOKING affines, and (b) the existence of separate junior and senior relationship terms within the Central Khoe Bushman categories GRANDRELATIVE and PARENT/CHILD and separate male and female terms within senior category GRANDRELATIVE. These differences do not affect higher-level (JOKING and AVOIDANCE) categorization. The third difference is the existence of the special category RESPECT RELATIVE in the Khoekhoe systems. This is by far the most significant difference, for kinship behaviour as well as for categorization and relationship terminology. Each of these differences will be taken in turn.

The first difference stems from the Central Khoe Bushman custom of referring to all in-laws, whether JOKING or AVOIDANCE, as */wi* or */ui*. This is, of course, both a terminological and a lower-level categorical distinction, but not a jural or behavioural one. Central Khoe Bushmen treat their spouses' same-sex siblings and same-sex siblings' spouses in the same way as do Western Khoe Bushmen. A Central Khoe Bushman JOKING IN-LAW is also a classificatory 'spouse' and therefore also a member of the lower-level category SPOUSE. Levirate and sororate are jurally preferred forms of marriage, although rare in practice (see, for example, Silberbauer 1981: 158–9). In terms of jural rules and behavioural norms, Central Khoe Bushman JOKING IN-LAWS are apparently identical with Western Khoe Bushman and probably also Khoekhoe same-age or same-generation GRANDRELATIVES. (On the Khoekhoe, see Hoernlé 1925: 19–20, 21; Engelbrecht 1936: 150, 153.) In fact, even a few Nharo use the JOKING IN-LAW / GRANDRELATIVE compound *ti-/wi-tsxõ*, for 'affinal GRANDRELATIVES'. This first difference, then, is of linguistic but not of sociological significance.

The second difference, concerning the senior/junior distinctions, is a more complicated matter. Relative age and generation are sociologically significant among the Khoe-speakers, even among those peoples whose relationship terminologies do not distinguish between senior and junior referents. For example, a man does not behave in the same way towards his elderly grandmother as he does towards his marriageable cross-cousin, though both may be called by the same term. With regard to GRANDRELATIVE egocentric terminology, we can summarize the Khoe systems diagramatically (table 10.4).

In table 10.4, *senior* relatives are defined as those in generations above ego's (for example, grandparents, cross-uncles or cross-aunts), *equal* relatives are those in ego's own generation, (for example, cross-cousins), and *junior* relatives are those in generations below ego's (for example, grandchildren, cross-nephews or cross-nieces). Other, more distant, cross-relatives are also included in each of these three subcategories.

The Western Khoe Bushmen use one term for all individuals in the GRANDRELATIVE category, the Central Khoe Bushmen use three, and the

TABLE 10.4   Khoe egocentric GRANDRELATIVE terminologies

	Western Khoe Bushman	Central Khoe Bushman	Khoekhoe
Senior	tsxõ	baba (m.), mama (f.)	//nao
Equal	tsxõ	n//odi	//nuri
Junior	tsxõ	n//odi	//nuri

Khoekhoe use two. Terms may be said to be 'structurally identical' when relationships traced through one are always the same as relationships traced through the other; they may be said to be 'structurally significant' when this is *not* the case. In this sense, Central Khoe Bushman *baba* and *mama* are structurally identical since the difference between them is only one of real sex, which, like number-gender suffixes and like relative age distinctions in both the Western and the Central Khoe Bushman terminologies presented here, is not structurally significant. Relationships traced through a *baba* are equivalent to relationships traced through a *mama*: e.g., the wife of a *baba* is always *mama*, and the husband of a *mama* is always *baba*. The G/wi relationship terms *ki-baba-ma* (*baba*, with appropriate prefix and suffix) and *ki-mama-sa* (*mama*, with prefix and suffix) may be translated exactly into Nama as *ti-//nao-b* ('my senior male GRANDRELATIVE') and *ti-//nao-s* ('my senior female GRANDRELATIVE'), wherever the Nama genealogical referents are in the GRANDRELATIVE category. Thus the real distinction here is between two, and not three, structural types: the Western Khoe Bushman type, with one structurally significant term, and the Central Khoe Bushman and Khoekhoe type, with two structurally significant terms.

The third difference among these systems is the one which is truly significant: the existence of the specific category RESPECT RELATIVE for the Khoekhoe. This category is important first because, by its very existence, its primary genealogical referent, FZ, is placed in the 'wrong' higher-level category (in other systems she is a GRANDRELATIVE and therefore a JOKING partner), and secondly because its defining morpheme *tàra* denotes a very distinct attitude and mode of behaviour towards those in the relationship.

With regard to the first point, the general rule that an opposite-sex sibling link changes higher-level category is superseded by a special rule which is dependent upon the patrilineal descent system of the Khoekhoe. The former is an element of the underlying structure of all Khoe and certain other Khoisan systems, and the latter is a surface-structural feature attributable to the role of the FZ in Khoekhoe society. Ego's FZ, rather than being distinguished from ego's F because of her AVOIDANCE relationship to him, is herself classified as AVOIDANCE because of her role as ego's senior female agnate. She is like a 'female father'. In fact, *tàra* is a polysemous morpheme, which apparently may sometimes be glossed, man speaking, 'any female AVOIDANCE partner of my patrilineal localized group' (see Engelbrecht 1936: 127, 130—1). Among the Central Khoe Bushmen, the Western Khoe Bushmen and the many modern Nama groups who today lack patrilineal kin groups, there is no equivalent of this term or the lower-level category it designates. The FZ's special categorization is dependent upon her role within ego's patrilineal kin group, and where such kin groups do not exist, her role is transformed to that of a sort of 'female mother's brother' and her category to that of GRANDRELATIVE.

With regard to the second point, it is a man's *tàra*, i.e. his Z or FBD, who is responsible for keeping discipline in the household, among her brothers and ultimately her brothers' sons:

> A sister was a *tàras*, that is, a person to be respected, not to be spoken to or of lightly. In the old days an oath by a sister was one of the greatest oaths a man could take, and a sister could generally be relied on to stop any fight in which her brother was taking part. . . . The eldest sister of a man is his *Gei Tàras*, his great respected one.
>
> (Hoernlé 1925: 22)

The term *tàra* always implies respect and very often implies authority. In some Korana tribes, a man's *tàra* was responsible for bestowing him in marriage (Engelbrecht 1936: 130–1). Among the Nama the term *tàra* was traditionally applied, at least by men, to their FZs, their Zs, and presumably also their parallel cousins, who were all classificatory 'sisters' (see Hoernlé 1925: 21–2). The FZs and 'sisters' alike reciprocated with the same term but with the diminutive suffix *-õa* ('child') added. Hoernlé (1925: 19) lists the term for FZH as '*Tatab*' (modern orthography: *dada-b*), which is also a word for 'father'. She also lists an archaic term for FZ, namely '*Éis Geis*' (modern orthography: *ai-s kai-s*), literally 'great mother' (1925: 19). In its most general sense, *tàra* seems to mean 'AVOIDANCE partner', a sense which in fact it retains today with the dissolution of the Nama clans and the resulting transformation of relationships of the RESPECT RELATIVE category earlier this century. In Hoernlé's two examples it overlaps categories AVOIDANCE SIBLING and PARENT/CHILD.

Finally, there is evidence that among the Korana a man's *tàra-s* is any woman who is not his *tará-s* ('wife'). According to Engelbrecht (1936: 127), 'a general term for the class of person one is not allowed to marry is *táras* [*sic*] for the female and *≠xana-khoeb* for the male.' Engelbrecht (1936: 127) goes on to say that some Korana non-marriageable people do not use these terms but instead call each other 'sister' and 'brother'. In contrast, MBD and FZS term each other 'husband' and 'wife', and there is evidence of generalized exchange. Men of a 'kraal' marry the women of their 'great kraal', and the women marry the men of their 'little kraal' (see Engelbrecht 1936: 3, 127, 153; Barnard 1975). Apparently, to a Korana man there are only two kinds of women, or at least only two kinds of same-age women: 'sisters' and 'wives'.

CONCLUSIONS

To summarize, in spite of differences with regard to rules of descent, marriage and other aspects of social organization, the kinship systems of the Khoe-speaking peoples exhibit considerable uniformity with regard to kin categorization and relationship terminology. This is not really surprising, given the common origin of their languages and the small number of reciprocal categories in existence within these systems. The general rules which determine higher-level, or JOKING and AVOIDANCE, categorization are the same for all Khoe-speaking peoples. In any Khoe kinship system there are also up to four lower-level categories, and sometimes several egocentric relationship terms may be applied within each of these. With accountable differences, both the genealogical definition of the categories and the terms which name them are very much the same throughout Khoe-speaking southern Africa.

There is however one important categorical difference. The category RESPECT RELATIVE occurs only among the patrilineal Khoekhoe. Its defining morpheme, *tàra* in Nama, emphasizes the AVOIDANCE relationship of members of this category. The term is also associated with the rights of Khoekhoe women over their male agnates. This is the category of the Khoekhoe FZ, and in a wider sense seems to be congruent with the higher-level category AVOIDANCE, which in turn is the category of Khoekhoe non-marriageable women and men. The Khoekhoe are the only Khoisan who possess such a category, and its existence is a result of the surface structural feature of patrilineal organization.

Of particular interest for comparative purposes is the rule that same-sex sibling, spouse and same-sex namesake links retain higher-level category, and that parent/child, opposite-sex sibling and opposite-sex namesake links change higher-level category. The absolute distinction between JOKING and AVOIDANCE on this level is nearly universal among Khoisan peoples, including both Khoe-speaking and non-Khoe-speaking groups. A very strong case could be made for this rule as an underlying structural principle of classification in virtually all known systems apart from Eastern ≠Hoã. Certainly its existence has been demonstrated as a principle of kinship behaviour for groups as diverse as the Nharo (Barnard 1978), !Kung (Marshall 1957; 1976: 201–51), and !xõ (Heinz 1966: 153–86). In addition, the recognition of such a distinction as an underlying principle of kin classification allows us to explain the otherwise unique !xõ practice of designating cross-cousins as 'classificatory CHILDREN' and forbidding marriage or intimate relationships with them. The !xõ system takes the principle of higher-level categorization to its logical limit, classifying AVOIDANCE partners' AVOIDANCE partners' AVOIDANCE partners as AVOIDANCE, even within the range of direct links through consanguineous kin. It is this, and not the formal distinction of parallel and cross-relatives, which orders the classification of !xõ close consanguines (see Barnard 1981: 231—4).

Even the elusive Eastern ≠Hoã system, the subject of Gruber's (1973) rather cumbersome 'transformational-generative' analysis, is clear and simple when seen as a transformation of a common Khoisan structure (see table 10.5). A striking feature of the Eastern ≠Hoã system, particularly by comparison with those of the Khoe-speaking peoples, is the seeming ambiguity of the categorization of the FeB and MeZ, and semi-reciprocally, that of the yGC, FyBCC and MyZCC. This 'ambiguity' is in fact two-fold, but may not be

TABLE 10.5   The Eastern ≠Hoã relationship terminology

Term	Gloss	Referents
Primary terms		
kyxana	'senior male grandrelative'	FF, MF, FeB, MB
kyxoõ	'senior female grandrelative' or 'junior grandrelative'	FM, MM, MeZ, FZ, yGC, CC, GCC, FyBCC, MyZCC
cu	'father'	F
cu-≠gao	'classificatory father'	FyB
gye	'mother'	M
gye-≠gao	'classificatory mother'	MyZ
ki-si	'senior sibling'	eG, FeBC, MeZC
//kam	'junior sibling'	yG, FyBC, MyZC
si-m'zale	'cross-cousin'	FZC, MBC
//qo'oe	'child'	C, FZCC, MBCC
//qo'oe-≠gao	'classificatory child'	eGC, FeBC, MeZC
Composite terms		
cu ki-si	'father's elder same-sex sibling'	FeB
cu //kam	'father's younger same-sex sibling'	FyB
gye ki-si	'mother's elder same-sex sibling'	MeZ
gye //kam	'mother's younger same-sex sibling'	MyZ
ki-si //qo'oe	'elder sibling's child'	eGC, FeBCC, MeZCC
//kam //qo'oe	'younger sibling's child'	yGC, FyBCC, MyZCC

Source: Gruber 1973; glosses added

as problematic as it seems. In the first instance, relative sex in relation to linking siblings is only structurally significant when ego is tracing to a senior relative, not when tracing to a junior relative: 'the rule of uniform reciprocals' (see, for example, Scheffler 1977) does not hold true.

The second instance of 'ambiguity' here is of a different kind. It is represented by the possible dual categorization of the five genealogical referents mentioned above, as both *kyxana* or *kyxoõ* (in Khoe terms, GRANDRELATIVE), and at the same time *cu ki-si* or *gye ki-si* (senior PARENT/CHILD), or *//kam //qo'oe* (classificatory junior SIBLING). Assuming for the moment that the Khoe comparison is relevant, this is not unlike the option afforded by some Khoe systems, of the dual categorization of joking affines as both GRAND-RELATIVES and JOKING IN-LAWS, or the dual categorization of certain AVOIDANCE relatives as either both RESPECT RELATIVES and AVOIDANCE IN-LAWS or both RESPECT RELATIVES and PARENT/CHILD. The difference is that dual categorization among the Khoe-speaking peoples functions only within each respective higher-level category, JOKING and AVOIDANCE. The Eastern ≠ Hoã practice could reflect the fact that there exists no universal polar dichotomy between JOKING and AVOIDANCE categories, in that in their terminology the dual categorization of FeB, MeZ, yGC, FyBCC and MyZCC places these relatives in both of such would-be categories. If this interpretation is correct, then relative age is what matters most, not category; and the choice between a usage indicating category GRANDRELATIVE and one indicating category PARENT/CHILD probably depends on the social context.

Of course many more examples could be given. My thesis is that Khoisan kinship systems are best seen as products of a regionally specific underlying structure which is neither 'emic' nor 'etic', but in between. I make no claims for the cognitive reality of the structures I have described, except that they are real to me. My method is one which I believe can account, with great precision, for the differences and similarities between Khoisan kinship systems, and beyond that, perhaps be helpful as a source of ideas in a wider range of comparative concerns within social anthropology.

REFERENCES

Barnard, A. 1975. Australian models in the South West African highlands. *African Studies* 34: 9—18.
___ 1978. The kin terminology system of the Nharo Bushmen. *Cahiers d'Etudes africaines* 18: 607—29.
___ 1980. Kin terminology systems of the Khoe-speaking peoples. In *Bushman and Hottentot Linguistic Studies, 1979* (ed.) J. W. Snyman. Pretoria: University of South Africa.

___ 1981. Universal kin categorization in four Bushman societies. *L'Uomo* 5: 219—37.

Barnard, A. and A. Good. 1984. *Research Practices in the Study of Kinship.* London: Academic Press.

Eggan, F. 1950. *Social Organization of the Western Pueblos.* Chicago: University of Chicago Press.

Engelbrecht, J. A. 1936. *The Korana.* Cape Town: Maskew Miller.

Goody, J. 1959. The mother's brother and the sister's son in West Africa. *Journal of the Royal Anthropological Institute* 89: 59—88.

Gruber, J. 1973. ǂHoã kinship terms. *Linguistic Inquiry* 4: 427—49.

Heinz, H. J. 1966. The social organization of the !kõ Bushmen. M.A. thesis, University of South Africa, Pretoria.

Hoernlé, A. W. 1925. The social organization of the Nama Hottentots of Southwest Africa. *American Anthropologist* 27: 1—24.

Josselin de Jong, J. P. B. de. 1977 [1935]. The Malay Archipelago as a field of ethnological study. In *Structural Anthropology in the Netherlands* (ed.) P. E. de Josselin de Jong. The Hague: Nijhoff.

Kuper, A. 1982. *Wives for Cattle.* London: Routledge and Kegan Paul.

Marshall, L. 1957. The kin terminology system of the !Kung Bushmen. *Africa* 27: 1—25.

___ 1976. *The !Kung of Nyae Nyae.* Cambridge, Mass.: Harvard University Press.

Needham, R. 1973. Prescription. *Oceania* 42: 166—81.

Radcliffe-Brown, A. R. 1913. Three tribes of Western Australia. *Journal of the Royal Anthropological Institute* 43: 143—70.

___ 1930—1. The social organization of Australian tribes. *Oceania* 1: 34—63, 206—46, 322—41, 426—56.

Schapera, I. 1930. *The Khoisan peoples of South Africa.* London: Routledge.

___ 1939. A survey of the Bushman question. *Race Relations* 6: 68—83.

Scheffler, H. W. 1977. On the 'rule of uniform reciprocals' in systems of kin classification. *Anthropological Linguistics* 19: 245—59.

Schultze [Schultze-Jena], L. 1907. *Aus Namaland und Kalahari.* Jena: Gustav Fischer.

Silberbauer, G. B. 1972. The G/wi Bushmen. In *Hunters and Gatherers Today* (ed.) M. G. Bicchieri. New York: Holt, Rinehart and Winston.

___ 1981. *Hunter and Habitat in the Central Kalahari Desert.* Cambridge: Cambridge University Press.

11

The Use of Ethnographic Parallels in Interpreting Upper Palaeolithic Rock Art

Robert Layton

with an appendix by Malcolm Smith

One of the animals painted at Lascaux is a horse, superimposed on which is a small brown motif made up of a slanting line and several diagonal strokes. A similar motif is slightly to the right of the horse. Kuhn described the panel as follows: 'there is . . . a pregnant wild mare that is especially striking. The soft, often broken outline is executed with a broad brush, as are also . . . the arrows directed against the body' (1956: 36). Marshack interpreted the panel rather differently: 'If we consider this horse to be female and pregnant — or female and potentially pregnant — then the ("feathered") image might be considered a branch and, therefore, a sign of late spring and the time of calving or, if the form is intended to represent a bare, sparse branch, it may be a sign of autumn-winter' (1972: 220). Leroi-Gourhan is sceptical: 'writers refer on every possible occasion to "pregnant" mares; but it would be interesting to know just how anyone can distinguish a well-fed equine on a cave wall from a pregnant one' (1968: 120). According to Leroi-Gourhan's general hypothesis animals represented in Palaeolithic cave art are sexual symbols. Deer, ibex and horse are 'male', bison and aurochs (wild cattle) are 'female'. The small brown motif is a stylized penis. Laming-Emperaire reaches the opposite conclusion; bovids represent a male principle, horses a female one. Comparing these theories, it seems fortunate that we can at least identify the figure as a horse. What is at issue is the place of the construct *horse* within a Palaeolithic culture.

The purpose of this paper is to consider what can undoubtedly be said of Palaeolithic art, what is probable and what is possible.[1] Any analysis of the art demands the assumption that, at some level, Palaeolithic cultures belong to the same order of phenomena as modern human cultures but we clearly cannot assume that rock paintings meant the same thing to them as they seem to, to us.

What kind of comparative framework can be derived from modern human cultures?

Piecemeal use of ethnographic parallels is unreliable because it depends on isolated similarities of form. The method ignores both the (potentially diverse) cultural contexts of the specific items compared and the fact that parallels with other items may suggest alternative explanations. A good example is Breuil's use of a photograph depicting a New Guinea dancer completely covered in a costume as the key to a triangular mass of lines at Lascaux, which he construed as the depiction of a Palaeolithic sorcerer (quoted in Ucko and Rosenfeld 1967: 152). Resort to universalistic concepts of primitive mentality is equally unhelpful. If a mode of thought or behaviour is held to be universal among non-literate cultures, it tells us nothing specific about the Palaeolithic to assert that here too there existed a fear of the dark or a belief in sympathetic magic; to claim that there *must* have been such beliefs does not even test the hypothesis (compare Lévi-Strauss's criticism of Malinowski's theory of totemism, Lévi-Strauss 1962: 58). The weaknesses of both methods led Leroi-Gourhan and Laming to reject the use of ethnographic parallels in the study of Palaeolithic rock art. Unfortunately these authors seem unconsciously to have substituted their own culturally conditioned preconceptions of what the art 'means'. As Ucko and Rosenfeld point out, this *can* only be avoided by an awareness of the diversity of human cultures (1967: 151).

What is needed is 'the systematic application of a coherent body of comparative material to the elucidation of particular archaeological phenomena' (Orme 1981: 24). As Orme suggests, a start may be made by collecting as many ethnographic parallels as may be found for the particular practices deduced from the archaeological record. Ultimately, however, such parallels need to be co-ordinated so that a variety of cultures can be compared according to certain defined axes of variation. If, for example, hunter-gatherers can be shown consistently to exhibit territoriality in certain environments, and to establish territories whose size varies with the availability of key resources, then this model could be tested against evidence for territoriality in the Upper Palaeolithic. On the other hand, clan totemism and cross-cousin marriage, although they are both characteristic of some hunter-gatherer cultures, are not exclusive to this category of human societies and cannot therefore be simply predicted from the production economy (see Burnham, this volume, on the category of 'pastoral nomads' and Davis 1984 on African rock art).

One of the principal difficulties in the use of ethnographic parallels is that human cultures are not simply diverse; they have an inherent tendency to generate variation in behaviour and to diversify. To this extent they are unpredictable. Buckley pointed out that this capacity distinguished both human cultures and genetic populations from lower-order systems (Buckley 1967: 14). In the 1950s Lévi-Strauss recognized this (Lévi-Strauss 1963: 296, 303) and took language as the best-studied cultural system, which has the capacity to generate an indefinite variety of verbal statements. Lévi-Strauss argued that anthropology should learn from linguistics and look for regularities of structure underlying the diversity of form in the telling of myth or the transaction of marriage exchanges. Goodenough also later wrote that he thought it useful to view social relationships as containing 'vocabularies' of units of behaviour and a 'syntax' or 'set of rules for their composition into (and interpretation as) meaningful sequences of social events' (Goodenough 1965: 1).

Parallel developments have taken place in archaeological theory, where it has been argued that stone tool manufacture requires the same basic cognitive skills as language use (Holloway 1969; Hewes 1973; Kitahara-Frisch 1980; Gowlett 1984). The mechanisms culture embodies for generating variety in behaviour are central to its evolutionary value; in a functional sense these parallel the role of mutations in a genetic system. The content of any culture at any period is thus relatively unpredictable, but cultures do have a characteristic structure.

A useful framework for comparing Palaeolithic with extant hunter-gatherer rock art would allow the capacity of these traditions to generate a diversity of 'visual statements' to be measured. Ultimately this would be of most interest if the above writers are correct in thinking social behaviour is in general governed by the same generative processes as symbolic communication. An analysis of the structure of Palaeolithic art revealed in the surviving 'texts' is likely to be more revealing than attempts to penetrate the exact meaning of any single motif. How may this structure be envisaged?

Two axes can be distinguished in the rules for using a system of signs which, for convenience, I will describe as *sequential* and *analogical*. For instance, a picture which states the story 'Three hunters attacked a herd of eland', makes a sequential statement (i.e. tells a story). A picture which embodies a visual metaphor makes an analogical statement: the king is a lion; our ancestor is that rock. It is by analogy that parallel structures are perceived between different areas of experience, making possible the construction of general explanatory schemes, either religious or scientific (Horton 1960; 1964; Lévi-Strauss 1966; Layton 1985).

Since Saussure's time it has been recognized that cultural systems generate many classes of behaviour: sequences of social action (from the manufacture of stone tools to the practice of cross-cousin marriage), speech, mathematical calculations (using a vocabulary of numbers or symbols and a grammar of operations), and visual representation (for example, cartography) using a vocabulary of motifs and a grammar of compositions (see Piaget 1971). The data anthropologists work with are performances; the underlying structure is inferred. It is notable that many analyses of Palaeolithic art tend to go straight to the inferred structure of meaning (cf. Parkin's remarks on essence and appearance, this volume). An alternative is to examine the complexity of the performances themselves, and to compare them with parallel data from recent hunter-gatherer cultures (compare Parkin's concept of variations on themes). Several useful questions may be asked with respect to Palaeolithic art, although not all are equally easily answered.

What was the character of the cultural subsystem which generated the sequences of paintings observed in the caves? The caves may be said to contain sets of paintings which constitute performances or texts created within the artistic system, and to a certain extent the complexity of their structuring is a matter for empirical analysis. However, differential preservation may have destroyed some of the original corpus; there may have been complementary subsystems which leave no record (for example, ritual) and classifying paintings as representations of 'the same motif' (for example, 'Bison', 'Claviform') is often difficult. The treatment of each cave as a single unit of analysis is also questionable, since in some cases (notably Altamira and Niaux) one large area of concentrated paintings stands out from a scatter of less visually spectacular motifs which may reflect a complementary cultural theme or may be entirely unrelated to the large panel.

What purpose did the art serve? This is a matter for inference. There is no *a priori* reason to suppose that Upper Palaeolithic man painted animals or geometric motifs for the same reason as recent Aboriginal or San artists. Indeed, comparative surveys show a multiplicity of functions which rock art may serve. Perhaps the most reasonable line of inference to follow is to consider whether certain functional contexts impose characteristic constraints on the free exercise of artistic creativity (see Layton 1985). If comparable degrees of complexity or parallel structures can be identified in both Palaeolithic and recent bodies of material it may be possible to show that on the balance of probabilities Palaeolithic art performed similar functions to ethnographically documented rock art traditions.

What was the specific content of the belief system? Fascinating though an answer to this question would be, it is probably impossible to deduce. Moreover, in the general context of the development of human cultural systems the specific content seems less important than the structural complexity of the system.

ANALOGICAL AND SEQUENTIAL RELATIONSHIPS IN RECENT ROCK ART

The simplest communication systems are those which Hockett and Ascher called 'closed-signal call systems' (1964: 139). In such systems there is no grammar. Each sign is mutually exclusive. The user can only respond with one or another of the signs, or with silence. Several signs cannot be combined in a single message. Some contemporary human rituals operate this way: the ritual acts 'position' the actor at a certain point along a series of alternative statuses, as when wearing a body painting in an Australian Aboriginal ritual (Bern and Layton 1984: 71–5). The frequency and context in which signs are 'called' will tell us something about how the system works. More complex systems of communication, exemplified by language, may combine elements in two ways: in the 'double level of articulation' represented by phoneme and morpheme (Mounin 1970: 74) and by the use of syntax (Reynolds 1968: 303) which allows both sequential and analogical relationships to be expressed.

In Australian Aboriginal culture it is possible to think of a set of conceptual relationships between a series of clans, articulated through marriage exchanges, and a parallel series of relationships between points in the landscape imbued with the creative power of the ancestral heroes (sacred sites), articulated by the routes of the ancestors from site to site. Each clan has an analogical relationship with the cluster of sites delimiting its estate. These relationships are frequently expressed in art motifs. For instance, in the Gulf Country of Northern Australia these are body paintings, each motif being the possession of a particular clan. They may appear in caves as an assertion of territory, but ceremonies, not cave paintings, are the focus for the production of motifs. The motif a man wears signifies his clan affiliation (Elkin 1961; Maddock 1982; Bern and Layton 1984). In the Western Kimberleys, cave paintings are central to the traditional religion (Crawford 1968; Blundell 1982; Layton 1985). Ancestral heroes specific to each clan are painted in rock shelters together with totemic animal species, carefully delineated in red and white. Small 'trickster' figures also appear, but these are generally poorly executed, in monochrome and often oriented upside down in relation to the totemic figures. Painted rock shelters tend to be well spaced, and correspond to the focal points of clan estates. In some the hero is depicted in semi-human form as a 'Wandjina'; in others there are multiple representations of the particular animal species with which he is associated, or into which he was transformed.

Not all Aboriginal art, however, is totemic. In the Kakadu area east of Darwin, beautifully painted animals and fish showing internal organs in 'X-ray' style simply represent species for which people traditionally forage. These paintings occur in a virtually unbroken line of rock shelters, extending along more than 250 km of the Arnhem Land Escarpment (Fox, Kelleher and Ker 1977: 37). The spacing evident in the totemic art of the Kimberleys is absent.

San (Bushman) rock art reflects quite a different cognitive system. The San lack local group totemism; all San groups in the Drakensberg appear to have shared a cosmology in which one animal species, the eland, is particularly important and this is said to explain the eland's predominance in the rock art of the Drakensberg Mountains (Vinnicombe 1975; Lewis-Williams 1981).

Is the different structure of Aboriginal and San cosmology reflected in any measurable way in their rock art?

The Kimberley material implies a *segmentary* system. A number of animal species are depicted, but each is associated with the territory of a particular social group, and will (in the model) only appear in that group's territory. A regional survey would show that each species appears with relatively equal frequency but only at a restricted number of locations. The San material implies a *unitary* system. A number of animal species are depicted, but certain species are of pre-eminent importance for all groups. A regional survey would show that certain species are depicted more frequently than others, but all will appear at a relatively high number of locations.

An Aboriginal Case

There is no comprehensive regional survey available of the distribution of motifs in Kimberley rock shelters, so I propose to use the data available from a survey of rock shelters in the Laura area of North Queensland, and consider how well it fits the 'Kimberley model'. Trezise's survey of 16 rock shelter complexes in the Laura area reveals an art tradition in which representations of humans and animals predominate (Trezise 1971). If each species represented is treated as a single unit of visual signification, this indicates a set of 22 motifs, or signifying units, including human, kangaroo, wallaby, tortoise, echidna and two introduced species, horse and pig. This is a minimum count; human figures may be divisible into at least two representational categories: capricious spirits in human form and headdressed, ceremonial figures. The report of Macintosh (1977) illustrates how difficult it may be correctly to identify the subject matter of Aboriginal rock art: when Elkin returned to a shelter with the Aboriginal custodian, Macintosh found that he had wrongly identified fifteen out of twenty-two motifs, and been only superficially correct in the other seven cases. Trezise identifies three discrete species of fish and three of bird, but lumps other representations together as 'fish' or 'bird'. A few species only occur once in the sample (for example, bêche-de-mer). How fair is it to count a signifying unit which only appears once? Perhaps the most interesting interpretation would be that they show these artistic traditions to be open systems: since the art is representational, an artist could utilize existing stylistic conventions to introduce a new 'sign' which can be 'read' as part of the existing system. This is exemplified by the depiction of introduced species in both San and Australian Aboriginal material. Rosenfeld demonstrates how horses are depicted at Laura in a form derived from the existing motif representing kangaroo (1982: 209).

The Laura sample (see table 11.1) conforms relatively well to the totemic model derived from the Kimberleys. There are many animal species which appear with relatively equal frequency. On average, each species occurs in 26 per cent of the shelters surveyed. On the other hand, the evidence that the Laura animal paintings really do depict totemic species is much less convincing than Trezise suggests, since he rarely visited caves with local informants, and those whom he did consult provided very generalized information (Rosenfeld, Horton and Winter 1981: 3). The most that can reasonably be said is that this is an art tradition consistent with a segmentary cognitive system. It may be that the segmentary structure of the art derives from different shelters being utilized for different purposes (secular foraging records, sorcery, ancestral themes) each of which was associated with a discrete set of motifs; Trezise is inclined to interpret catfish, eel and snake as indicative of sorcery (Trezise 1971: 14). Rosenfeld found from her re-examination of the Laura material that certain motif types tended to occur in association with one another, and that within each geographical cluster of shelters, each of these identifiable sub-sets was represented. This, she concludes, 'is indicative of the existence of differential cultural connotations for the shelters within a cluster' (Rosenfeld 1982: 216). The implication is that, in contrast to the Kimberleys, each territorial unit contains a shelter representative of each segment of the cognitive system (see Appendix).

A San Case

Lewis-Williams's survey of 38 San rock art sites in the Drakensberg (1981: 134—5) indicates, again, an art tradition in which humans and animals predominate. In his sample 12 species are represented. Vinnicombe's larger sample contains 26 species, but many occur very infrequently (Vinnicombe 1975: 363—4). In terms of the frequency with which particular species appear, the Drakensberg data reveal quite a different pattern to that seen at Laura. A few animal species predominate, each present with progressively decreasing frequencies. The eland far outnumber other species. Both Vinnicombe and Lewis-Williams convincingly link this with the pre-eminence of the eland in San cosmology. Both draw attention to aspects of eland behaviour which make it an appropriate image of social interaction. Vinnicombe suggests that as a herd animal which aggregated in the wet season, with demonstrably different behaviour patterns between males, females and young, eland herd structure was perceived to reflect Bushman band structure (Vinnicombe 1975: 163). Lewis-Williams documents eland imagery in San *rites de passage* (girl's puberty, boy's first kill, marriage) and possession dances. The San do not have a system of local group totemism and this appears clearly reflected in the relative frequency with which animal species are represented in the art.

Unfortunately there is little data on the distribution of Drakensberg motifs shelter by shelter, although Vinnicombe writes that despite the numerical preponderance of human over animal paintings, more shelters contain only animals (21 out of 150) than contain only humans (eight out of 150) (Vinnicombe 1975: 135).

In analysing these two art traditions simply in terms of the frequency with which motifs appear, I have implied that they are 'call systems' without a visual grammar. The question of sequential relationships will be considered later in the paper; visual 'stories' are much more characteristic of San than of recent Aboriginal art. They appear to depict ceremonies, hunting scenes, etc.

San and Aboriginal art possess distinctive modes for representing analogical relationships. Munn (1964, 1973) originally demonstrated how the simple geometric style of many Aboriginal art traditions uses motifs capable of simultaneously representing several items in what is referred to here as an analogical set. An arc may represent an ancestral hero sitting in his camp, the natural feature which now marks the site (a waterhole or cave), and it signifies in an heraldic fashion that the bearer of this motif in ceremony is a member of the clan owning that site (see Layton 1985: 438).

A different way of codifying an analogical set is suggested by Lewis-Williams's analysis of Bushman rock art. Lewis-Williams details the many contexts in which San draw parallels between human and eland behaviour and reproduces paintings of eland-headed humans. He argues that such 'conflation', in which elements of different models are combined in a single motif, is indicative of a perceived analogy between man and animal (Lewis-Williams 1981: 22, 65). The same technique occurs in other art traditions (see Layton 1981a: 21–3).

CONTENT OF UPPER PALAEOLITHIC ART

What can be said about sequential and analogical relationships in Palaeolithic rock art? There are a number of difficulties to be faced. It cannot be assumed that the relationships we observe fully document those that existed in a prehistoric culture, because the art is like a fossil, preserving only the 'hard parts' of a more complex organism. Just as organisms evolved to some complexity before developing parts capable of fossilization, so human cultures almost certainly began by developing systems of cognition and communication which leave no archaeological record. Nor are the patterns we observe necessarily the product of human culture. Leroi-Gourhan ingeniously argued that the so-called Palaeolithic 'Bear Cult', postulated from apparently intentional arrangements of bear skulls and bones in caves, was non-existent; really, he argues, it was the movement of bears themselves through the caves that destroyed certain bones and pushed others into fissures in the rock (Leroi-Gourhan 1964: 32—3). A similar apparent structuring is seen in the tendency for much Palaeolithic rock art, particularly paintings, to be located well beyond daylight. Only bas-reliefs and deep carvings are normally found at cave entrances. Human intention, symptomatic of the art's significance, has been inferred since the time of Reinach (1903, cited in Ucko and Rosenfeld 1967: 124). However in 1972 a Palaeolithic cave entrance blocked by scree was discovered at Fontanet in the French Pyrenees. In this instance the entrance chamber was itself decorated with paintings which the rock fall had protected from erosion (Delteil, Durbas and Wahl 1972). Finally, there is substantial difficulty in assessing how much of the cave art may be regarded as part of a single synchronic system. Breuil, who paid little attention to the internal structuring of the art but considerably more to the concept of cultural evolution, regarded it as extending over forty thousand years (Breuil 1952). Leroi-Gourhan, who saw the art as the expression of a single Palaeolithic world view (1968: 44, 48) considers that most of the underground art was executed during the middle phases of the Magdalenian, a period of less than 5,000 years (1968: 52). Leroi-Gourhan's dating is probably more accurate. Most of the cave art probably belongs to the Magdalenian, the period between 17,000 and 10,000 B.P., although many open-air bas-relief representations date from the Solutrian, from 22,000 B.P. onwards (Leroi-Gourhan 1964: 48—51; Ucko and Rosenfeld 1967: 26—7).

There is, as far as I know, no ethnographic evidence which would make it possible to predict how likely the cognitive structures of a non-literate culture are to undergo change during a period of five to seven thousand years. The significance of such evidence would, in any case, depend on how specific were the structures one deduced from Palaeolithic art.

THE CORPUS OF MOTIFS

Animal Art

The best known and more easily construed body of Palaeolithic art is that of animal silhouettes, depicted as painted or engraved outlines, or solid figures in one or more colours. Taken as a whole, this body of material is composed of many discrete signifying units, identifiable because even 17,000 to 10,000 years later it is possible to recognize what the motifs represent: horse, bison, aurochs, mammoth, deer, ibex, reindeer. Some recur frequently, others are unique, such as the goose (?) at La Bastide and the marten/weasel/polecat at Niaux (Clottes and Simonnet 1972). Some writers have argued that subspecies of horse, feline, deer etc. can be distinguished on anatomical grounds, but beyond a certain point it becomes difficult to distinguish anatomical from stylistic traits. Notwithstanding this, when one looks at animal representations one can tolerate a considerable variation in the mode of portrayal; some outline figures are as readily identifiable as are solid polychromes. The significance of differences in the shape of heads, horns, backlines etc., can be appreciated by knowing that these are features diagnostic of bison, deer or horse. Beyond a certain point, however, identifications become increasingly subjective (Ucko and Layton in press). For instance, Breuil, who emphasized the animal component of the art and believed it exhibited long cycles of stylistic development, was prone to identify amorphous motifs as primitive or degenerate animal representations (see Ucko 1977: 8).

If one takes this material as evidence for a minimum of 18 signifying units (see table 11.1) it is possible to compare the animal art of the Palaeolithic with similar traditions among recent hunter-gatherers. The first point of interest is that the number of signifying units is of the same order as that seen among the Aboriginal and San samples; the apparently slightly lower number of motifs may simply be due to the greater difficulty of identifying what is represented.

'Signs'

In addition to the animal silhouettes of the Palaeolithic there exists an acknowledged, apparently separate stylistic tradition of 'signs' which co-existed with it. It is extremely difficult to assess what these 'signs' may signify, and consequently much harder to identify discrete signifying units. It may well be, in fact, that what we treat as a discrete set of motifs is actually a subjectively defined, residual category distinguished by our inability to be certain what they signify. Palaeolithic 'signs' range from large, complex designs to simple dots, vertical strokes and grids.

Because their significance is uncertain, an intuitive understanding of subject matter cannot be used to identify signs. It is extremely difficult to classify the numerous, often unique motifs into sets which can be said to constitute signifying units. Until recently this problem was largely sidestepped. Researchers adopted two approaches. One was to postulate a meaning which the artist is supposed to have intended, so that any design that could be interpreted as a hut or windbreak, for instance, is classified as a 'tectiform', regardless of the degree of visual similarity between the motifs lumped together in this way.

The second solution frequently adopted is to assimilate sets of signs to a model that suggests itself to the researcher but which is not alleged to have been in the mind of the artist, as with claviforms (perceived as key shapes) or aviforms (perceived as bird shapes). Even with this approach it is hard to delimit discrete sign types.

The most satisfactory method is that of Sauvet, Sauvet and Wlodarczyk (1977), who classify signs on strictly formal grounds and deliberately reject any attempt to identify what the motifs signify. They divide signs into 12 types or 'clés', each of which is *posited* to constitute a discrete signifying unit.

There are still problems, particularly among the simplest of motif 'classes'. Is it fair to consider, for instance, that all rectangular grids belong to a single signifying unit? Might not the grid be spontaneously rediscovered by several doodlers of the Palaeolithic?

Probably the most important question to ask is, do signs constitute a separate mode of representation to the animal and human silhouettes? The Aboriginal rock art of Laura includes depictions of plants and artefacts (spears, dilly bags, digging sticks . . .). The Bushman rock art of the Drakensberg includes similar artefacts. It may be, and it has often been assumed, that some or all of Palaeolithic 'signs' represent artefacts by means of stylistic conventions similar to those embodied in the animal art. On the other hand, there are also cases where hunter-gatherer cultures utilize two distinct modes of representation to achieve different goals in visual communication. One example is the contrasting use of split representation and portrait masks on the north-west coast, another the use of geometric and animal silhouette art by the Yolngu of Northern Australia (both are discussed in Layton 1977 and Layton 1981a: chapter 4). Simple, geometric motifs may serve a variety of functions; allowing the rapid communication of information, or deliberately exploiting visual ambiguity to convey several messages. Geometric motifs need not necessarily have any representational value (see the essay on heraldry in Mounin 1970: 103—15). If 'signs' are considered to belong to the same stylistic set as the animal motifs, their association with animals will be construed as a sequential one (animals hit by weapons etc.); if they are considered to belong to a discrete mode of representation, associations with animal motifs are more likely to indicate an analogical relationship between subsets of the cognitive system (conceivably, animals and social categories). Does the juxtaposition say 'the bison fell into this trap' or 'these people are bison'?

Amorphous Motifs

Unfortunately for the study of Palaeolithic art, the corpus of figures is not exhausted by animals and 'signs'. There exist many more which are too faded, incomplete or irregular to classify. There is a repeated tendency by researchers either to perceive these as 'poorly executed', or to rely on natural cracks and fissures in the rock surface to 'complete' them. There is no doubt that Palaeolithic artists did sometimes rely on natural features of the cave wall to provide part of a figure, but it is unsafe to assume this was always the case.

The figures which can be attributed beyond reasonable doubt to the categories 'animal' or 'sign' lie at either end of a continuum of visual forms, many of which cannot be classified.

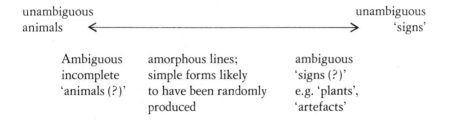

unambiguous animals	←	→	unambiguous 'signs'
Ambiguous incomplete 'animals (?)'	amorphous lines; simple forms likely to have been randomly produced	ambiguous 'signs (?)' e.g. 'plants', 'artefacts'	

Performance in Palaeolithic Art

Can any useful evidence be obtained by considering the frequency and context of production of Palaeolithic motifs? Given the difficulty of identifying the signifying units among Palaeolithic 'signs', it is easier to ask this question of animal motifs.

Table 11.1 compares the Laura and Drakensberg data with a *sample* from the Palaeolithic.[2]

What pattern emerges from the Palaeolithic sample? In terms of frequency of occurrence, distributions seem more closely to resemble the Drakensberg pattern. Certain animal species (horse, bison) are numerically preponderant and even less well represented species such as deer or bear occur with a high

TABLE 11.1   The Laura and Drakensberg data compared with a sample from the Palaeolithic

	Laura		Drakensberg		Palaeolithic	
Motif	Occurrence %	Shelters in which represented %	Motif	Occurrence %	Motif	Occurrence %	Shelters in which represented %
Human	55.0	1.00	Human	55.0	Horse	40.0	0.80
Catfish	6.4	0.70	Eland	12.0	Bison	19.0	0.80
Kangaroo	5.8	0.60	Unidentifiable antelope	6.90	Auroch	7.0	0.70
Fish generally[a]	5.1	0.40	Rhebuck	6.40	Reindeer	6.0	0.30
Flying fox	3.4	0.20	Fish	5.60	Mammoth	5.6	0.30
Bird generally[a]	3.1	0.30	Hartebeest	0.90	Anthropomorph	5.4	0.60
Emu	2.9	0.40	Baboon	0.70	Ibex	5.3	0.80
Tortoise	2.9	0.50	Feline	0.50	Deer	4.4	0.70
Snake	2.5	0.40	Serpent	0.30	Bear	2.7	0.40
Echidna	2.3	0.30	Winged	0.30	Lion	1.3	0.30
Crocodile	1.9	0.40	Small carnivore	0.20	Fish	0.5	0.30
Scrub turkey	1.8	0.30	Pig/warthog	0.10	Megaceros	0.5	0.20
Dingo	1.6	0.30	Elephant	0.07	Wolf	0.4	0.20

Laura			Drakensberg		Palaeolithic		
Shark	1.5	0.30	Hippopotamus	0.07	Rhinoceros	0.3	0.20
Wallaby	1.3	0.20	Reedbuck	0.05	Bird	0.3	0.20
Lizard, goanna	0.8	0.20	Wildebeest	0.04	Wild boar	0.3	0.20
Sting ray	0.3	0.06	Jackal	0.04	Caprid	0.2	0.10
Jabiru	0.3	0.06	Antbear	0.04	Compound/imaginary	0.1	0.05
Eelfish	0.2	0.03	Wild dog	0.04			
Ibis	0.2	0.06	Roan antelope	0.03	(956 motifs)		(18 caves)
Brolga	0.1	0.03	Bushbuck	0.03			
Bêche-de-mer	0.1	0.03	Oribi	0.03			
Shrimp	0.1	0.03	Hyena	0.03			
			Rhinoceros	0.01			
(997 motifs) (32 shelters)			Buffalo	0.01			
			Hare	0.01			
			Lizard	0.01			
			(6,951 motifs) (150 shelters)				

a Excludes specific identifications listed separately.

Sources: Laura (Trezise 1971); Drakensberg (Vinnicombe 1975: 364); Palaeolithic (as in note 2 of text)

frequency among different caves. Each species occurs, on average, in 42 per cent of the caves surveyed. The evidence seems to suggest a cognitive structure rather like that of the San, in which a variety of animal species hold the same position throughout the region surveyed, rather than a segmented structure analogous to the Australian system of local totemism.

It is significant that the frequency with which species figure in the rock art does not seem to correspond to their importance in Palaeolithic diet. While there is some controversy about how to interpret dietary evidence, it appears the animals most often hunted for food throughout the Magdalenian were, in south-west France, reindeer; in Northern Spain red deer (Mellors 1973: 262; Clark and Strauss 1983: 138, 144—95). Vinnicombe makes a similar point about the discrepancy between the dietary importance of species on the Drakensberg, and the frequency with which they appear in the rock art (1975: 151, 164).

A second striking point about the distribution of decorated caves in south-west France and northern Spain is that it is discontinuous: heavily decorated caves tend to occur at intervals, separated or surrounded by caves containing few or no paintings (figure 11.1; see table 11.2). Thirty kilometre circles tend to define areas containing one major and several minor caves. The pattern parallels the distribution of decorated shelters in both the Drakensberg (Vinnicombe 1975: 137—9) and the Laura area (Rosenfeld 1982: 214), but contrasts with that noted for the Kakadu region. This provides additional evidence to support the hypothesis that Palaeolithic art was not simply a record of subsistence activities. It suggests that directly or indirectly the art may have performed some function in demarcating territorial units (compare the conclusions Conkey reached from her analysis of decoration on artefacts excavated in some of these caves: Conkey 1980). Bailey (1983) has used the length of site habitation to make a parallel distinction between major and minor site clusters on the coastal plain, 'distributed so as to form almost contiguous site exploitation territories'. He notes that this clustering does not depend on the availability of habitable caves (1983: 155). Bailey derives his boundaries from a two-hour walking range out of the putative base camp. This yields smaller territories, giving an additional one based on Meaza (cave 8) between Altamira and Pindal, and one based on El Pendo (cave 12) north of Castillo.

A comparison of the content of Palaeolithic caves with few and many motifs (table 11.2) suggests the same motifs occur in both types, although 'signs' perhaps constitute a greater proportion of the work in caves with few motifs. Thus the Palaeolithic pattern is apparently not like that Rosenfeld found at Laura, where there were several opposed types of cave in any cluster.

A striking feature, which differentiates the Palaeolithic from both recent

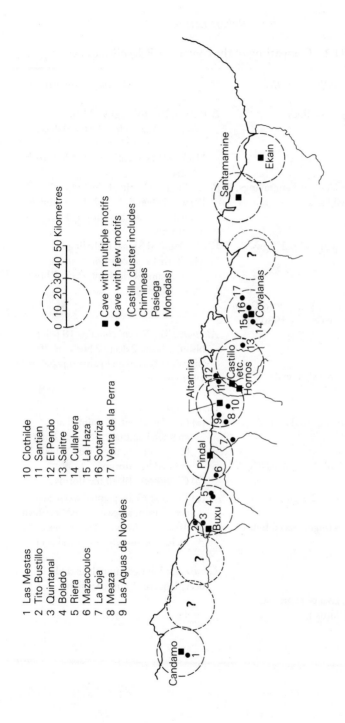

1 Las Mestas
2 Tito Bustillo
3 Quintanal
4 Bolado
5 Riera
6 Mazacoulos
7 La Loja
8 Meaza
9 Las Aguas de Novales

10 Clothilde
11 Santian
12 El Pendo
13 Salitre
14 Cullalvera
15 La Haza
16 Sotarriza
17 Venta de la Perra

0 10 20 30 40 50 Kilometres

■ Cave with multiple motifs
● Cave with few motifs

(Castillo cluster includes
Chimineas
Pasiega
Monedas)

Candamo

Buxu

Pindal

Altamira

Castillo
etc.
Hornos

Covalanas

Santamamine

Ekain

Figure 11.1 Distribution of decorated caves in northern Spain

TABLE 11.2 Comparison of the content of Palaeolithic caves

Caves with few motifs	Caves with multiple motifs
Las Mestas: engraved lines	*Candamo*: Painted 'signs': 11 horse, 10 stag, 15 auroch, 5 bison, 4 ibex; engravings including stag, hind, 3 bison; black outline paintings include auroch, 2 horses
Quintanal: 2 unidentified engravings, 1 engraved wild boar	*Buxu*: Engraved animals including 7 horses, 5 stag, 3 deer, 1 ibex; painted animals include ibex, bison; 15 engraved 'tectiforms'
Bolado: 10 foot panel of red 'signs'	*Pindal*: Painted 'signs' including 6 'claviforms', 'placentiform' and 'scutiforms', painted elephant, deer, 3 bison, engraved fish
Riera: painted dots. Adjacent to *Cueto de la Mina*: (see Conkey 1980 and Clark and Strauss 1983)	*Altamira*: 'Big Room' contains 18 painted bison, 3 boar, 2 deer, 2 horse, wolf; 'signs'; engraved and painted panels elsewhere in cave
Mazacoulos: faded red animals and 'signs'	
La Loja: about 6 engraved animals	*Castillo Complex*
	(a) *Castillo*: about 75 painted and engraved animals including horse, bison, auroch, deer, ibex. About 15 painted 'tectiforms'
Meaza: 1 red 'sign', 1 engraved 'sign'	(b) *Chimineas*: Black tectiforms
Las Aguas: 2 bison, 2 'signs', 1 amorphous	(c) *Pasiega*: Many painted horse and deer, bison; at least 20 red 'tectiforms'
Clothilde: 7 or 8 finger-traced figures	(d) *Monedas*: About 30 paintings including auroch, bison and deer
Santian: about 15 red 'signs'	*Covalanas*: Painted animals include 17 deer, 1 horse, 1 auroch; 'signs'
El Pendo: one panel of engravings (including 2 'birds')	

Table 11.2 continued

	Santamamine: Black painted animals including 26 bison, 4 horse, 2 ibex, 1 stag, 1 bear
Salitre: about 4 painted animals. including deer and bovid	
Cullalvera: red dots, panel of 'claviforms' and 2 painted horses	*Ekain*: 30 painted horse, 7 bison, 2 bear, 2 deer, 1 caprid, 1 fish
La Haza: 3 painted horses	
Sotarriza: 1 painted horse; some other paintings in adjacent cave	
Venta de la Perra: 3 engraved bison, 1 engraved bear	

traditions, is the much greater frequency with which humans were portrayed at Laura and in the Drakensberg: they constitute over half of both samples; in the Palaeolithic case they only make up 5.4 per cent. There are, in fact, problems in identifying many human representations in the Palaeolithic which will be outlined below; 5.4 per cent is unlikely to be an overestimate.

While the analysis of Palaeolithic art as a 'call system' appears to reveal some interesting patterns, there are difficulties in this approach. Should all occurrences of a unit such as 'horse' be treated as equal in value? Peche Merle contains more depictions of mammoth than horse, but two of the horses form an impressive display on an upstanding slab embellished with green dots and red 'signs'. Should these be given greater weight than small, black outline mammoths? Is the proper unit of analysis the whole cave? Caves such as Les Combarelles and Gabillou appear to be continuously decorated passages. Others, like Altamira and Niaux, contain a scattering of paintings and engravings in conjunction with one large panel covered with representations in a unified style. Beltran argues that the 'big room' at Altamira containing the unified panel of bison also contains earlier red paintings entirely different in 'style and conception' while other engravings and paintings, in the linear part of the cave, are also the product of several periods (1980: 621). Would changes in the Palaeolithic cognitive system over a period of 7,000 years weaken or obliterate a pattern represented in the art of a single phase? The curve of diminishing frequency of animal representations by species for the Palaeolithic (see table 11.1) could be construed as the superimposition of a 'San' pattern upon an earlier 'Aboriginal' one (or vice versa!).

If Palaeolithic 'mobiliary' art (decorated objects excavated from habitation debris) were shown to preserve a different structure of 'performance' this would strengthen the hypothesis that rock art occupied a particular place in

Upper Palaeolithic culture. A preliminary survey based on artefacts illustrated in Marshack (1972) suggests deer and humans are the *most* frequent motifs in this selective sample of mobile art, and that signs of the Sauvets' classes 3, 4, 5 and 6 are virtually absent. This includes all the types classically described as tectiforms, aviforms, and claviforms. While claviforms are similar in appearance over a wide area, tectiforms and aviforms show conspicuous local variation (Leroi-Gourhan 1958a: 320). It is possible that *if* the rock art were directly concerned with demarcating territorial units, this function is reflected in local variations of rectangular 'signs'. There is however some problem in treating all the mobile art as contemporaneous with the cave art; the decoration of artefacts may have persisted after the cave art ceased (Leroi-Gourhan 1968: 52), and therefore potentially reflect a different cognitive system. Since many of the open-air bas-reliefs probably predate the deeper cave art, Laming-Emperaire's suggestion that a structural contrast can be drawn between their respective subject matter also suffers from this objection (Laming-Emperaire 1962: 291–3).

Compositions: Animal Art

Lewis-Williams introduces a useful typology in his study of the Drakensberg art. *Juxtapositioning* puts together elements not seen in nature. It is significant that Lewis-Williams does not attempt to quantify this, on the grounds that intentional juxtapositioning is hard to verify (1981: 20). *Superpositioning*, perhaps intended, involved 20.6 per cent of eland and 4.6 per cent of human figures in one area. *Activity groups* constitute identifiable 'scenes', compositions in which figures are engaged in complementary activities (hunter and hunted, dancers in *ensemble*). Lewis-Williams identified 66 out of 1798 human figures as participants in such groups. *Conflation* combines elements of different models in a single motif, such as a human body with the head and feet of an eland, indicative of a perceived analogy between human and animal. Lewis-Williams found 72 examples in a sample of 3436 paintings (1981: 10–11, 19–22, 130). Vinnicombe had already recognized many of these types of association (1975: 330, 350). Activity groups most clearly belong in the category of 'sequential' relations; conflation in the category 'analogical' relations.

Is it possible to identify 'statements' in Palaeolithic rock art in which more than one signifying unit are combined? It is simplest to answer this question with respect to the most complex compositions, scenes. Identifiable scenes are virtually absent from the cave art. The most plausible candidate from the sample of 18 caves used in this paper is the Lascaux Pit 'Scene', apparently combining a bison, a human, a weapon, a stick and a rhinoceros. It has been variously interpreted (Ucko and Rosenfeld 1967: 41—4). Has the man disembowelled the bison or did the rhinoceros do it? Has the man died or is he in a shamanistic trance? Is it allegorical, or the record of an actual event? Does the rhinoceros have anything to do with the other figures?

The overwhelming majority of Palaeolithic cave paintings and engravings do not appear to be composed into scenes. The art resembles recent Aboriginal rock art in 'the static nature of figurative items, and their apparently hieratic distribution' (Rosenfeld 1982: 203). This is not the case with Drakensberg rock art. According to Lewis-Williams, most of the human figures are depicted in social groups, walking, running, dancing, fighting and hunting. Single human figures are comparatively rare (1981: 19). Vinnicombe tabulates 20 per cent of human compositions as 'scenes' (hunting, dancing, fighting, other) (1975: 363). Many paintings show humans and eland in conjunction.

On the balance of probabilities, it would seem that the absence of complex compositions in Palaeolithic and recent Aboriginal rock art is not the consequence of lack of skill on the artists' part, but an inherent feature of the art's cultural role (Layton 1985).

Less complex associations between motifs in Palaeolithic rock art have frequently been proposed. Laming-Emperaire suggested a typology for the association of animals on the basis of her work at Lascaux. Three types are recognized. First, the linear association of a number of animals of the same species; second, the linear association of animals of different species, unlikely to be seen together in nature. Many panels at Lascaux seemed to repeat the same juxtaposition: horse and bison; mammoth and auroch (Laming-Emperaire 1962: 280—4). Predatory animals seemed to be confined to inaccessible locations (1962: 271, 285). Sometimes Laming-Emperaire also detects *association by deliberate superpositioning* (Laming-Emperaire 1959: 162—4; 1962: 274).

Compositions: Signs

Sauvet, Sauvet and Wlodarczyk (1977) claim to have found regular associations between 'signs' belonging to different categories. They recognize three types of association: juxtaposition, superpositioning and integration (where two motifs have been combined to form a more complex form). They report that only certain combinations among those mathematically possible are found.

Analogical Relationships in Palaeolithic Art

Vinnicombe (1975) and Lewis-Williams (1981) argued convincingly that the repeated association of human and eland in San rock art provided a key to analogies drawn by San culture. Probably the most provocative type of association in Palaeolithic art is that between animal and 'sign'. Curiously enough, it is usually the more ambiguous 'sign' which is thought to provide the key to understanding the association (see introduction). Leroi-Gourhan, the great combiner in this field, goes to the extreme 'when each set of signs was analysed separately, it *leaped to the eye* that the ovals, triangle and quadrangular signs were all more or less abstract variations on the vulvas which appear among the earliest works of prehistoric art. As for the dots and strokes, it was *obvious* that they are male signs, although their degree of abstraction is beyond any simple similarity of form' (1968: 137; my emphasis). The conjunction of these signs with animals is argued to reveal that certain species (deer, ibex, horse) represent a male principle, others (large herbivores) a female principle. It seems clear, however, that for such representations simply to 'leap to the eye' is inadequate. Leroi-Gourhan's analysis sometimes depends on distinctions being made between what are formally very similar configurations. A 'scutiform' at Castillo (1958b: fig. 149) is inferred to be a 'female' sign because it is adjacent to rows of 'male' dots, while a similar 'scutiform' at Lascaux which occurs in isolation (fig. 170) is said, on the basis of an entirely hypothetical evolutionary sequence, to be a double sign containing both male and female elements (1958b: 386, 388).

Laming-Emperaire was led by her conclusion that particular species are consistently juxtaposed to argue that the art did not consist of the infinite repetition of single motifs: rather 'where one has read juxtaposition or superposition, one should read composition' (1962: 262). Her key for unlocking an analogical relationship is found in the association of human with animal representations. Open air friezes consist largely of horses. With them are realistic portrayals of women. The impression is one of familiarity and peacefulness (1962: 293). Down in the caves 'signs' abound, imaginary animals are depicted, silence creates an air of mystery. Small human figures cower among the teeming animals. It seems that although Laming-Emperaire rejected particular ethnographic parallels as a means of explaining the art, she has allowed her own preconceptions to take their place.

Leroi-Gourhan also rejected the use of 'a few ethnographic comparisons, taken from the most diverse of peoples' (1958a: 307), and tried to find a key in the art itself. Despite his desire 'not to impose on Palaeolithic thought our own categories or those of the Australians' (1958a: 307, 321), Leroi-Gourhan's classification also depends ultimately on subjective judgement. Nor does his division of caves into entrance/central panel/end stand up to re-examination; by no means all caves are so neatly divided, by no means all animals or signs occur where they should (Ucko and Rosenfeld 1967: 207–12, 234–9; Lorblanchet et al. 1973: 314).

The fact that Laming-Emperaire and Leroi-Gourhan construed the analogical value of the horse in opposite ways 'dealt a trump card to the critics of this new vision of Palaeolithic art' (Laming-Emperaire 1969: 1261). Laming-Emperaire's response was to formulate a new and ingenious explanation based explicitly on Lévi-Strauss's work. She rightly emphasized that the importance of Lévi-Strauss's analysis is its concern with cultural universals, thus potentially overcoming the difficulty of matching Palaeolithic art against specific ethnographic parallels. Lévi-Strauss showed that all conceivable human societies are built on reciprocal exchange, exemplified by the exchange of women between kin-based groups (1263). Perhaps this is what Palaeolithic art depicts?

The problem is that while reciprocity may be universal, cross-cousin marriage is merely one manifestation of it in any culture, and only occurs in some. There is no necessary reason why it, in particular, should be the subject of Palaeolithic art.

Does this mean that no analogical relationships can be inferred from Palaeolithic art? Not quite, perhaps. Laming-Emperaire drew attention to the special interest of the occasional imaginary creatures that appear: composite animals or hybrid figures with human body and animal head (1962: 287). It is a curious feature of Palaeolithic rock art that many alleged 'human' figures are particularly ambiguous. Ucko and Rosenfeld (1972) have attributed this to the fact that humans have few diagnostic features: neither tail, trunk, hoofs, wings nor horns. This does not prevent us from identifying convincing human figures in Aboriginal or San rock art; nor, in the latter, composite human-antelope figures. While nothing definite can be said about amorphous shapes, many of which may not be human, there are a few striking instances in the Palaeolithic where a figure more clearly suggests a composite human-animal: apparently bison-headed figures at Gabillou and Trois Frères, an apparently deer-headed figure at Trois Frères, a curious human body with a horned (?) head at Pergouset. Other motifs have been interpreted in similar terms (see, for example, Laming-Emperaire 1962: 232–5), but often they prove to be as ambiguous as the 'bison women' of Peche-Merle or the headless, two (?) legged animal at Bedeilhac. These figures may be hunters disguised, they may be masked dancers or they may be beings from a Palaeolithic cosmology. If they are *not* disguised hunters then it would seem they are evidence that *at some level* the Palaeolithic cognitive structure embodied a metaphorical relationship between human and animal: that, like the human-eland figures of the Drakensberg, they are symptoms of some perceived analogy between man and animal. What that analogy was, is obscure. The fact that the art concentrated on herd animals which were not the primary source of meat suggests that Upper Palaeolithic culture may, like that of the San, have perceived a parallel between human and animal social behaviour. To say more than this would be rash.

CONCLUSION

A comparison of Upper Palaeolithic cave art in Western Europe with that of recent Australian Aboriginal and Southern African San cultures, shows that while the Palaeolithic material is in some respects unique, it also exhibits interesting parallels with the modern traditions. The number of animal species portrayed is comparable. Some species are portrayed more often than others, and in this the Palaeolithic material resembles the San. Decorated caves are not randomly distributed but cluster in a fashion which suggests a correspondence with territorial units. Although the animal art seems to indicate that species held the same significance at all localities, variation in rectangular signs may relate directly to the differentiation of local areas. Scenes are not typical of Palaeolithic rock art and in this, it resembles recent Aboriginal art rather than that of the Drakensberg; apparently simply making 'positional' statements where the significant feature is the presence or absence of single motifs. There may, however, be some significant association of motifs at a level below that of the true 'scenes'. Plausible evidence for analogical relationships is hard to find, but there may be some parallel drawn between human and animal in the Palaeolithic cognitive system.

Looking for specific meanings in Palaeolithic motifs is frustrating and relatively unproductive. Looking for structure is easier, although there are problems in being sure that the structures we measure are always the direct reflection of Palaeolithic culture. Given the nature of human cognitive systems, however, it is surely less interesting to know whether, for example, the horse exemplified masculinity or femininity, than to show that Palaeolithic rock art has a structure comparable, in its complexity, to that of modern hunter-gatherers.

If we select a few key variables it is possible to visualize Upper Palaeolithic rock art, and the art of the modern hunter-gatherer cultures referred to in the paper, as occupying particular locations in a matrix, rather in the manner employed by Howe and Barnard (this volume) in their analysis of related cultures. Such a matrix (table 11.3) emphasizes that the Palaeolithic art presents a unique configuration, which counters the tendency for it to emerge as the lowest common denominator of better understood traditions.

Wobst (1978), Gamble (1982) and Mellars (1973), have all made the point that what was new about the Upper Palaeolithic in Europe was essentially a development in human culture, not a simple change in technology: art appears, subsistence 'strategies' become more specialized and more complex,

TABLE 11.3   Matrix comparing content of rock art traditions

Trait	Occurrence	
	Frequent	*Rare*
Humans	Kimberleys Drakensberg	Palaeolithic Kakadu x-ray
Scenes	Drakensberg	Kimberleys Palaeolithic Kakadu x-ray
	Clustered	*Not clustered*
Site distribution	Kimberleys Drakensberg Palaeolithic	Kakadu x-ray

the land is more densely populated, residential and hunting patterns are less affected by climatic change (see also Strauss and Clark 1983). If Lévi-Strauss, Piaget and Goodenough are right about the parallel structure of systems of communication and systems of social behaviour, a more fundamental point may be made: the structure seen in the art system would be evidence of cognitive capacities that would also permit more complex patterns in social relationships. I do not mean this in the precise sense of Laming's interpretation of the art at Lascaux as marriage exchange, but rather in the general sense of systems which can embody more units of meaning and conduct more complex logical operations on those units. Could it indeed be that in the Upper Palaeolithic changes in thought were taking place which were to be as important for human cultural development as those which were later achieved in classical Athens?

APPENDIX: COMPUTER ANALYSIS OF ROCK ART MOTIFS
M. T. Smith

Our approach to the analysis of motifs has been drawn from the formal analogy between the distribution of motifs in a number of rock art sites and the distribution of surnames in populations, a prominent theme in recent biological anthropology of historical and living populations.

The relationship between two populations is calculated from surname frequencies according to Lasker's (1977) extension of the original genetic model of isonomy within populations, proposed by Crow and Mange (1965). Several workers including myself (Smith and Hudson, 1984; Smith, Smith and Williams, in press) have subsequently employed the technique to estimate the genetic relationship between populations.

Formally, the relationship is described thus:

$$Ri = \sum \frac{nia}{2\,Na} \frac{nib}{Nb}$$

where nia is the frequency of the *ith* name in population a, and nib its frequency in population b. Na and Nb are the numbers of individuals in populations a and b respectively.

A coefficient of relationship within a population, or of a population with itself, can also be computed as

$$Raa = \sum \frac{(nia)^2}{2(Na)^2}$$

though this has the drawback of being dependent on population size.

In terms of the analysis of motifs

$$Ri = \sum \frac{nia}{2Na} \frac{nib}{Nb}$$

where nia is the frequency of the *ith* motif in site a and nib its frequency in site b. Na and Nb are the total number of images in sites a and b respectively.

There is no doubt that other coefficients of relationship would be adequate for this analysis. The isonymic model came to mind and to hand readily simply because I was already using it. It does have, however, some properties which make it particularly apt in the present situation. It takes into account (a) the types of motif, (b) the numbers of each motif and (c) the distribution of types and their frequency within and between sites. It thus retains much more detailed information than previous analyses.

After the matrix of relationships has been computed, a visual 'map' of it is produced by means of Kruskal's non-metric multidimensional scaling algorithm implemented in the SPACES analysis package. Such a visual plot allows a clear distinction to be seen between the European cave art and the Australian rock art. Whereas the former has the same highly repeated motifs (e.g. horse, bison) in many sites, yielding a tight cluster due to high relationships between sites, the Australian pattern of lower frequency of motifs and greater variation in their choice between sites yields lower relationships and a more dispersed 'map' of sites (figures 11.2 and 11.3).

Rosenfeld's (1982) claim that there are different types of Aboriginal shelter, each with a different and characteristic constellation of motifs, suggests that a 'map' of relationships among Aboriginal sites should cluster, not according to

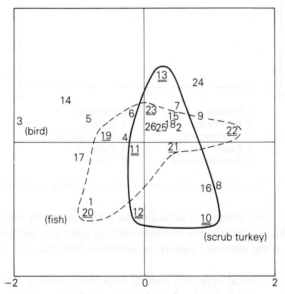

(bird) example of location of particular motif type

Ref.
no. Site name

1	Above Pig	10	Horse 1 ⎫	19 Quinkan ⎫
2	Bull	11	H 2 ⎬ Giant Horse	20 Q 2 ⎬ Quinkan
3	Croc	12	H 3 ⎭ site complex	21 Q 3 ⎬ site complex
4	Emu	13	H 4	22 Q 5 ⎭
5	Ginger CK 1	14	Mungin	23 Q 6
6	Ginger CK 2–6	15	Mushroom	24 Red Bluff
7	Gugu Y 1–6	16	Norm	25 Split Rock
8	G Y 7	17	Pig	26 Sp 2
9	Hopev T'Off	18	Plat	

Figure 11.2 Clustering of Laura sites according to motifs present

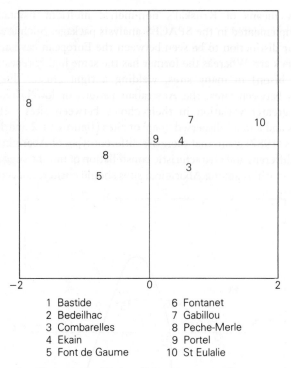

8		
	7	10
	9 4	
8	3	
5		

-2   0   2

1 Bastide   6 Fontanet
2 Bedeilhac   7 Gabillou
3 Combarelles   8 Peche-Merle
4 Ekain   9 Portel
5 Font de Gaume   10 St Eulalie

Figure 11.3   Clustering of Palaeolithic sites according to motifs present

geography or clan estate but according to particular motif complexes. An analysis of this situation by the methods outlined suggests that this is indeed a component of the observed pattern of variation, but that it is not the sole determinant.

A further analytical approach seeking Rosenfeld's shelter types has been made by factor analysis, but has been less than perfectly satisfactory owing to the high factor scores given to some unique or rare motifs. However, some of the lower-scoring factors do seem to represent clusters with relevance to the real world as well as to the computer.

NOTES

1   The Palaeolithic data discussed here were collected during a research project directed by Peter Ucko from University College London, between 1971 and 1973. The 1973 fieldwork was financed by a grant from the Social Science Research

Council. In proposing an analysis of Palaeolithic art I have been greatly influenced by Peter Ucko; specifically, I am grateful for his comments on an earlier version of this paper. In revising the paper I have also taken into account Alan Rumsey's helpful comments on Layton 1985.

2   Lascaux, Ekain, Peche-Merle, Fontanet, Ste Eulalie (original publications), Gabillou, Font de Gaume, Combarelles (Ucko and Rosenfeld 1967: 232—9); Hornos de la Pena (our survey), Mas d'Azil, La Bastide, Portel, Bedeilhac (original publications checked by us during survey). Pair-non-pair, La Greze, Gorge d'Enfer, Villars, Cougnac (Leroi-Gourhan 1968).

REFERENCES

Bailey, G. 1983. Economic change in late Pleistocene Cantabria. In *Hunter-gatherer Economy in Prehistory: a European Perspective* (ed.) G. Bailey. Cambridge: Cambridge University Press.

Beltran, A. 1980. Comments on Conkey 1980. *Current Anthropology* 21: 621—2.

Bern, J. and R. Layton. 1984. The local descent group and the division of labour in the Cox River land claim. In *Aboriginal Landowners* (ed.) L. R. Hiatt. Sydney: Oceania Monographs (27).

Blundell, V. 1982. Symbolic systems and cultural continuity in Northwest Australia: a consideration of Aboriginal cave art. *Culture* 2: 3—20.

Breuil, H. 1952. *Quatre cents siècles d'art pariétal*. Montignac: Windels.

Buckley, W. 1967. *Sociology and Modern Systems Theory*. Englewood Cliffs, New Jersey: Prentice Hall.

Clark, G. A. and Strauss, L. G. 1983. Late Pleistocene hunter-gatherer adaptations in Cantabrian Spain. In *Hunter-gatherer Economy in Prehistory: a European perspective* (ed.) G. Bailey. Cambridge: Cambridge University Press.

Conkey, M. 1980. The identification of prehistoric hunter-gatherer aggregation sites: the case of Altamira. *Current Anthropology* 21: 609—20.

Crawford, I. 1968. *The Art of the Wandjina*. London: Oxford University Press.

Crow, J. F. and A. P. Mange. 1965. Measurement of inbreeding from the frequency of marriages between persons of the same surname. *Eugenics Quarterly* 12: 199—203.

Davis, W. 1984. Representation and knowledge in the prehistoric rock art of Africa. *African Archaeological Review* 2: 7—35.

Delteil, J., P. Durbas and L. Wahl. 1972. Présentation de la galerie ornée de Fontanet. *Bul. Soc. Pre. Ariège* 27.

Elkin, A. P. 1961. The Yabaduruwa. *Oceania* 31: 166—209.

Fox, R. W., G. G. Kelleher and C. B. Kerr. 1977. *Ranger Uranium Environmental Inquiry, second report*. Canberra: Australian Government Publishing Service.

Gamble, C. S. 1982. Interaction and alliance in Palaeolithic society. *Man* (N.S.) 17: 92—107.

Goodenough, W. H. 1965. Rethinking status and role. In *The Relevance of Models for Social Anthropology* (ed.) M. Banton. London: Tavistock.

Gowlett, J. A. J. 1984. Mental abilities of early man: a look at some hard evidence. In *Hominid Evolution and Community Ecology* (ed.) R. Foley. London: Academic Press.

Hewes, G. W. 1973. An explicit formulation of the relationship between tool-using, tool-making, and the emergence of language. *Visible Language* 7: 101–27.

Hockett, C. and R. Ascher. 1964. The human revolution. *Current Anthropology* 5: 135–47.

Holloway, R. L. 1969. Culture: a *human* domain. *Current Anthropology* 10: 395–412.

Horton, R. 1960. A definition of religion and its uses. *Journal of the Royal Anthropological Institute* 90: 201–26.

—— 1964. Ritual man in Africa. *Africa* 34: 85–104.

Kitahara-Frisch, J. 1980. Symbolizing technology as a key to human evolution. In *Symbol as sense* (eds) M. L. Foster and S. H. Brandes. New York: Academic Press.

Kuhn, H. 1956. *The Rock Pictures of Europe*. London: Sidgwick.

Laming-Emperaire, A. 1959. *Lascaux*. Paris: Voici Science Information.

—— 1962. *La Signification de l'Art Rupestre Paléolithique*. Paris: Picard.

—— 1969. Pour une nouvelle approche des sociétés préhistoriques. *Annales* 5: 1261–9.

Lasker, G. W. 1977. A coefficient of relationship by isonymy: A method for estimating the genetic relationship between populations. *Human Biology* 49: 489–93.

Layton, R. 1977. Naturalism and cultural relativity in art. In *Form in indigenous art* (ed.) P. J. Ucko. Canberra: Institute of Aboriginal Studies.

—— 1981a. *The Anthropology of Art*. London: Granada.

—— 1981b. Communication in ritual: two examples and their social context. *Canberra Anthropology* 4: 110–24.

1985. The cultural context of hunter-gatherer rock art. *Man* (N.S.) 20: 434–53.

Leroi-Gourhan, A. 1958a. La fonction des signes dans les sanctuaires paléolithiques. *Bul. Soc. Pré. Française* 55: 307–21.

—— 1958b. Le symbolisme des grands signes dans l'art pariétal paléolithique. *Bul. Soc. Pré. Française* 55: 384–98.

—— 1964. *Les Religions de la Préhistoire*. Paris: Presses Universitaires de France.

—— 1968. *The Art of Prehistoric Man in Western Europe* (trans.) N. Guterman. London: Thames and Hudson.

Lévi-Strauss, C. 1962. *Totemism* (trans.) R. Needham. London: Merlin.

—— 1963. *Structural Anthropology* (trans.) C. Jacobson and B. G. Schoepf. New York: Basic Books.

—— 1966. *The Savage Mind*. London: Weidenfeld.

Lewis-Williams, D. 1981. *Believing and Seeing: symbolic meanings in southern San rock paintings*. London: Academic Press.

Lorblanchet, M., F. Delpech, P. Renault and C. Andrieux. 1973. La grotte de Sainte-Eulalie à Espagnac. *Gallia Préhistoire* 16: 233–325.

Macintosh, N. W. G. 1977. Beswick Creek cave two decades later: a reappraisal. In *Form in Indigenous Art* (ed.) P. J. Ucko. Canberra: Australian Institute of Aboriginal Studies.

Maddock, K. 1982. *The Australian Aborigines*. 2nd edn. London: Penguin.

Marshack, A. 1972. *The Roots of Civilization*. London: Weidenfeld.

Mellars, P. A. 1973. The character of the middle-upper Palaeolithic divide in southwest France. In *The explanation of culture change* (ed.) C. Renfrew. London: Duckworth.

Mounin, G. 1970. *Introduction à la Sémiologie*. Paris: Minuit.

Munn, N. D. 1964. Totemic designs and group continuity in Walbiri cosmology. In *Aborigines now* (ed.) M. Reay. Sydney: Angus and Robertson.

___ 1973. *Walpiri Iconography*. Ithaca: Cornell University Press.

Orme, B. 1981. *Anthropology for Archaeologists*. London: Duckworth.

Piaget, J. 1971. *Structuralism*. London: Routledge and Kegan Paul.

Rosenfeld, A. 1982. Style and meaning in Laura art. *Mankind* 13: 199—217.

Rosenfeld, A., D. Horton and J. Winter. 1981. *Early Man in North Queensland*. Terra Australis, 6, Department of Prehistory, Research School of Pacific Studies, Australian National University.

Sauvet, G., S. Sauvet and A. Wlodarczyk. 1977. Essai de sémiologie préhistorique *Bul. Soc. Pré. Française* 74: 545—58.

Smith, M. T. and B. L. Hudson. 1984. Isonymic relationships in the parish of Fylingdales, North Yorkshire in 1851. *Annals of Human Biology* 11: 141—8.

Smith, M. T., B. L. Smith and W. R. Williams. (in press). Changing isonymic relationships in the parish of Fylingdales, North Yorkshire, 1841—1881. *Annals of Human Biology*.

Trezise, P. J. 1971. *Rock Art of South-East Cape York*. Canberra: Australian Institute of Aboriginal Studies.

Ucko, P. J. 1977. Opening remarks. In *Form in indigenous art* (ed.) P. J. Ucko. Canberra: Australian Institute of Aboriginal Studies.

Ucko, P. J. and R. H. Layton. (in press). Subjectivity and the recording of Palaeolithic cave art. To appear in proceedings of the International Colloquium on Palaeolithic rock art held in Perigeux, November 1984.

Ucko, P. J. and A. Rosenfeld. 1967. *Palaeolithic Cave Art*. London: Weidenfeld.

___ 1972. Anthropomorphic representations in Palaeolithic art. *Actas del Symposium de Arte Rupestre*, Santander 1972.

Vinnicombe, P. 1975. *People of the Eland*. Pietermaritzburg: University of Natal Press.

Wobst, H. M. 1978. The Archaeo-ethnology of hunter-gatherers or the tyranny of the ethnographic record in archaeology. *American Antiquity* 43: 303—9.

Index

Abimbola, W., 111
Abuja people, 91
Africa, 91, 100—1
  ethnicity, 174, 178—83, 185
  history and culture, 88—118
  kinship and marriage, 55—6, 57,
    58—60, 63, 95—6, 98—9
  pastoralism, 155, 158—60, 163—5
  political systems, 95, 100—8
  religion, 88—9, 94—7, 106—8,
    110—11, 163, 180
agriculture, 31, 143, 147
Akan people, 88—9, 107, 110—11, 112
  see also Asante
Allan, W., 157
alliance see under kinship
Amerindians, 77—80, 83—4, 90
amorphous rock art, 221
analogical relationships in rock art,
    214—17, 229—32
anarchist/dadaist methodology, 70—1
ancestor cult, 95, 97—8, 143
Anderson, B., 170, 177, 178
Anderson, P., 109, 110
animals in art see rock art
Ardener, E., 61
art, 64—5, 66
  see also rock art
Asad, T., 155, 157, 160
Asante kingdom, 102—8, 110, 113

Ascher, R., 214
Asdiwal, 27
Asia
  kinship, 56, 57, 129—30
  time and colour concepts, 123—8
    passim
Australian aborigines, 124—5, 193
  rock art of, 213—17, 219—20,
    223—4, 227, 229—35 passim
avoidance category in Khoisan kinship
    terms, 194—208
Azande people, 55

Bailey, G., 224
Baines, J., 130
Bali
  caste system, 135—52
  cultural concepts and language,
    30—1, 36, 39—44, 47, 59, 139
  kinship and marriage, 34—5, 143,
    145
  politics, 31, 33
  witchcraft, 35, 46
Bambara people, 105
Bantu people, 57, 59, 61, 91, 96,
    98—9, 190
Barley, N. F., 36
Barnard, A.: on Khoisan kinship, 15,
    17, 189—209, 232

Barnes, B., 24, 71, 75—6, 78, 134, 150
Barnes, R. H., 45, 121, 125, 129—30,
    141
  on comparison, 10, 15, 17, 19—34,
    153
Barth, F., 145, 149, 157, 158,
    159—60, 161—3, 165, 185
Bartlett, H. H., 126
Bascom, W. R., 111
Basseri people, 159—60
Basso, K. H., 7
Batak people, 126
Bateson, G., 45
believing, kinds of, 36
Beltran, A., 227
Bendix, R., 109
Benin kingdom, 102—5
Bennett, P., 179
Benoist, J.—M., 45
Beowulf translations, 74—5, 80
Bergdama *see* Damara
Berghe, P. van den, 169, 176,
    184, 185
Berlin, B., 121—4, 126
Berlin, L. A., 123
Bern, J., 214
Beteille, A., 7
bilocality, 57
binary *see* duality
Binsbergen, W. van, 89, 178, 183
Bloch, M., 30—1, 34, 45—6, 109, 121,
    126—9
Bloor, D., 71, 75—6, 78, 151
Blumer, H., 6
Blundell, V., 214
Boas, F., 93
Boon, J., 16, 136, 138, 142
Bornstein, M. H., 126
Bosch, F. D. K., 40, 143
Botswana, 190
Bouglé, C., 142
boundaries, ethnic, 176
Bourdieu, P., 25, 154
Bourdillon, M. F. C., 30
Bradbury, R. E., 98, 102, 104—5, 112

Brain, R., 185
branching, concrete history and culture
    (West Africa), 90, 91
Brandstetter, R., 126
Breton, R., 173
Breuil, H., 211, 218
bridgeheads *see* universality
Brown, C. H., 123
Brush, S., 6, 157
Buckley, W., 212
Buddhism, 138, 143
Bura people, 185
Burghart, R., 141
Burke, K., 26, 43
Burnham, P., 57
  on pastoralism, 15, 17, 153—67,
    237
Burton, R. F., 107
Bushmen/San people, 190—208 *passim*
  rock art of, 213, 215—17, 219—24,
    227—33 *passim*
Bushong people, 99
Busia, K. A., 107

call systems, 214, 217, 227
Cameroon, 163, 185
  see also Chamba
Cancian, F., 7
caste system, 39, 42, 52, 59, 92
  in Bali and India, comparison of,
    135—52
  conceptual level, 137—41
  institutional level, 141—4
  interactional level, 144—9
categories in Khoisan relationship
    terms, 194—7
caves *see* rock art
centralization, political, 101—6
Cesara, M., 7
Cézanne, P., 64—6
Chamba people, 179—82
chant language, 79
children
  Khoisan terms for, 194—208 *passim*
  marriage payments and, 58—9

Chilver, E. M., 181
Christianity, 107, 112
Cicourel, A., 6
Clark, G. A., 224, 226, 233
Clifford, J., 185
closed-signal call systems *see*
    call systems
co-activity, standardized modes of, 34
Cohen, A., 30, 184
Cohen, P. S., 45
Cohen, R., 3, 170, 172, 184, 185
Cohn, B. S., 100
Colby, B. N., 7
collective representations, 35, 36—7
Collingwood, R. G., 24, 30, 32, 44, 45,
    46
colour concepts, 17, 121—6, 140
Colson, E., 4—5
coming of age of anthropology, 22—51
    science and, 23—8
    translation, 37—42
commensurability, 71
    see also incommensurability
comparative anthropology, 119—34
    continuity, search for, 52—69
comparison
    contemporary problems, 15—18
    cross-cultural, 9—12
    definition, 29
    functional correlations established, 9
    and generalization, 1, 12—15
    intra-cultural, 12
    styles of, 9—12
compositions in rock art, 228—9
computer analysis of rock art, 233—6
Comte, A., 67, 92
conceptual level of caste system,
    137—41
concrete history and culture, 90, 91
Conkey, M., 224, 226
Conklin, H. C., 122, 123, 125
constructions, social facts as, 5, 7, 10
continuity, comparison as search for,
    52—69

convention and nature, distinction
    between, 29—30
Coppet, D. de, 121, 130
Coquery-Vidrovitch, C., 185
Crabb, R. G., 32
Crawford, I., 214
creativity *see* translation
Crick, M., 6, 52
Croce, B., 45
cross-cousin marriage, 57
cross-cultural correlations facilitating
    description, 9—12
crossing over, 61
Crow, J. F., 234
cubism, 65—6
Culler, J., 26, 45, 85
culture and nature linked, 30, 34
    see also history and culture
Cunningham, C., 60
Curr, E. M., 124

dadaism, 66
    methodological, 70—1
Dahl, G., 156—7
Dahomey kingdom, 102—8, 112
Daka language (Chamba), 179—82
Damara people, 190—1
dams *see* water
Dani people, 124
Das, V., 141
Davis, W., 211
deconstruction, 65—6, 74, 85
Delteil, J., 218
derogatory objections and growth of
    ethnicity concept, 173—4
Derrida, J., 45, 62, 65
descent *see under* kinship
description
    and comparison, 9—12
    and generalization, 1, 2—9
deviance, 35
dichotomy *see* duality
differences *see* similarities
Dinka people, 185

discourse, 17, 23, 32—3, 53—4
  see also language
Divinity as regularity, 30
divorce rates, 112
Dolgin, J. L., 6
Donato, E., 45
Donoghue, D., 26
Douglas, J. D., 6
Douglas, M., 98, 99
Dracula legend, 26—8
Drakensberg *see* Kimberley
Driver, H. E., 4, 5, 120
duality, 12, 32, 36, 46, 58—63,
  124—5, 142
Duff-Cooper, A., 30
Dumézil, G., 91
Dumont, L., 120—1, 123, 125, 137—8,
  141—2
Dupire, M., 57, 163—4
Durbas, P., 218
Durbin, M., 123
Durkheim, E., 2, 31, 64, 127, 130—1
Dyson-Hudson, N., 156, 157, 162
Dyson-Hudson, R., 155, 162

Eades, J. S., 104
eating, 39—40, 224
Echols, J. M., 40
Edo people, 98, 102—5
Edwards, A. C., 95
Eggan, F., 3, 93, 96, 119, 193
egocentric Khoisan relationship terms,
  199—205
Egypt, ancient, 92
Elkin, A. P., 214, 215
Ellen, R. F., 7
Elster, J., 113
Engelbrecht, J. A., 203, 204, 205
Epstein, A. L., 62, 184
essences, 24, 40—2
Ethiopia, 123
ethnicity, limits to comparability of,
  17, 168—88
  African ethnogenesis, 182—3

Chamba ethnogenesis, 179—82
comparative anthropology and,
  168—9
growth of concept, 171—4
nationalism and autonomization of,
  170, 177—8, 184
subjective and objective, 174—7
Evans-Pritchard, E. E., 8, 45, 82, 95,
  99, 101
  on comparative method, 2—3, 52, 90,
  97, 119—21, 135, 153—4
  on generalization, 154, 156
  on history, 97, 100, 154
  on participant observation, 120
  on rationality and the mystical, 83
  on realism, 78
  on time, 128—9
  on universal laws, 81
everyday judgements, 16, 17, 55
evil, 35
evolution, 90—1, 93, 94, 155, 173
explanation, 89, 100

Fabian, J., 44, 173
facts, social, 5, 23, 24, 28—9, 31—2,
  34, 154
family *see* kinship; marriage systems
Fardon, R., 57, 96
  on ethnicity, 15, 16, 17, 168—88
Ferguson, A., 90
Feyerabend, P., 24, 28, 45, 70—3, 75,
  76, 78, 80, 81—2
Filmer, P., 6
Firth, R., 34
Fon people, 99
food, 39—40, 224
Forde, C. D., 95, 100, 101
Fortes, M., 94—5, 97—8, 101, 103,
  172
Foucault, M., 26
Fox, J. J., 141
Fox, R. W., 215
France: rock art, 218, 224, 231
Frankenstein legend, 27—8

Frazer, Sir J., 94
Fremantle, J. M., 182
Friedman, J., 161
Frobenius, L., 181
Fulani people, 105, 155, 158, 160,
    163—5, 180
Fuller, C., 141
functionalism, 9, 96—7, 158—61,
    173, 174

Galton, F., 4, 93, 184
Gamble, C. S., 233
game analogy, 59
Ganda people, 100
Gandonu, A., 185
Garbosa, B. S., 182
Garfinkel, H., 6, 154
Gbadamosi, T. G. O., 111
Geertz, C., 7, 45—6, 53, 131, 134, 142
    on kinship, 34, 143, 144
    on politics, 31, 33, 36
    on religion, 106, 137—8
Geertz, H., 34, 136, 142—4
Gellner, E., 177, 184
generalization, 154, 156
    and comparison, 1, 12—15
    and description, 1, 2—9
generative models of pastoralism,
    159—62
Ginsberg, M., 90, 91
Girard, R., 26
Giriama language, 61
Glaser, B. G., 6, 8
Glazer, N., 173
global comparisons, 56—60, 64
Gluckman, M., 98—9, 102, 184
Godelier, M., 174
Goldschmidt, W., 158—9, 160
Gonja kingdom, 103
Good, A., 194
Goodenough, W. H., 1, 212, 233
Goodman, N., 28—9, 32, 46, 71, 84
Goody, J., 9, 45, 102, 103, 105, 106,
    193
Gowing, L., 65

Gowlett, J. A. J., 212
Grice, H. P., 46—7
grounded theory, 8
Gruber, J., 192, 207
Guinea, 164
Gwiwi people, 198—201

Habermas, J., 154
Hacking, I., 45, 74, 76
Hai—//om people, 191—2, 195—6
Hallpike, C. R., 45
Hammel, E. A., 89, 93
Hanson, F. A., 7
Hanunóo people, 123, 125
Hausa-Fulani people *see* fulani
Hawkes, T., 71
Hayes, E. N. and T. A., 45
Hays, D. G., 123
Heider, E. R., 124
Heinz, H. J., 206
herd size, minimum *see under*
    pastoralism
Héritier, F., 56, 57, 130
Herskovits, M. J., 104, 107, 108
Hesse, M., 43, 72
Heusch, L. de, 57, 60, 91, 96
Hewes, G. W., 212
Hickerson, N. P., 122
Hinduism, 123
    see also caste system
Hirsch, E. R., 38
history and culture (West Africa),
    88—118
    branching, concrete, 90, 91
    ideal, universal, 90—1, 92—3
    ignored, 90, 94—5
    not societies, 99, 108—10
    regional comparative studies, 90,
        95—108
Hjort, A., 156—7
≠ Hoa people, 192, 207
Hobart, M., 59, 60, 71, 136, 139,
    142, 145
    on coming of age of anthropology, 4,
        13, 15, 16, 17, 22—51

Hobhouse, L. T., 91
Hobsbawm, E., 177
Hocart, A. M., 91, 92
Hockett, C., 214
Hoernlé, A. W., 198, 201, 203, 205
holistic presentism, 97, 99
Hollis, M., 30, 37—8, 71, 75, 78
Holloway, R. L., 212
Holy, L.: on description, generalization
    and comparison, 1—21
homesteads *see* houses
Horton, D., 216
Horton, R., 30, 88—9, 91, 107, 112,
    212
Hottentots *see* Khoekhoe
houses/homesteads
    concept, 77—8
    property complex, 98—9
    spatial organization, 59
Howe, L., 30
    on caste, 15, 16, 17, 135—52, 232
Hudson, B. L., 234
Humboldt, Von, 91
hunter-gatherers *see* Bushman;
    Khoisan; rock art

Ibn Khaldun, 155
ideal
    type, concept of, 162—3
    universal, history and culture (West
        Africa), 90—1, 92—3
idealization of pastoralism, 155
ideological errors, 175
ideology, religion and state, 106—8
Ifa cult, 110—12
Ife *see* Yoruba
Igbo people, 99
Ilesha kingdom, 104
Iliffe, J., 110
impressionism, 64—5, 66
incoherences, 28—32
incommensurability, 71—6, 81—2
    see also translation
Inden, R., 26

India, 57, 123, 124
    caste system, 130, 135—47 *passim*
Indo-European as ancestral language, 91
Indonesia, 47, 58, 125—6, 137,
    143, 193
    see also Bali
induction, 24
Ingold, T., 157, 159, 161
inheritance *see under* kinship
institutional level of caste system
    comparison, 141—4
institutions, social, 34
interactional level of caste system
    comparison, 144—9
intergenerational transfer of livestock,
    163—4
interpretative anthropology: description
    and generalization, 5—9
intra-cultural comparison, 12
inversion, 35
Ions, E., 25—6, 45
Iran, 160, 161
Irons, W., 156
irrationality, 75
irrigation *see* water
Isajiw, W. W., 170
Islam *see* Muslim

Jacobson-Widding, A., 123
Java, 40, 47, 137, 143
Johnson, M., 72, 105, 106
joking category in Khoisan kinship
    terms, 194—208
Jones, G. L., 91, 100
Jorgensen, J. G., 4
Josselin de Jong, J. P. B. de, 130, 193
Josselin de Jong, P. E. de, 130

Kaberry, P., 100, 101, 181
Kant, I., 128—9
Kaplan, A., 7
Kaplan, D., 78
Kaplan, M. R., 84
Karim, W. — J. B., 26
Karo Batak people, 126

Kay, P., 121—4, 126
Kédang people, 125, 126
Kedourie, E., 178, 184
Kelleher, G. G., 215
Kemnitzer, D. S., 6
Kenya, 58, 63
Kerr, C. B., 215
Kersten, J., 40
Khoekhoe (Nama/Hottentots) people,
    189—92, 195—6, 198—204, 206
Khoe-speaking people *see* Khoisan
Khoisan kinship: regional comparison
    and underlying structures,
    189—209
  interpretation and comparison,
    192—4
  peoples, 189—91
  relationship terms: categories and,
    194—7; egocentric, 199—205;
    reciprocal, 197—9
Kikuyu people, 63—4
Kimball, S., 7
Kimberley and Drakensberg rock art,
    215—17, 220—3, 227—9, 231—5
kinship 8, 34
  concept, 74, 79—80, 122, 129—30
  other concepts: alliance, 56, 74,
    81, 129—30; descent, 55—6,
    62—3, 74, 81, 129—30;
    inheritance, 163—4; lineage, 98,
    101, 104, 106, 112—13
  see also marriage
Kitahara-Frisch, J., 212
Klein, A. M., 113
Köbben, A. J. F., 2, 3, 9, 119—20, 185
Kopytoff, I., 185
Korana people, 191, 205
Korn, V. E., 137
Korongo people, 67
Kripke, S., 46
Kroeber, A. L., 120—1
Kuhn, T., 6, 24, 25, 72—3, 135
!Kung people, 190, 192, 202, 206
Kuper, A., 45, 59, 60, 96, 112, 193
Kuper, L., 170

labelling, 83—4
  power of, 73—6
  see also ethnicity
Lakatos, I., 24
Lakoff, G., 72
Laming-Emperaire, A., 211, 228, 229,
    230—1, 233
Lancaster, C. S., 179
language
  colour and, 122—3
  ethnicity and, 179—82
  food and eating, 39—40
  Indo-European as ancestral, 91
  'material-object', 30
  rock art and, 212—15, 217
  signs and, 36
  see also discourse: Khoisan;
    metaphor; motifs; translation
Lascaux rock art, 210, 211, 228, 229
Lasker, G. W., 234
Laura rock art, 215—16, 220—4, 227,
    235
law
  in Bali, 140
  natural, 24
Law, R. C. C., 102, 104, 106
Layton, R.: on rock art, 16, 210—39
Leach, E., 45, 55
  on descent, 56
  on inversion, 35
  on marriage, 34, 74, 129
  rubber sheet metaphor, 55, 57, 67
  on statistics and reification, 3, 154
Leech, G., 122
Lekkerkerker, C., 136
Leko language (Chamba), 179—81
Lele people, 99
Leroi-Gourhan, A., 210, 211, 218, 228,
    230—1
Leur, J. C. van, 143
Lévi-Strauss, C., 45, 55, 64, 67, 91, 95
  on generalization and comparison, 25
  on models, 34
  on myths, 26—7, 57, 169
  on 'Omaha alliance', 130

on rock art, 211—12, 231, 233
on time, 127
on totemism, 52, 74
Levin, S. R., 26
Lewis, I. M., 92, 97, 100, 112
Lewis-Williams, D., 215, 216—17, 228—9
lineage *see under* kinship
linguistics *see* language
Littlejohn, J., 60
Littleton, C. S., 91
livestock *see* pastoralism
Lloyd, G. E. R., 26, 45
Lloyd, P. C., 100, 102—4, 112
Lorblanchet, M., 231
Losee, J., 24
Lounsbury, F., 79
Lozi people, 99, 102
Lukes, S., 75, 78, 130—1
Luo people, 11, 63—4

McCaskie, T. C., 107, 108, 110, 112
Macintosh, N. W. G., 215—16
Macksey, R., 45
Maasai people, 158
Madan, T. N., 7
Maddock, K., 214
magic, 94
    concept, 83—4, 85
    see also witchcraft
Maitland, F. W., 92—3, 109
Mali, 164
Malinowski, B., 97, 211
Manchester School, 174
Mange, A. P., 234
marriage systems and family type, 34, 52, 143, 145
    concept, 11, 74
    cross-cousin, 57
    dual, 58
    matrilineal, 103, 113
    matrilocal, 57
    monogamous, 63
    nuclear, 122
    pastoralists, 163

patrilineal, 99
patrilocal, 57
payments, 58—9
polygynous, 63
rock art and, 214
see also kinship
Marshack, A., 210, 228
Marshall, L., 206
Masina state, 105, 106
'material-object' language, 30
matrilineage, 103, 113
matrilocality, 57
Maupoil, B., 107, 112
Mayer, A., 142, 147
Mazrui, A., 183
meaning, 6—7, 10, 63
medicines, 35
Meek, C. K., 179—80
Meek, R. L., 90
Mellars, P. A., 224, 233
men
    Khoisan terms for, 194—208 *passim*
    marriage payments and, 58—9
Mercier, P., 107
Mesakin people, 67
metaphors, 26, 46, 72
    of society, 52—5, 61—2, 66—7
metaphysical ideas, different *see* incommensurability
method, modes of comparative *see* history and culture
metonymy, 26
Middleton, J., 98, 113, 172
Mijikenda people, 11, 58
Mill, J. S., 89, 92, 94
minimum herd size *see under* pastoralism
Mitchell, J. C., 184
modes of comparative method, *see* history and culture
Monod, T., 156—7
monogamy, 63
Montesquieu, C. Baron de, 155
Moore, B., 109, 110
Morgan, L. H., 101

Morton-Williams, P., 101, 102—3, 112
Mossi kingdom, 103
motifs of rock art, 219—32
    amorphous, 221
    analogical relationships, 229—32
    animals, 219, 228—9
    compositions, 228—9
    computer analysis of, 233—6
    performance in, 221—8
    'signs', 219—21, 229
Mounin, G., 214, 220
Moynihan, D., 173
Muller, J. C., 57
Munn, N. D., 217
Murdock, G. P. 3, 15, 45
Mursi people, 123
music, 44
Muslim societies in Africa, 98, 106,
    110, 163, 180
myths, 57, 91, 111
    structure of, 26—8

Nadel, S. F., 34, 46, 67, 95—6, 98,
    134, 172
Nagel, E., 45
Nairn, T., 178
Nama people *see* Khoekhoe
name, power of *see* translation
naming *see* labelling
Naroll, R., 3, 93, 120, 185
nationalism and autonomization of
    ethnicity, 170, 177—8, 184
'natural' category, pastoralism as,
    155—6
natural history of society, 90—1, 100
natural law, 24
nature
    and convention, distinction between,
        29—30
    and culture linked, 30, 34
Ndembu people, 123
Needham, R., 45
    on Bali, 41
    on comparative method, 3, 8, 13—14,
        95, 135

on ethnicity, 170
on inversion, 35
on kinship, 34, 52, 74, 194—8
on polythetic classification, 62
on Purum classification, 12
on reification, 154
New Calabar, 91
New Guinea, 124
Nguni people, 59, 60
Nharo people, 197—201, 203, 206
Nietzsche, F., 170, 182
Niger, 91, 105, 163
Nigeria, 163
    see also Chamba; Yoruba
Ñnakenyaré identity, 180—1
nomadism, 155, 156—7, 165, 190
nominal objections and growth of
    ethnicity concept, 172
Northrup, D., 106
nourishment, 39—40, 224
Nuba people, 96
nuclear family, 122
Nuer people, 127—8, 185
numerical system, 124—5

objectivity, 4, 174—7
observation, participant, 120
occupation *see* caste
Oedipus myth, 26—7
Okamura, J., 185
Okely, J., 7
Omaha people, 129—30
Ondo kingdom, 104
Onvlee, L., 124, 125
!Ora people, 191
order, 30
Orme, B., 211
Ortner, S. B., 10
Ortony, A., 72
Otite, O., 105
Overing, J., 15, 26, 30, 41, 131
    on translation, 6, 12, 16, 17, 43,
        70—87
Overing Kaplan, J., 76, 77, 81
Ovo kingdom *see* Yoruba

Pabir people, 185
Palaeolithic *see* rock art
Panoff-Eliet, F., 123
Parkin, D., 6, 11, 14, 31, 35, 53, 61—2
 on continuity, 12, 15, 17, 43,
  52—69, 149, 213
Parkin, R. J., 121, 130
Parry, J., 141—2, 147
participant observation, 120
pastoralism, 153—67
 as comparative category, 155—7
 Fulani example, 163—4
 generative models, 159—62
 minimum herd size, 157—9, 160, 162,
  163, 164
 see also Khoisan
patrilinearity, 99
patrilocality, 57
payments, marriage, 58—9
Peel, J. D. Y., 100, 101, 104—5,
 112, 113
 on history and culture, 15, 88—118
Peirce, C. S., 67
Pepper, S. C., 28
performance in rock art, 221—8
perspectives, endless, 67, 149
 see also continuity
Phillips, D. L., 7
Phillipson, M., 7
Piaget, J., 64, 213, 233
Piaroa people, 77—80, 83—4
political centralization, 105—6
politics and agriculture, 31
polygyny, 63
Pontie, G., 185
Popper, K., 24, 134
positivistic anthropology
 comparison and generalization,
  12—15
 description and generalization 1, 2—5
power, 30, 33, 46
 of labelling, 73—6
 of name *see* translation
 see also caste
presentism, holistic, 97, 99

punning, 79
pure and impure, 142
'pure' pastoralism, 155, 156
Purum people, 12

quantification, 2—3, 5, 124—5
Quine, W. V. O., 24, 28, 41, 42, 45,
 76, 77

Rabinow, P., 7
race concept, 184
Radcliffe-Brown, A. R., 45, 81, 97, 99,
 100, 193
 on comparative method, 2, 23—4
 on facts, 29
 on generalization, 94—5
Ranger, T., 178, 185
rank *see* caste
rationality shared, assumed *see*
 universality
Rattray, R. S., 103, 107
Ray, V. F., 123
Read, K., 7
reciprocal Khoisan relationship terms,
 197—9
reductionism, sociological 97—8
Reff, T., 65
regional comparisons, 56—9, 64
 history and culture (West Africa), 90,
  95—108
 see also Khoisan
regularity and Divinity, 30
reificatory objections and growth of
 ethnicity concept, 172—3, 174
relativism, 121
religion
 ancestor cult, 95, 97—8, 143
 Buddhism, 138, 143
 Christianity, 107, 112
 as classification system, 52
 concept, 83
 Hinduism, 123; *see also*
  caste
 ideology and state, 106—8
 Islam, 98, 106, 110, 165, 180

regularity and, 30
world, conversion in Africa, 89, 107, 110, 112
see also witchcraft *and under* Africa
revival of history in anthropology, 99—101
Richards, A., 55
Ricoeur, P., 26, 72
Riesman, D., 173
Rivers, W. H. R., 126
Rivière, P., 34, 52, 57
rock art
analogical and sequential relationships in recent examples, 214—17
context of Upper Palaeolithic examples, 217—18
interpreting: ethnography in, 16, 66, 210—39
see also motifs
Rosenfeld, A., 211, 216, 218, 224, 229, 231, 235—6
Ruggles, C., 128
Runciman, W. G., 89

Sahel drought, 158
Sahlins, M., 89, 122, 124
Said, E., 185
Salmond, A., 53
Sama/Samba people *see* Chamba
Samo people, 130
San people *see* Bushmen
Sanskrit, 143
Sarana, G., 4
Saussure, F. de, 64, 66
Sauvet, G. and S., 220, 229
scale of forms, 44
Schapera, I., 3, 45, 96, 100, 189—90
Scheffler, H., 74, 208
Schneider, D. M., 6, 11, 12, 14
Schulte-Nordholt, H. G., 141
Schultze (Schultze-Jena), L., 198, 201
Schutz, A., 154
science, 3, 23—8, 74
methodology, 70—2
progression from magic to, 94

segmentary systems and rock art, 215
Selby, H. A., 7
semantics, 6—7, 62—3
see also language
Senegal, 164
sequential relationships in recent rock art, 214—17
Seton-Watson, H., 170
Shadily, H., 40
shamanism, 84
see also witchcraft
Shaw, T., 111
signification, endless, 63, 65
signs, 36
in rock art, 219—21, 229
Silberbauer, G. B., 201, 203
Silverman, D., 3
similarities and differences, 16, 120—1, 135, 169
see also comparative; ethnicity
Simmel, G., 169, 177
Simpson, G. G., 45
situational objections and growth of ethnicity concept, 174
Skillen, A., 33
Skocpol, T., 109, 113
Smart, J. J. C., 128
Smith, A., 90, 173, 177
Smith, B. L., 234
Smith, B. T., 234
Smith, M. G., 90, 91, 100—1, 161, 185
Smith, P., 90
social institutions, 34
sociological reductionism, 97—8
sociological time, 101
Somali people, 100
Somers, M., 113
sorcery *see* magic; witchcraft
Sotho people, 59, 60
South America, 57, 77—80, 83—4
Southall, A. W., 55, 62, 172, 185
Southwold, M., 52, 170
space and time, 128—9
Spain: rock art, 219, 224—7
spatial organization, 59—60

Spencer, H., 90, 92, 100
Sperber, D., 30, 36—7, 45, 46—7
Spradley, J. P., 6
Sri Lanka, 57
state
  definitions of, 33
  formation, 101—5
  religion and ideology, 106—8
  see also nationalism
statistics, 2—3
status *see* caste
Steiner, F., 3
Stenning, D., 155, 157, 160, 163
Stocking, G., 93
Strathern, M., 10—11
Strauss, A. L., 6, 8
Strauss, L. G., 224, 226, 233
Strawson, P., 46, 128
structuralism, 25—8, 33, 53, 56—60,
  64—5, 80, 96, 100—1, 161, 173,
  174
Stryker, S., 6
Sturtevant, W., 7
subjective ethnicity, 174—7
Sumatra, 58
Sumba people, 124, 125
surplus meaning, 63
Swahili people and language, 58, 61
Swellengrebel, J. L., 137, 143
Swidler, W., 159—60
symbolism, 6—7, 11, 35—6, 85
  see also motifs

Tallensi people, 94, 97, 99
Tambiah, S. J., 137
Thompson, E. P., 128
Tidy, M., 183
time
  concepts, 31, 121—2, 126—9
  sociological, 101
  see also history
Toba Batak people, 126
Tonkin, E., 185
totemism, 52, 74, 214, 216
Touraine, A., 109

tourism, 44
transformation, 17
translation as creative process
  definitions and power of labelling,
    73—6
  knowledge and creativity: methodology
    of revolt, 81—5
  power of name, 15, 37, 44, 45, 47,
    70—87
  problem of, 76—81
Trezise, P. J., 215, 216, 223
tribe: objections to term, 171—4, 183
Tswana people, 100
Turner, V., 35
Turton, A., 60
Turton, D., 123, 128
Tuuk, H. N. van der, 40—1, 47
Tyler, S. A., 13
Tylor, E. B., 93

Ucko, P. J., 211, 218, 219, 229, 231,
  236—7
universality, 30—1, 34, 38, 41, 46, 75,
  81, 94, 121—2, 90—1, 92—3, 211
Upper Volta, 164

variation, 17, 64—5
Vinnicombe, P., 215—17, 223, 224,
  228—9

Wahl, L., 218
Wallace, A. F. C., 38
Ward, B. E., 45
Warna, W., 40
water control/irrigation, 124, 143, 147
Watson, J., 7
Weber, M., 92, 93, 109, 110, 154, 162
Weck, W., 35, 40
Werbner, R., 184
Wheeler, G. C., 91
Whitehead, H., 10
Wijk, H. A. C. W. van, 126
Wilden, A., 45
Wilks, I., 103, 106—8
Williams, W. R., 234

Wilson, B. R., 7
Wilson, D., 47
Wilson, M., 98
Winch, P., 72, 134
Winter, E. H., 98
Winter, J., 216
witchcraft, 35, 40, 52, 67, 84, 95—6, 98
    see also magic; religion
Witkowski, S. R., 123
Wittgenstein, L., 29, 72, 129
Wlodarczyk, A., 220, 229
Wobst, H. M., 233
Wodaabe people, 163
women, 10—11
    Khoisan terms for, 194—208 *passim*
    marriage and, 58—9, 61, 63
    word for, 78
world views, different *see*
    incommensurability

Wouden, F. A. E. van, 140
Wraneck, J., 126
Wyllie, R. W., 112

/Xam people, 192
!xo people, 192, 206

Yalman, N., 57—8, 59
Yolngu people, 220
Yoruba people, 88—9, 99, 100,
    102—7, 110—12
Young, C., 172

Zaria people, 91
Zoetmulder, P. J., 30, 40, 47
Zulu people, 99, 102
Zwernemann, J., 91

Index by Ann Hall